The Butterfly Fleet

Laurence, J. Cook,
"Who would fish
for free!"
Smooth sailing always,
Dena Johnson
Nov. 1, 1997

The Butterfly Fleet

Salmon, Sails and Oars
on the
Columbia River

Dena Johnson

 **BookPartners, Inc.**
Wilsonville, Oregon

BookPartners, Inc.
P.O. Box 922
Wilsonville, Oregon 97070

Dedication

*To my father, Emil Aldin Pearson,
whose pride in his gillnetting heritage
inspired this work;
and to my husband, Dennis Johnson,
whose faith in its completion
proved invaluable.*

Introduction

~ ~

The Baltic Sea
October 24, 1874

As the small fishing boat inched its way through the open waters toward Stockholm, the air stiffened, forecasting snow. An hour earlier the sky and sea had been distinguishable swaths of blues and grays and the shoreline had stood out as a substantial reference point upon the horizon, but ominous white clouds were beginning to encroach upon the scene and were altering the recognizable. Rightfully apprehensive in this changeable environment, Ingrid Nilsdotter, sitting in the stern of the boat, pulled her woolen scarf more securely around her face, and the book she had nestled on her lap fell open on the floorboards.

"It'll do you no good out here, anyway," her father remarked as he observed the vulnerable position of her prized possession.

Ingrid retrieved her *Bibeln* (Bible) and clutched it firmly to her chest. Small snowflakes began swirling in the air. The scene was thick with impending winter, but Ingrid did exactly what her father did and ignored the light flurries to ponder a more precipitous situation. Today, on her twenty-fifth birthday, she had attained the age of majority and was free to sail to America to be joined in wedlock with her beloved, Olof Andersson. Being no longer classed along with children and the insane, she was rid of parental guardianship forever. Her blonde hair and blue eyes would belong to another man, and she would no longer think of herself as being Nils's *dotter.* The journey from her small fishing village to Stockholm, however, seemed to rival the most tedious moments in her life. She wished it over and her new life begun.

"What did you mean about The Lord's Book?" Ingrid asked her father, Nils Gustav Petersson.

His eyes twinkled in response. Set against the wintry background of the now silvery sea, he brought forth the image of an obliging *tomten,* an elfish creature of folklore, residing in the woods, and said to bring comfort to the people of Scandinavia during the long winter nights. But the fairy tale comparison was short-lived in Ingrid's immediate thinking, because the image of a cloistered forest canopy could not overshadow the omnipresent sea, nor could it deny Nils's reality as her father.

Always slow with his words, Nils observed both the solemnity and solid quality of the sea before answering. He was neither a large nor an overbearing man, yet aboard his fishing vessel, he could assume prophetic proportions. His graying temples and silver-inflected beard glistened from the snowdrops haloing his face, as if in the natural accord of things, he, too, was in a state of transition but traveling through time with the advantage of knowing where he was headed. "Out here," he responded gruffly, "The Lord is only an observer, and one must take responsibility for oneself. Frailty is seldom forgiven by the sea, and goodness is not equated with survival. The law of the land and the sea are applied quite differently. On law shall the land be built, but the sea ... the sea has rules of its own and will quickly weed out the weak in favor of the strong. Remember that, Ingrid." Nils paused from his rowing to glance over his shoulder and look directly at his daughter. "Do take heart, however, knowing that nature always reigns supreme, and that Mother Nature is the most worthy competitor given us by God. If you observe her warnings, you'll find that your journey through life will be more fruitful."

The sky interrupted any further insights from Nils by taking on a blinding iridescent quality, a goldish cast locked between the clouds and the sea. So bright was the shimmering reflection off the water's surface that it brought tears to the young woman's eyes. She took heed of the dynamic and changeable realm surrounding her, but her father seemed inured to any uncertainty, even when the Bible, again, slipped through her fingers. She felt estranged from her two guiding influences, suddenly cognizant of her own vulnerability.

Chapter One

~ ~ ~ ~ ~ ~ ~ ~ ~ ~ ~ ~ ~ ~ ~ ~ ~ ~ ~

The Columbia River Bar
Spring, 1875

The mouth of the Columbia River was spewing its watery backlog into the Pacific Ocean, while the wind's fury was adding to the unfolding drama. The three females aboard the coastal trader huddled together, enduring the storm aside from the frantic efforts of the male contingent. From all appearances, both sailors and passengers were too disorganized to know what the crisis was about, let alone how to correct it. In its final throes, the ship rose high on a steep wave and instinctively Ingrid, Elizabeth, and Elizabeth's daughter Jane grabbed for something solid as the ship plowed into the giant sand bar. The ship screeched and groaned, and the first fatality occurred as a seaman was swept overboard by a wall of water. "My God!" Elizabeth cried out, but her shrill voice was no competition for the roar of the waves or the wrenching sound of timbers being dislodged from the hull below. Ingrid was momentarily dumfounded. "How can this be?" she stammered, tripping over each absurd utterance. Elizabeth's horror-stricken expression was etched in stone, and eight-year-old Jane had already dropped to her knees and disappeared among the protective folds of her mother's skirt. Ingrid scoured the horizon for any signs of assistance beyond the embattled ship, but the wind and sea spray lashed at her face, blinding her. They were shipwrecked at the mouth of a tremendous river, a river so swollen with water that it could defy intervention until it had had its way with this insignificant ship. Having traveled thousands of tedious miles, the remaining dozen or so had possibly bested them.

Impulsively Ingrid opened her water-soaked Bible, seeking an avenue of escape. "That's a good idea," Elizabeth agreed over her shoulder. Elizabeth's steadfast demeanor was again discernible, although her integrity had been impaired by the force of the wind. Her dark tresses were in uncharacteristic disarray around her neck and shoulders. Nevertheless, she had regained her composure, and for that Ingrid was grateful. Ingrid's fingers fought with the wind and rain to keep the Bible open, but the pages were slippery and her endeavor futile. Too, Elizabeth had since turned her attention back to Jane, the young girl hiding in her mother's skirt folds. Ingrid shut the book and allowed her mind to wander. Her father's warning came to her as clearly as if he were next to her, on the quarterdeck of the sinking ship: "It'll do you no good out here! The Lord is only an observer, and one must take responsibility for oneself."

Elizabeth tugged Ingrid on the shoulder. "We're supposed to go forward!" She said: "See, they're waving at us!" Ingrid watched in numbed fascination as the captain ordered one of the small boats to be lowered into the churning water. "It can't be!" she thought. Ingrid clenched her Bible and made no effort to move. She observed the first officer making several thwarted attempts to board the small vessel. Her gut reaction told her she was witnessing an act of desperation. She looked over at Elizabeth through the lashing spindrift and grappled for any "American" words to explain her resolve. "No!" she said convincingly to Elizabeth. "No! Do not go!"

The rain and pounding swells failed to stop a few sailors from reaching them. Ingrid clung fiercely to her Bible as two deckhands grabbed her by either elbow and escorted her toward the crashing waves, imploding on the forecastle. She jerked herself free just short of their destination, but while she argued, Elizabeth acquiesced. Ingrid caught only a glimpse of the woman's ashen face and rigid body as the sailors grabbed her by the upper arms and lowered her into the small vessel. Before anyone could speculate as to the success of the effort, a giant swell lifted the unsteady craft upwards and flipped it over. Both the first officer and Elizabeth were gone. Jane screamed as her mother disappeared. Ingrid forced her way through the crowd of guilty sailors to draw the young girl close to her bosom. "No!" she shrieked, protecting both herself and Jane from anymore ill-conceived attempts at saving them.

The mayhem grew as swells continued coming at the coastal trader in thirty-foot walls, and wind tore across the deck in forty-knot gusts. The only thing left to ponder was the miniscule chance of survival. In a both burly and chivalrous presentation, the captain ordered everyone into the riggings, the two "ladies" included. Refusal meant certain death. Ingrid went first, with Jane grabbing at her ankles to steady her climb. They clung to the yardarm as ropes were secured around them. Ingrid placed a hand on Jane's shoulder and found it as rigid as the rigging to which they were bound. Jane made no effort to raise her head; instead she whimpered like a wounded animal, unable to adequately express her pain. Ingrid searched the horizon, able to find only two lighthouse beacons, points of reference appearing so far removed as to be stars, observing them from another galaxy. They were miles from anywhere.

Night thickened. Below, tons of water cascaded off the decks, while above, like spiders in a web, the crew in the riggings fell quiet so their hearing might quicken and guide them through the darkness. Ingrid could only guess, but in her mind's eye she associated the squeals and groans as coming from the small boats, being wrenched free by the force of the water. The crashing and banging were surely the work of the swells, crushing the boats against the hull of the ship. As the capstan broke loose, taking the steering wheel and binnacle overboard, Ingrid put a hand to her chest and realized her Bible was gone. Her mind began to wander, beyond the walls of reason and into the imaginary world she had hoped to share with Olof. She would pass out, yet he was there, waiting for her at the end of a plank walkway that stretched across a short distance of water. Purposely setting herself an easy goal, Ingrid intended to bridge the gap. She was meant to have the new life awaiting her.

At first the physical distance appeared a few yards in length. Her first few steps proved her wrong, however, for the intermediate planks were simply floating on the river's surface, and whenever she took a step forward, the water level rose up around her ankles and restricted her progress. Olof, a formidable young man with a reddish beard and emerald-green eyes, began to take on a Christ-like aura in

Ingrid's dream, creating additional zeal in Ingrid's desire to reach him. But as surely as she created the image, she had to be rid of it. Surely He would not approve of the wishful likeness she imagined in those soulful eyes of her betrothed. It was an act of desperation. Contrite, she lowered her eyes to study the narrow walkway separating her from her illusive lover, but when she failed to concentrate on Olof 's image, it faded away. Her dream was awash, relegated to obscurity by an impenetrable grayness clogging around her. All along she had expected as much, for both she and Olof were mere mortals, and neither of them was capable of walking on water. Her mind was just playing with her, giving her hope when there was none. As her father had warned her, the law of the land and the sea were quite different. Perhaps he had been trying to illustrate the folly of wandering too far from the familiar.

Thankfully the air was being drawn from the physical world around her and being supplanted by a peaceful numbness. Even the ropes binding her to the yardarm no longer seemed restrictive. She focused her waning energy on God's beneficence; as a certainty, she was dying. Somewhere a mournful tenor was singing a Swedish hymn as the last of any temporal resistance abandoned her body. However she had seen herself before, that vision would forever be altered. In a matter of seconds she was bereft of any substance, and any lingering terror was replaced by a winsome acceptance. Perhaps she had not made it across the Columbia River bar to experience the new life awaiting her, she thought, but Nils Gustav Petersson could have found little fault with her effort. Even a crowd of skilled men could not keep the ship afloat during such a violent storm. The water rose like cliffs too high to climb and fell with such force as to disintegrate anything in its path.

Before Ingrid could let it all go, she embraced her little sister, Hanna, in her thoughts. Hanna's image was quite vivid. She could hear her younger sister calling to her, telling her she must remain alive! At that very instant, death indeed seemed an unjust punishment. She could find only one transgression in her life on which to fix the blame ... wanting to come to America.

Astoria, Oregon

Olof lay in the bed and watched the rain beat mercilessly against the windowpanes. He was alone in the dimly lit room, half-expecting the woman to return. But after they had made love she had gotten up, put on her robe, and discreetly closed the door behind her. Apparently there was no romance involved in their fiscal arrangement; only a few fleeting instances of physical pleasure were to be had from the casual exchange of money. Olof crawled out from beneath the covers and slowly dressed. In the future the nights would move ahead on a more convincing and reassuring course; in the future Ingrid would pause long enough to hear his thoughts and protect his soul from such transient weaknesses.

Outside sheets of rain skidded sideways across Astor Street, driven by fierce gusts of wind. Olof pressed down on the crown of his hat and stepped cautiously beyond the brothel doors. Promptly the brusque weather swept him up, scooting him across the thick boards typical of the underlayments supporting the waterfront establishments built on piles. He cursed the foul weather as he turned into the rain-laden wind and headed toward a familiar saloon, supposing this storm would further delay Ingrid's long-awaited arrival from San Francisco. Surely the ship would be held offshore until this southwester blew through.

Even before Olof had hung up his outerwear on a nail, Henry Hihnala was there near the doorway, observing his fishing partner with curiosity. "You haven't heard, have you?" Henry offered rhetorically. By observing Olof's relaxed appearance, Henry knew his communication would come as a shock. "A coast-wise trader is hung up on the outer sand bar at the mouth of the river, and she's the bark Ingrid's supposed to be aboard."

Just like that, Henry had delivered the news. He grimaced slightly in anticipation of Olof's reaction, yet there was nothing anyone could do to assist those ship-wrecked in such a storm. It was foolishness to pretend otherwise. Olof eyed his best friend with bewilderment, completely taken off stride. Ingrid could be dead or, worse, she could have been dying while he was exploiting his status as a bachelor. Olof was stunned, incapable of speech. Henry turned and made his way to a circular table, a location preferable to the raucous gathering at the bar. He had something more to tell his friend, something he knew could very well raise the roof on the tavern.

The mouth of the Columbia was well on its way to earning the distinction of being the Graveyard of the Pacific, having swallowed five ships in one year alone. During stormy weather, prudent captains were known to wait offshore as long as six weeks before begging entrance through the shoal-laden waters. The Columbia River was deceptive, and it protected its five-mile-wide mouth with an obstacle course that constantly rearranged itself with the compilation of sediment, amassed from a drainage area of 259,000 square miles. The flow of water at the mouth could be as much as 1,000,000 cubic feet per second, and when storms accompanied this massive off-rush, inundating the giant sand deposits, there were cataclysmic results. Lives were lost, including those of trusting emigrants in transit, people exactly like Olof's sweet Ingrid.

Henry, a twenty-three-year-old Finnish emigrant, felt ill-equipped to pursue the conversation. Although his round face and dimpled smile bespoke an easygoing, jovial sort (someone who would rather downplay a crisis than exploit it), he could be as judgmental as any other gillnetter when considering the goings-on along the river. There was always more than met the eye, as well as things that needed rectifying. But in this case, an appraisal of the night's events might prove harmful. His two-year-long friendship with the tempestuous Swede had been a natural ... but this was not ... there was risk involved in explaining to a man why his dream had been swept off the face of the earth in one sorry incident.

Olof swung his leg over the chair back and reached for the whiskey bottle in one coordinated move. Henry was slower to be seated and refill his glass. He could communicate with Olof fluently, using American as a foundation and tossing in Finnish and Swedish for color. He held his tongue, however, wondering if Olof was prepared to accept the grisly details as he intended to relate them. With only a few ceiling lamps illuminating the overcrowded, smoke-filled room, Olof's facial expressions were secretive, overpowered by the outline of his shoulder-length hair and full beard. He appeared tough, unkempt and wild, akin to the ambience evoked by a roughly hewed saloon built on piles near the river's edge, in a crusty part of Astoria where kidnappers were known to lurk in the shadows, and black bear came to feed upon decaying fish carcasses. There could be no better setting for the telling of this tale and, by its telling, any further reference to Olof's Ingrid would be unnecessary. There was nothing to be gained by sidestepping the issue. Henry shoved his glass across the tabletop and allowed Olof to fill it.

Henry sought out a rather surly-looking fellow, leaning against the wall beneath one of the ceiling lanterns, and pointed him out to Olof. "That's the bar pilot right over there, repeating his tale of woe. I suppose it's been a long night for him, but if I've understood his story correctly, sooner or later it's going to come back to haunt him." Henry straightened himself in his chair, as if he were singularly prepared to approach the man with a few choice words. Olof drummed his fingers on the table's surface, anxious for Henry to get to the heart of the matter. He was confused by mixed messages, uncertain as to Ingrid's fate. Too, he was uncertain as to what part the bar pilot might have played in this tragic event. Olof was capable of busting a liar's jaw, but the river was a different matter. "Get on with it," he grumbled.

Henry's broad lips were pursed and ready to continue. "Seems he went out to meet the bark and a signal flag was raised. Instead of coming alongside, however, he changed his mind and began retracing the eighteen-mile return trip to Astoria. 'Any fool could see the storm building,' he claims. But the captain of the trader must have gotten the idea they were supposed to follow the pilot boat upriver. When the ship got well under way, the wind dropped off, and she was forced to drop anchor to avoid the Middle Sands. The pilot says she was clear at that time. No problems whatsoever! And the breeze returned, and the hooks were again weighed. Appears the bark tried to pick her way to a deep enough channel by following in the diminishing wake of the pilot boat and skirting the bar on the outside. Just what any good captain would do under those conditions, believing he was in the hands of a reputable bar pilot. But the wind died again, and the ship lost steerage. By this time she was drifting into shallow water. She struck stern first and clipped her rudder."[1]

Henry paused to catch his breath. Not only had he been speaking rapidly, but his voice was beginning to crack, trying to reach above the din. News of the wreck was spreading like a wildfire throughout the saloon, feeding on its own momentum. At each table, and along the crudely constructed bar where strangers came together with the closeness of bedfellows, the patrons were engendering it. Their voices continued to peak, rivaling the pulsating excitement garnered by a Fourth of July parade cascading through town.

From Olof's perspective, the scene was ghoulish: men showing too much willingness to participate in the celebration of a tragedy. He had the urge to rise up and show them what a six-foot-five-inch tall Swede could do to silence their loose talk, but instead his imagination took a different turn, and the story began replaying itself. He relaxed his grip on the shot glass and observed the amber liquid. He was alone with his thoughts and trying desperately to put them into a relevant context. He could draw the sea air into his lungs and taste the salt. Too, he could observe both the current and the wind working against the bark. He brought the mouth of the river into his vision, and the huge sand bar, a couple miles in length. To the south he scanned the channel used in the winter; to the north, the deeper and

---

1. The progression of events loosely detailed in the shipwreck are similar to those incurred by the American bark *Industry* in March 1865. The incident is memorialized on Astoria's Shark Rock. Seven lives were saved, while seventeen were lost, including that of a twelve-year-old girl who was swept overboard from a raft. Source: James A. Gibbs, *Pacific Graveyard* (Portland, 1964), pp. 88-91.

more reliable passage used in the summer. Doubtless, approaching from the south, the captain would have willingly stood offshore because the tide was slack. He would prefer waiting until flood tide and breach the river with depth to spare. Olof groaned. Even so, the north channel would have sufficed if the coast-wise trader hadn't paralleled the Middle Sands too closely, and then lost the wind. But the captain surely got mixed signals; the appearance of the bar pilot must have given him some false indication that there was ample room to skirt the sands. Damnable luck!

But luck wasn't the applicable term because the passengers were now lining the starboard side of the ship, witnessing the awesome beauty of the river unfolding. And Ingrid was among them in his imagination, appraising the size and wonderment of the gate to her new home, just as Olof had described it to her. Her blonde hair was radiant under the blazing sunshine, and her skirt was blowing freely in the wind. She was unchanged from their last meeting, still strikingly beautiful and confident. But she could not seem to take it all in because she was looking for someone near and dear to her heart, searching for someone she had traveled thousands of miles to meet in marriage.

Olof's lower jaw slid sideways. His eyes widened and his brows formed inquisitive arches. What could be done? The bark's only hope rested on the incoming tide. Perhaps she would float off the sands and be carried into the channel. Olof knew it wasn't possible. Even if she drifted some, the size of the Middle Sands precluded escape. "Finish the story," he said brusquely. "I'd like to hear all of it."

Henry took a deep breath in preparation. The fire was returning to his partner's eyes, but how Olof was interpreting his story remained a mystery. "The bar pilot watched from afar, now certain the rising tide would float the ship and bring her around. Then he'd be off the hook. That's the only saving grace in this entire story, that the tide tried to help some. The captain and crew got her freed temporarily, but by then the storm had moved in. She drifted a good 100 yards before driving ashore again, where she dislodged her false keel." Henry's voice suddenly became agitated as his objectivity failed him. "Mind you, Olof, that cocky son of a bitch, leaning against the wall over there, says that the cap'n of the ship ought to be landlocked! In my opinion, he's the one who got his wires crossed and beached that coast-wise trader. Sure as shooting, at this very instant that ship is getting its guts beat out because of his negligence, and those passengers from San Francisco will be swept into the Pacific."

Olof brushed his unkempt hair away from his neck. He was noticeably shaken. He lifted the bottle from the table and funneled whiskey directly down his throat. Henry watched in silence, wondering what his friend would do. Olof always did something. He was an-eye-for-an-eye and a-tooth-for-a-tooth man.

"So, my sweet Ingrid is dead," Olof thought to himself. "Some fools fouled up and killed her." His recollections of Ingrid's kindness and beauty were clear in his memory, while all hope for their future together appeared lost. There was a bitter irony here, in that he and Henry, who traversed the churning waters of the Columbia in their twenty-two-foot salmon boat with care and caution, could succeed where a 300-ton bark should fail. He had never taken Ingrid's ability to survive under consideration. He had intended to protect her from the river's domain, and recreate a semblance of the secure fishing village of their youth. His lack of foresight was a bitter pill to swallow. He stood on his feet, and the overturned chair clattered to the floor. He took the bottle by the neck and flung it across the room. It struck the wall a few inches from the bar pilot's head and shattered. Silence came over the room. The bar pilot appeared stunned, and the crowd parted as Olof approached him. Olof's green eyes were aglow and his face was tinged with a reddish hue. He threw a fist and the bar pilot reeled from the blow. "Hey, what are you doing?" the barkeep hollered. Olof swung again, this time missing his target and striking the wall with the full bore of his knuckles. A chair came crashing across his shoulders. He turned and saw Henry, subduing the irate barkeep in a headlock. Someone grabbed Olof by the arm, but Olof quickly pinned his assailant against the bar. The pilot had garnered supporters, and the fight quickly embroiled all willing participants. Bottles and fists flew. Olof purposely fanned the fire, expending the energy that couldn't be diverted to saving Ingrid.

At first her fellow travelers were extremely apologetic for allowing such a cruel fate to befall her. On the surface they had overcome the language barrier and learned to smile upon one another as vital people, emigrating in unison to the New World. As usual, their voices were soft, sympathetic and soothing, but then her mother's stringent opinions intervened, reminding them that Ingrid had brought it all upon herself by leaving her family, and that they should save their pity for someone more deserving, at least for someone more prudent. "There's no such thing as being one's own person ... there are only people ... duty bound to serve family and country." Ingrid tried to answer on her own behalf, but as usual she had no voice to raise; no absolute means of retaliation responded to her will. She could not dispute her mother's authority. "Personal feelings must be set aside," her mother reiterated for the hundredth time. "Love is something only the foolish and the frivolous pursue. Contentment is a far more realistic goal. Best to tend to your sister Hanna and accept the responsibilities already bestowed upon you. You can be such a singular and moody girl, Ingrid. Duty isn't a dirty word, and as a woman it will bring continuity to your life. Forget this nonsense called America. No one is ever free of the bondage called tradition. You'll find yourself alone and swallowed up by your dreams. Mark my words." Ingrid became angry. Her teeth locked onto flesh, and she tasted blood.

In the light of day, Ingrid tried to untangle herself from the heaps of ropes surrounding the fallen yard. Her fingertips were afire from the onset of frostbite, but one perusal of the ship's condition put her physical discomfort into perspective. She was stranded on a rapidly disintegrating platform amidst a swell-ridden river where it met up with the ocean. Memories were coming back to her with shocking clarity and, although the dismembered ship seemed to profess the opposite, Ingrid had the distinct feeling the ordeal was far from over. The little English girl, Jane, was entangled in the same mess of ropes, but the eight-year-old's body was doubled over at the waist while blood was seeping from her nose. She needed tending. Ingrid's heart beat at a frantic rate, yet she retained her composure, knowing she would gladly cut off her fingers if she believed the nubs would remove the ropes any faster. She continued to work methodically, intent on freeing themselves from the rubble before either of them died. Those who were ambulatory were distracted, reacting to the demands of the captain. She could hear him calling out ... it was imperative to build rafts! The terror returned. Memories of yesterday's groundings were running rampant in her mind. There had to be some logical reason for having graduated onto this new level of despair, but reason was no longer a reliable guidepost.

Pinching herself would do no good; it was all surreal. "It's only a nosebleed," she comforted Jane, though Jane's wounds were obviously internal because she continued to spit up blood. Ingrid pulled back her lower lip and showed the young English girl the gouge inside her own mouth. "See," she explained calmly, "we both have wounds that will eventually heal." Jane turned her head askew like a curious bird, seeking understanding. Ingrid meant nothing to her, and certainly wouldn't suffice as a replacement for her mother. "We should wrap you up in blankets and keep you warm," Ingrid said apologetically, "but we don't have any blankets, so my shawl will have to do." Jane accepted the waterlogged garment as Ingrid draped it over her shoulders.

Ingrid was afraid to count heads and acknowledge how few people actually remained aboard. If they hadn't died of drowning, they would certainly perish in the frigid air. Ingrid's dress was wringing wet and clinging to her body like a second skin, but it cut the wind, and for that one aspect of natural law she was grateful. She watched over her shoulder as two men came to take the yard. "We need everything remaining to construct the rafts, ma'am," one of them offered apologetically. Ingrid couldn't comprehend the words, but she understood the concept. She stepped aside, keeping Jane tucked under her arm. The deck of the ship was almost at water level. The swells were tame in size, compared to the previous evening's storm, but they continued to roll over the ship as if, in the end, they would still have their way. "I've got to go help the men," she said to Jane. "You stay close by my side, and we'll see our way through this together."

The first raft was breaking apart even as it met the swells. The few remaining square feet of surface space would have to do. Ingrid scanned the endless Pacific to the west and saw the raft pulling in that direction. The captain prodded her in the shoulder blades and said something to her backside she could neither comprehend or appreciate. The congenial travelers, as they were now, had forgotten how to face one another and express their genuineness through eye contact. The river continued to feed on the weak and the frail.

There were four men aboard the raft, one of them motioning her aboard. Ingrid squeezed Jane's hand firmly and led her to where the raft was waiting. The ship's railing was missing, and the river surged before her very eyes. The only encouragement came from the open area in the middle of the raft, a space adequate for both her and Jane. The other passengers had positioned themselves one at each corner. Two held boards in such a way as to indicate that they were meant to suffice as paddles; two held ropes in their hands, keeping the raft abreast of the ship. Ingrid watched the momentum of the raft as it rose and fell on the swells. She dropped Jane's hand and made a motion that the young girl was to follow. Ingrid leapt aboard. Two men grabbed her by either arm as she flew through the air and landed on her knees. The boards were as slippery and cold as polished stone, yet she managed to turn and extend her arms toward Jane. The raft lurched sideways, and Ingrid dropped on all fours. The captain had the young girl restrained and was pointing out the second raft being built from the ship's decking. Ingrid was helpless to change the situation. "Shove off!" he shouted.

Ingrid cried out for Jane, but the ropes had been released and the raft was quickly on its way. In words Jane could not understand, Ingrid offered the only support available to her: "You'll be all right! You'll be safer on the next raft!"

At times the water rolled gently beneath them. No one spoke. It was as if the Columbia was giving them a respite, a time to be lulled into believing they would be given safe haven, if they took it all for granted. But Ingrid's inner voice was telling her something different: that this great river of Olof's lied through its teeth; that the lullaby of the river was the song of the dead; and that it was far more imperative to keep her eye on the living and see to it that Jane's raft followed. Yet her eyes could not tolerate the sun's reflection off the water, and she found herself weeping. The river did not approve of her insolence. She caught a glimpse of another raft in their wake, but that raft tipped over and sent Jane to a watery grave.

The sky was becoming heavily overcast as they drifted out to sea on a south-southwesterly course. The Point Adams Lighthouse came into view, but the crosscurrents were too fierce to overcome with the makeshift paddles. Drizzle began and quickly changed to rain. At some point the current shifted and the raft, well south of the mouth of the river, started drifting toward the beach. Men in boats were rowing toward them from shore. Now ill, Ingrid was far too fevered to address the uniformed men from Fort Stevens who brought them safely through the surf. The rescuers were inquisitive about the nature of a woman who could have survived such a shipwreck, but Ingrid was distressed by their attentiveness. She took no pride in her own salvation, because the recollections of a young girl, swallowed up by the Columbia, weighed heavy on her conscience. Looking back at the waves, curling against the beach, she had a passing thought that chilled her to the bones. Perhaps she was being punished for coming to the New World to wed her beloved; perhaps placing love ahead of duty to family and country had precipitated such a senseless tragedy.

∞

During the lengthy buckboard ride around Youngs Bay to Astoria, Olof kept his eyes trained on the rutted and muddied road as it twisted and turned through disparate groves of gnarled spruce. His recent reunion with Ingrid directed his thoughts elsewhere. Public displays of affection were something to which he was unaccustomed, yet any word of recognition would have been welcomed. He steadied Ingrid with one arm placed around her shoulder, but he dared not caress her cheeks or marvel at the depth of her blue eyes. Her only words were a puzzlement to him, sounding like remonstrances aimed solely at herself. Occasionally she made mention of her sister Hanna in concert with two of the drowning victims, Elizabeth and Jane, but no words of appreciation for his being there were offered. And he was a proud man, incapable of projecting himself into her seeming quandary unless invited.

∞

Molly Bochau was the closest thing to a female confidant that Astoria could afford Ingrid. Unlike the Englishwoman Elizabeth, Molly had a rough edge about her and was not one to mince words or closet her opinions. For two weeks, Ingrid fought back the effects of pneumonia in Molly Bochau's boardinghouse, accepting the timely offer of private accommodations down the hall from Olof's. Ingrid was becoming more proficient in American, but the thinking behind the language was a far more complicated process to master, and she took it in graduated steps. Though their conversations were admittedly lopsided, Ingrid was gleaning more than she had hoped for from this heavyset woman in her mid-forties, with dark facial hair rimming her upper lip and hair drawn so tightly into a bun that her eyes bulged forth from their sockets. As Ingrid's health improved, sharing tea with Molly became a daily ritual. Molly's ready font of information was all Ingrid could rely upon to help her arrive at a decision.

This morning, Ingrid served the tea. Molly was seated at the large table, reading *The Daily Astorian.* "They'll be arriving soon," she commented. "It says here, under Vessels on the Way, that three ships are expected from San Francisco shortly. The fishing season's about to begin. We'll fill up overnight and stay that way for four months. Can't say I look forward to all of them boarders, however. Some of them's not worth much. Your fisherman, Olof, now he's a real gillnetter. He's a good cap'n, and he's got an able boat puller. The two of them tend to business, unlike many of them hooligans."

Ingrid pulled out a chair and sat across from her hostess. The tea was too hot for simple sipping, so she folded her hands on the table and waited, hoping to learn more about this strange phenomenon about to occur when the gillnetters arrived. Molly continued: "Astoria will soon be bursting at the seams with transients — some coming from failed mining efforts; some coming from the railroads; and some just wandering around, looking for an easy buck. Most come through California. Seems every man's got to try striking it rich before heading north. Then they arrive here and blow all their hard-earned money on whiskey and women. Only a few ... like your Olof ... seem to have a head for fishing. I'd keep a close eye on him, nevertheless, cuz he's a looker. The women in Swilltown like to bed him. Two handsome people such as yourselves are bound to have beautiful babies, unless one of the other women picks him off. Just warning you. He makes good money and tends to save it better than most. Never had a problem getting rent out of Olof, or his boat puller, for that matter. They're a different breed, taking fishing seriously. A lot of the Scandihoovians are noted for that. But then again, one never knows the worth of a man until the times get rough, and times do get rough in Astoria."

Ingrid lifted her cup to her lips and blew across the steamy liquid. Outside the window she could see several ships at anchor. "More are coming?" she queried.

"Dozens," Molly replied. "When the fish migrate up the Columbia, ships come and go like fleas on a hound. And they're building more canneries as we speak. See, right here in the paper, piles are being driven in Upper Astoria for another. There's big money in owning a cannery. Labor's cheap and the fish are so plentiful they literally leap into the cans. Astoria is bound to be the salmon capital of the world. Mark my words."

Ingrid noted the excitement in Molly's voice when she spoke of Astoria's future, and it reminded her of those men aboard the bark who had equated the possibility of heroism with the ship's actual foundering. In their desire to rise above the norm, they had failed to weigh their own integrity against the river's mighty spirit — the real contest. It was something Ingrid was incapable of explaining, and even if she could, she suspected Molly would be deeply offended if she begged to differ. As their friendship strengthened, it was prudent to keep her thoughts to herself. On the surface it seemed that Molly's appraisal of the future was as ill-founded as was the captain's decision to lower a boat into the churning Columbia and send an innocent woman to her death. Ingrid bit her tongue, reserving her insights. They wouldn't matter to Molly anyway. Her only female friend in America was a different sort. At times she could be as rough and garish as the gillnetters she mocked. Her mannerisms and criticisms did little to raise Ingrid's hopes.

The rise in Molly's voice interrupted the sadness beginning to encompass Ingrid. Her sudden explosion into voluminous laughter couldn't help but shake Ingrid from her thoughts. "Can you believe this!" Molly howled. "Mrs. Sorensen has dubbed her new boardinghouse the Weston Hotel! That building is a rathole waiting to burn. Can you imagine the gall of that woman? New, my eye! Her husband bought an old warehouse and they put in two-seaters. Tsk! I can't believe they call that news. Everybody's just looking to get some free publicity. Can't pull the wool over my eyes!"

The back door opened and in walked Olof. Ingrid eyed him with extreme caution, as if meeting him for the first time. He was part and parcel of this new world, and she was not, nor did she intend to be. What she remembered of him had surely been defiled.

He dropped into the seat next to her casually, accepting these odd surroundings as his home. "Feeling better?" he asked in Swedish.

"Much," Ingrid replied in American, "very much."

Olof's eyes surveyed her from head to toe. Just as it had been in Sweden, he was hungry for her, lusting for her touch at that very instant.

Ingrid looked away, uncertain how long she could keep up this facade. She wanted answers from him, some guarantee she was doing the prudent thing.

"Marry me today?" he asked in Swedish.

Molly glanced up from the newspaper, and her bulging eyes leveled themselves upon Olof. "Nothing so rude as someone talking behind your back. Either say it straight out, or keep your mouth shut. Only American spoken here!"

Although the comment hadn't been meant for her, Ingrid gritted her teeth. Molly had a way of putting her nose in where it wasn't wanted. Already, Ingrid had forfeited her Bible and few other possessions to the Columbia. Now it was her self-respect being threatened. Everywhere Ingrid turned, she found reason to be suspicious.

Olof rose from his chair and walked around the table. He rested his hands on Molly's shoulders and gently massaged them. "Getting ready for their arrival?" he asked.

"Yeah," Molly replied. "A lot of fuss in the future. Don't see as how an old woman such as myself can keep pace with it all."

Ingrid watched with amazement as Molly slumped comfortably in her chair. She was old enough to be Olof's mother, yet the relationship here was clearly not maternal. Her smile was sensual and flirtatious, though it emphasized a mouth filled with yellowed teeth. She placed a hand atop Olof's, pressing it to her shoulder blade. "You'll not be drinking too much whiskey and getting yourself drowned on the river this year, will you?"

"Never," Olof replied. "That river will never take me."

"You see to that, Olof," Molly replied. "You've got the best salmon boat and boat puller on the river."

"What's new in the paper today?" Olof asked.

"Nothing important," Molly replied. "Just some complainers, itching to get a road into the cemetery. Seems to me the dead don't much care where they're buried, do they Ingrid? If you can't reserve a place in life, why should you expect as much in death? Better to drift out to sea where a shark can benefit from your stupidity."

Ingrid was offended. Her survival had somehow upset the natural accord of things, and Molly enjoyed pointing that out. Ingrid could have been shark bait herself, and that would have suited Molly just fine. The lack of civility and compassion in Olof's world was something Ingrid could not tolerate. She got up from the table and carried her teacup to the drainboard. "And to think I likened him to Christ," she thought in disgust.

Olof watched as Ingrid slipped away one more time. His frustration level was again peaking. His fingertips dug into Molly Bochau's shoulder blades. She tensed for a moment, and Olof eased up. His eyes were glued to Ingrid. She was far more beautiful than he recalled, but she was cold ... oh, so cold! She had bested the Columbia but forfeited much in the doing. Olof had no idea how to get through to her, other than to keep his distance. Had he changed so much in the three years he had spent in America that he had become unrecognizable?

He watched as Ingrid rinsed and dried the cup. She started for the door. He needed to keep her from leaving. For some reason, he had the feeling she was curing herself of pneumonia so she could walk out for good.

"In a few days the fishing season will start," he said in Swedish. Ingrid knew the comment was for her benefit, but she didn't know why he'd bother when Molly Bochau was eager to carry on such a conversation. "I'll be gone most of the time," he continued, "and you'll be left to fend for yourself." Molly started to say something, but Olof ignored her and was quickly at Ingrid's side. "Let's step outside and discuss it in private."

Ingrid waited to hear what he had to say. She could tell it was difficult for him to express himself, for he and she were both foundering. Outside, she refused to take the seat offered to her. Instead she leaned against the porch railing and observed the sea gulls circling overhead. She did not know how to put it, but she felt it prudent to return to Sweden. Perhaps it was the coward's way out, but in that far-off land was a little sister who needed her guidance, and a family that spoke her language as well as years of tradition that showed compassion for the dead. America was uncivilized; neither land nor sea were what she had imagined. She could not be her own person here, or even speak the proper words to defend herself. She would trade love for duty if it would bring her some peace of mind.

"Molly's a strange woman," Olof began, "but she runs the best boardinghouse in town."

Ingrid kept her eyes focused on the sea gulls. No words could suffice to describe her misgivings, and talk of Molly Bochau merely added to the problem. Ever since Olof had left Sweden and come to this place called Astoria, she had nurtured visions of how it was going to be ... free and uncluttered, lending itself to a new Sweden rather than a new world. But freedom here meant something different: survival of the fittest, rather than a fostering of the weakest. Perhaps Molly Bochau was not the best example when it came to predicting what Ingrid might become, but Ingrid needed to extricate herself from such uncertainty before her life was indelibly linked to such a male-dominated world. Her mother had warned her that love could blind a woman to foreseeing her future, but at the time Ingrid had thought differently. Now, with the shipwreck ever-present in her thoughts, she had come to respect the wisdom of her mother's words. Love had brought her this far, but where in the world would it lead her next? Ingrid was not one to fail a commitment, but indecision had been firmly planted in her mind, and when it came to a moment such as this, she was without the courage to face it squarely. "This isn't the place where I once hoped to raise my children," she said meekly. "It all seems ... ungodly."

"At times it is," Olof agreed, "but God is in the eye of the beholder." As usual, Olof's words were clear and thoughtful, expressing beliefs Ingrid also shared. They certainly weren't strangers, but people estranged by different expectations. "A man has to live by his own rules and raise his children the best way he sees fit. At least, here on the Columbia, there's an opportunity for a man to better himself and look toward the future. I can earn money here; I can put food on the table. I don't think I have much to do with God, however, so if you're looking for a man with Biblical notions, I'd not be the one to suit you. I don't pretend to know much more than fishing. I thought you understood that."

All their cards were on the table. There would be no ethereal promises from this man who conducted his life according to defined aspirations. Ingrid turned around and looked squarely at Olof. She wanted something other than memories of the shipwreck and her fear of this strange new land influencing her dreams; she wanted to come back to earth and feel the ground beneath her feet. "Hanna," she said, "my little sister Hanna could use my guidance."

Olof turned toward the river, and Ingrid's eyes followed his. If there was something larger for them on the horizon, something more meaningful than old family ties, only he could see it. "I suppose that's true, but I believe America will eventually provide whatever you need, be it comfort or comforting. A person who has bested the Columbia should never fear again. Put it behind you. Forget about Jane and Elizabeth — their time had come; and Hanna will grow and become her own woman, regardless of your concern."

For Ingrid, that was easier said than done. She had wagered her future on one person, a man whose sole desire in life was to fish a river that killed indiscriminately. She was incapable of forgetting the terror. Moreover, her mother had warned her. Childbirth and rearing a family were sufficient responsibility for any woman, and coming to America, estranged from her family, that responsibility appeared overwhelming. "Do you promise to stay alive?" she asked. The question sounded casual, but Ingrid didn't mean it to be flippant. She needed to know he was stronger than the rest, and he wouldn't suddenly disappear from her life like Elizabeth and Jane had done. Without Olof's promise, Ingrid was determined to place duty ahead of love and rid herself of the guilt for being the one left alive. Her mind formed such excuses because she was afraid of continuing down this untraditional path and discovering anymore pitfalls. She had lost her self-confidence.

"Whatever decision you make, I'll always love you," Olof said solemnly. The oath was short while sincere, because any lengthy promises concerning the life he had chosen could end in a lie. She was correct in her observations. Life along the lower river was rough around the edges and certainly a world apart from anything she had known. Olof reached out and laid a hand on her shoulder, hoping somehow to share the strength of his resolve. Ingrid trembled, remembering. They had trusted each other from childhood, each believing in the integrity of the other. Ingrid had to say yes to his proposal or become one of the frail creatures who, according to her father, could be swept away as easily as Elizabeth and Jane had been.

Ingrid gave thoughtful consideration to her final answer. She had come all this way to America, seeking the new life awaiting her. Oddly enough, with that opportunity near at hand, she was shrinking from it. It was incumbent upon her to free herself from outside influences, and resurrect the determination that had bonded her with Olof in the first place. "Well, you can see that I'm here!" she blurted out nervously. "I've traveled all this distance, and a promise made should be a promise kept." That said, she and Olof embraced. It wasn't like any of the childhood hugs they had shared in the past. They were wrapped securely in each other's arms, enjoying the moment for what it would lead to.

The small group walking up the street toward the Finnish Evangelical Lutheran Church created quite a stir. Everyone was staring at them and, in particular, the mismatched coupling of Henry and Molly, who lagged ten paces behind. Ingrid dropped Olof's arm and fidgeted with the pink and blue wild flowers she had affixed to the golden braids crowning her head. Though the skies were clear, the afternoon wind was a nuisance. Molly's voice was typically critical, cursing both her petticoats and the corset that made the event too restrictive to suit her fluid style. Nevertheless, the broad smile on Henry's face evidenced the fact that he was unabashed by the whole affair. At times he dipped into the basket of rose petals Molly had brought along, and strewed them across the planked street to the delight of the young women who watched from the windows of the whorehouses. A gillnetter was getting hitched. The small wedding party was history in the making.

The pastor, J.J. Hoikka, was there to greet them. The church was cozy and new and, to Ingrid's surprise, filled with witnesses. It was a social affair, something to pique the curiosity of many. The ladies were outnumbered, but Molly's presence was sufficient to tip the scales. She made no bones about preceding the couple up the aisle and exchanging her "How have you been?" with old acquaintances and strangers alike. Ingrid had expected as much; propriety was not one of Molly's long suits.

Ingrid, truly beautiful this day, restrained Olof until Molly had cleared a space for herself in the front pew and given Henry a jerk on his coat sleeve to demand his presence alongside her on the bench seat. His buttocks hit the pew with a thud and raised a few snickers, but Ingrid stood her ground. She was not going to relinquish this cherished moment for anything. The fire in her was resurfacing, and Olof liked what he saw. Together they made a stately couple, covering the short distance arm in arm and meeting the pastor in front of a respectful audience.

The pastor spoke in Finnish, but from the cadence of his chosen sermon it was clear he was repeating something taken from the Bible. Ingrid watched his lips and supplied her own meaning. He hesitated briefly, long enough to allow one of Molly's grumbles to surface in the background. Ingrid quickly supplied Molly's exact thoughts: "Only American spoken here!" But at the moment, the language in use was irrelevant. Ingrid concentrated on Olof's solemn face, certain the pastor's words had not been lost on him, he deeming them appropriate for the occasion. The exchanging of vows went quickly. Olof translated the brief list into Swedish, and Ingrid supplied a "yes" in American, causing those in attendance to leap to their feet and cheer. The newlyweds each signed their names to an official document, and the ceremony concluded with a shower of rose petals supplied by Molly. Henry discreetly disappeared.

There was no such thing as an extended honeymoon with the fishing season under way. Olof joined the ranks of gillnetters on the river, and Ingrid applied herself to the process of becoming assimilated. She earned their board and room by cooking and cleaning for the male tenants, who occupied every bed available at the boardinghouse, just as Molly had predicted. The two women rubbed elbows from time to time, but Ingrid was regaining the courage to stand up for herself. Some of the men eyed her askance and needed to be put in their places. Her desire to fulfill her wifely duties outweighed the displeasure of what she saw and heard in Olof's absence. Astoria was a strange place, with the best and the worst vying for attention. "It is better not to judge what one cannot understand," she reassured herself. "If Olof is content with this life, then so be it."

Chapter Two

~ ~ ~ ~ ~ ~ ~ ~ ~ ~ ~ ~ ~ ~ ~ ~ ~ ~ ~

1876

During the first month of the fishing season, the spring freshets swelled the Columbia River, and every drift was bountiful beyond belief. The fast-moving, silty waters inspired the migration of fish upriver, and runs of forty-pound chinook salmon could be found most anytime, or anyplace, the gillnetters laid out their nets. When the fishing boats regaled the river by running downwind under full sail, they boasted of their easy compensation while succeeding to the appellation Butterfly Fleet.[2] But moving into the month of June, the river was not as generous with its silver wealth. As the mountain run-offs diminished and the river's

---

2. When the term Butterfly Fleet actually came into use remains undocumented. It applied to those instances when the boats ran downwind with a second spritsail or large jib set opposite the main. If fishing, the single spritsail rigging was the norm.

clarity returned to normal, night fishing became the best method to coax the wily salmon into the nets. With this change in methodology, other things also underwent revision. The cover of night provided an opportunity for the unscrupulous ranks of fishermen to defy common law and impinge on what were rumored to be greener pastures. More and more unwelcomed boats from competing canneries converged upon the lower river's fifth drift, a prime fishing ground that began west of Booth's Cannery and terminated off Smith's Point.

Olof cursed the uninvited competitors as he lent Henry a hand and they dismantled the spritsail and stowed it forward in the open fishing boat. He tossed the gaff hook into the stern, although the prospect of landing a forty-pounder was highly improbable. Not only would the net have to be laid out in a zigzag pattern to feed it into a limited area, but the ebb tide, in combination with a westerly wind, resulted in steep, choppy waves that made handling it a difficult venture. Henry laid to the oars, pitting his muscular upper arms against the river; Olof balanced himself in the stern and overhauled the net, being careful to keep the corkline free from the leadline so it would act as a wall in the water. He motioned with his hand when he wanted Henry to change directions. Overhead the appearance of stars, making overtures in the sky, seemed insignificant when compared to the number of salmon boats scattered across this section of the Columbia's surface. Olof, the one responsible for filling the fishlocker, had a sour note of reproach stuck in his throat.

Eventually the double-ended salmon boat turned stern first, aligning itself with the net as it drifted downriver. Henry relaxed his rowing and put a harmonica to his lips. He blew a few chords, then spoke to his partner. "You might as well settle down," he said confidently. "We've never been skunked yet."

Olof couldn't afford such certainty. He was the fisherman of the two, and laying out the net in such a pattern wasn't his intention. It wouldn't provide the optimum coverage needed to outwit the wily salmon, yet the number of nets crisscrossing their drift made it impossible to do otherwise. The captain of another boat had usurped Olof's position, a position rightfully belonging to him. He tensed up, worried about the future implications of this congestion on the lower river. The salmon canning industry, only a decade old, was already out of control, employing opportunists to do an honest man's work. Olof was bracing himself against something more unsettling than the river's chop; he was fortifying himself against the inevitability of war. Henry shared his captain's concern, though he couched his predictions in less-ominous terms. "We'll still make a buck or two," he said soberly. "In spite of these other salmon boats, there'll always be enough fish to go around."

Olof remained unconvinced. This very evening, time was waning. At thirty-eight minutes into the following day, the tide would go slack and a good effort would be wasted. Still, there was little he could do about the situation, other than to heed Henry's advice and assume that the abundance of fish moving upriver would compensate for their poor positioning in an overcrowded drift. It was time to alter the mood. He spat over the stern and tried focusing his thoughts elsewhere. "How much money have you got set aside by now?" he asked Henry.

"Enough for one passage," Henry answered. "Two more years of good fishing, and I'll be able to send for the whole family."

Being part of the success engendered by the newly burgeoning fishing industry, a gillnetter might easily become too Americanized; so independent that old promises could be easily discarded in the shuffle. Such was not the case with Henry; Henry had both his head and heart in the right place. He was indentured to a cause larger than himself, and he was not ashamed to divulge his enthusiasm. "The old folks make quite the couple," he said proudly. "In the Old Country, everyone says they're like Siamese twins, joined at the jawbone. Pa says something, and Ma is bound to repeat it word-for-word. I know they won't leave the Old Country separately; they'd rather die together than live apart. And my two younger brothers are much the same: where one goes, so goes the other. They have jobs in the homeland, hoping to set aside enough income to help out with their passage. As soon as they arrive, I suspect they'll be canvassing the waterfront, looking for a cannery to rent them a boat. They are hard workers and honest by nature." Henry paused momentarily and scratched at the woolen cap where it rubbed against his forehead. He had just stumbled across another aspect of his family's character requiring edification. He got that boyish homesick look on his face; the one that said he was emotionally involved in each and every aspect of bringing his family to America. "But my mother won't take to boardinghouse life, because she's the one in the family who's determined to do for herself. She'll insist on having potatoes from her own garden, and a place to air the laundry where the neighbors can't see it. She's a sturdy Finnish woman and doesn't take criticism from anyone ... other than Pa. But her heart is in the right place, like your Ingrid's, though she's not so sweet. I suppose being the only female in the family, she had to toughen up a mite, expected to split wood and wear a few unsightly calluses."

Olof began to relax. The idea of Mrs. Hihnala and Molly Bochau in the same town tickled his funny bone: Molly Bochau would be inspecting the Hihnala's laundry no matter where it got hung. He wondered if his partner had thought about the unlikely combination, and what would ensue when Molly began insinuating her rather strange set of standards on someone of her own generation. Still, Henry's well-thought-out plans were to be commended, and he would overcome any minor conflicts as they arose. There were few like Henry; only a handful of young men considered themselves in light of a bigger picture. Olof could almost bring himself to believe in such generosity. There were reasons for fishing that far outweighed the requirements of the male ego, including the betterment of people like Henry's soon-to-emigrate family. A mediocre catch was better than none, and every evening's drift counted for something. Henry was a font of good advice: there were things worth fighting for, and minor tribulations, such as this evening's discouragement, that weren't worth worrying about. Tomorrow evening would be different. Henry cupped his harmonica in his hands and started off on the lively wanderings of a Scandinavian polka. Olof took a seat next to him and watched the pale light of the moon highlighting the depression in Saddle Mountain. The river could be either crowded or serene, depending on one's outlook. Henry's optimism had a way of putting things into perspective.

The tide had gone slack before they reached the bottom of the drift; nevertheless, it was time to haul in the net or the fish would back out of the diamond-shaped webbing. Henry applied himself to the oars and kept the boat in line as Olof overhanded the gillnet aboard. Nothing. Not one salmon. *"Gud in himmel!"* Olof exploded. Henry was too aghast to speak. They'd never been skunked before.

Olof shook his fists at the stars. The cannery required one-third of the boat's gross income in payment for the boat and net rental, and, of the remainder, the boat puller received only a third. Henry could ill-afford fishing for a captain who came up empty-handed. Olof was disgusted with himself. From the evening's outset, he'd known they were poorly positioned. His experience had taught him better; a man was responsible for designing his own luck. A firm hand fell on his shoulder. "Don't take it too hard," Henry said judiciously. "It can happen to the best of them."

"But not to me," Olof responded sharply. "Not to me."

∞

Henry considered taking along his revolver, but on second thought, he stowed it beneath the three-foot-deep decking at the bow of the boat. They tied up to the whiskey scow, stern first, and heaved the anchor off the bow. Theirs was the only boat moored at the floating establishment; it appeared their bad luck was a unique event and would die its own death unbeknownst to others. True, it wasn't like this Swedish-Finnish partnership to frequent a drinking establishment midweek, but it wasn't like them to come up empty-handed, either. "You're certain Ingrid won't get worried?" Henry quizzed his lanky partner. Olof curled his lower lip and let it go at that. The means by which a man came to terms with himself were of no concern to a woman.

The floating scow was moored in quiet water just inside the eastern tip of Desdemona Sands, not far from the hazy after-hour lights of Astoria. The barkeep was asleep in a chair next to the wood stove. The environment appeared completely innocuous except for the stagnant air, saturated with eye-irritating smoke. Olof propped the door open with a chunk of cedar, borrowed from a woodpile that was neatly stacked along the deck surrounding the outside perimeter of the one-room structure. Henry sauntered over to a makeshift bar constructed from parallel boards laid end to end across three oak barrels. He picked up a bottle that had been left mid-span of the boards and consumed a full swig of whiskey before passing it off to Olof. The barkeep squinted at them for a while but maintained the pretense of being asleep. When the time was right, he leapt to his feet. "Did you young bucks plan on paying before you backwashed into that bottle? Or did you just figure on getting roaring drunk and leaving here on the toe of a boot? Well ... I've got the boot, mind ya'. Either pay up first, or get the hell off these premises before I'm obliged to remove you forcibly."

Olof chuckled. The barkeep's ferocity belied his physique. In a word, the middle-aged man was puny; at best, his robust threats were comical. Regardless, he strolled the length of the bar with an air of confidence and took a stance directly beneath the kerosene wall lamp. Still, the lantern light only confirmed the obvious discrepancy between the man's appearance and behavior. His mouth was small and pinched ... good for little more than dispensing spittle. His shoulders were half the width of Henry's, indicating a man incapable of mustering a good defense. His hair was greasy and matted to his head — a sign that women also paid him little heed. Yet, both of his ears were misshapen and ragged around the edges. Olof couldn't help but stare at the cauliflowered appendages, looking for something more substantial.

"They're from years of being in the ring," the barkeep growled, "and unless you want to partake in a little demonstration of my boxing prowess, I suggest you demonstrate your ability to pay by placing some coins on the counter."

Olof held firmly onto the neck of the bottle as he dug around in his pants pocket to withdraw a couple of quarters, the equivalent of two forty-pound salmon. He slapped them down flat-handed on the bar with a thud. He was in a foul mood to begin with and did not appreciate this man who seemed eager to test his constitution on a night when it had already suffered a great indignity. The barkeep was a nuisance, like a fly attracted to his sweat. "You own this place?" Olof asked abruptly.

The barkeep slid the quarters off the bar and into a can. "Certainly not," he replied tartly, apparently relieved not to have that particular distinction. "It belongs to Danny, the man who runs the Dockside Tavern on Astor Street."

Henry noted one obvious discrepancy, however, and said as much. "But the Dockside Tavern provides drinking glasses along with its whiskey."

The barkeep shifted his attention from the tall, red-headed Swedish immigrant onto Henry. Henry was of a much stockier build. It was obvious which of the two was the boat puller and which was the captain. They were a pair of transient gillnetters, men who would not be readily missed. It was not even worth the effort to check on the rented salmon boat assuredly moored outside. "In this establishment, you always pay before you're served anything," the barkeep retorted. "I think I've said as much before."

Henry obliged by placing two additional quarters on the bar while Olof filled the two glasses set before them, yet the completion of the transaction failed to interrupt the barkeep's study of Henry's physique. Being sized up in such a manner was the normal precursor to a fight, yet there was nothing in evidence to bring them to blows. Henry, like Olof, felt uncomfortable in this man's presence — he was surely a strange one. "Where were you fighting?" Henry queried. "Boxing isn't popular around these parts."

The barkeep had to rethink his first impressions. For a moment his eyes strayed and his words were less certain. "So, you're from around here and still know something about the sport of boxing?"

Henry had no desire to share his personal history, but it seemed the barkeep was determined to stick his nose in where it was not wanted. "Name's Henry and my partner's is Olof. And you are...?"

There was a pause prior to the barkeep's reply. "They call me Jim. Jim Harney."

"Well, Jim Harney, I guess I'm from around here as much as anybody else is," Henry replied. He considered his answer more than generous and raised his glass and drained it.

Olof thought better of refilling his glass and raised the bottle directly to his lips. The consumption of each measured glassful was akin to the loss of another salmon. The barkeep had what Molly would term gall, asking too much for something worth so little. The bottle wasn't even labeled, meaning it came dirt cheap from the moonshiners who lived in the mountains. "So, what's this so-called sport of boxing?" Olof grumbled, half-slurring his words. "Can't you answer Henry's question straight out? The man asked you where you were fighting."

The timing was impeccable. Jim Harney pursed his lips and diplomatically tabled Olof's request. "I'd be glad to explain all about it, but it seems I've got other customers waiting."

Both Henry and Olof glanced over their shoulders. Four men were coming through the open doorway, meandering casually toward the makeshift bar. Henry kept track of their arrival, while Olof perused the interior of this nondescript establishment. The floating structure, rectangular in shape, had but one entrance cramped in the corner of a longer wall. The bar, then the wood stove, stood opposite the entrance, occupying most of that side of the room. Two square tables and a dozen chairs were in the area of the wood stove and beyond, stuck back from the inadequate light provided by the single kerosene lamp which illuminated the area behind the bar. There were no windows; not even a crude ornament had been hung to dress up the rough-hewn walls. It was a dark and dingy place, having only the lure of whiskey to bring it business.

Eventually, three men came forward and lined up at the bar to Henry's left. Henry watched as the fourth member of the party lagged behind, and with a polished boot kicked aside the wood block wedging the door open. It struck the narrow walkway outside before splashing into the river. When the door slammed shut, the last entrant connected with Henry's look of disapproval, but he made a point of rubbing his open palms up and down the sleeves of his jacket, sending the message that the chilly night air was the offender ... not him. He then approached the bar resolutely and elbowed himself between his fellow companions and Henry. He reeked of cologne.

Olof observed Jim Harney as he served the new customers. There were marked differences in his routine, beginning with the presentation of a labeled bottle of whiskey which was displayed for the customers' approval, followed by the unsolicited appearance of four accompanying shot glasses. The once-menacing barkeep happened to overfill a glass and the resulting puddle elicited an apologetic grin, directed at the man who stood to Henry's left. This customer immediately diverted the attention away from Jim Harney by drawing his companions into a stilted conversation. In the meantime, the barkeep lifted the glass from the makeshift bar and used his shirt sleeve to wipe up the spill. Olof was confused by Jim Harney's sudden change in attitude. The barkeep had been demoted to an obscure and bumbling nobody, begging the sufferance of these strangers. Olof was about to say as much to Henry when the man at the far end of the bar motioned to the one drenched in cologne, and all four of the new arrivals took their drinks and departed for a table in the far depths of the room. Olof kept his eyes trained on Jim Harney, however, because he'd failed to collect money from these customers, either before or after filling their requests. Olof was incensed by the inequity.

Jim picked up the same bottle that Olof and Henry had been drinking from and refilled their glasses. "For such good customers," he muttered, "a free round."

Olof pushed aside both his glass and the bottle. "I always pay my way," he replied in a guttural voice. "I don't take something for nothing." He reached into a pocket and withdrew a tin of chewing tobacco.

Henry turned a deaf ear on whatever was transpiring between Olof and the barkeep, and kept a vigilant eye on the other patrons. Since they had chosen to convene as far away from the lamp light as was possible, it was difficult to assess them individually, but fortunately two of them were so alike that they could be thought of as being one and the same. Each of these twins was thick through the upper torso, much like Henry, and both were slovenly attired in ill-fitting, wrinkled clothes. The third man was slim, wiry and awkward, at times waving his hands in the air with childish abandon. The fourth, smelling like a dandy, was over-dressed for the occasion. He continually ran his fingers along the lapels of his suit jacket, appreciating the quality of the fabric. None of the quartet was a gillnetter, not one of them smelled like fish flesh. "Are you acquainted with them?" Henry turned to the barkeep. The tone of his voice conveyed a forcefulness, meant to exact the truth from the spent boxer, regardless of the man's evasive tactics. Henry felt uneasy, suddenly mistrustful of his immediate environment. There were kidnappers lurking along the Astoria waterfront, and for each seaman who jumped ship to become a gillnetter, an unsuspecting fisherman or farmer was found to take his place. It was a sordid business and probably transpired in places such as this.

The barkeep was glad to be diverted from Olof's riveting stare. "Haven't the slightest idea who they'd be," he answered calmly. "I've never laid eyes on them before."

Henry tried rephrasing his inquiry, though he was tiring of the man's lies. He, too, had noticed Jim Harney's obsequious behavior when the so-called strangers walked in. "Well, they've sure come a fair distance in the middle of the night to wet their whistles!" Henry exclaimed cynically. "You must have quite a reputation to draw those landlubbers way out here. What's your secret? Your whiskey is of the local variety. In fact, it has a bitter taste to it."

Olof rested a hand on Henry's shoulder to steady himself. He was light-headed, feeling woozy. The scow was listing sideways on a twenty-foot swell, and he was perspiring unnaturally. He could drink any man under the table; a half-bottle of whiskey should not have this effect. He careened across the room toward the door and ran headlong into one of two slovenly dressed henchmen blocking his path. His opponent responded with a sinister grin. Olof returned the challenge by grazing the stranger's cheek with a wad of chewing tobacco, then shoving him aside. The two assailants immediately came together, wrestling Olof by his upper arms and pressing him to his knees. Olof freed one arm and locked onto an ankle and twisted it. One of the men fell, striking his head against the wall as he buckled under.

Henry had a gun barrel thrust into his chest. He was temporarily at the mercy of the dandy. The man's foul breath co-mingled with his own excited gasps as he heard the pronouncement: "You'll sign some papers and earn $30 dollars a month for four months. Room and board included. It's the only deal you're going to get. I suggest you take it."

Across the room, Olof was securely pinned to the floor by both the wiry fellow and a brawny companion. One of the assailants was apparently unconscious, crumpled up where he had collapsed. From Henry's perspective the scene lacked credibility, particularly Olof's unnatural posture on the floor. Jim Harney had disappeared. Henry considered his options. What reply would buy him and Olof some time? "Sure," he replied as the walls began moving, "sure thing. So, where do we sign? I could use some guaranteed income. My fishing partner, over there, ain't got the touch."

There was urgency in the dandy's voice. "Not here! You'll sign the papers later." As the dandy delivered his answer, Henry tried stepping out of the line of fire, but his balance was impaired. He heard the gun being cocked and thought better of relying on his coordination. He stayed put, waiting for further instructions. Flight was not a viable alternative until he could bring the effect of the whiskey under control. The nameless dandy waved his gun at Olof. "Get up and get moving!" he shouted.

Through blurred vision, Olof saw nothing of the gun and was dragged to his feet. The two men kept him under control, gripping him by the upper arms and applying pressure to his shoulder blades. The wiry man opened the door, and he was escorted into the night. He recognized the shape of a longboat immediately. No way in hell was he going for a ship ride! Even in his drunken stupor, he wasn't about to leave his sweet Ingrid for ports in China, Australia or South Africa. He thrashed around violently, driving the wiry man into the woodpile and sending the other escort backward into Henry. A gunshot rang out. Olof was incapable of regaining his equilibrium. He fell forward and landed in the salmon boat. Another shot was fired, grazing his shoulder. He could make out Henry's garbled voice trying to rise above a struggle taking place on the narrow walkway fringing the scow. He rose up on his knees, but someone grabbed him by the neck and choked off his air. Henry's gun was in the bow of the boat, while he was in the stern. His assailant, a man heavier than himself, was getting the better of him. Olof tried to wrench himself free of the stranglehold, but the fingers bearing down on his windpipe were too strong for his weakened state. His hands fumbled around the floorboards until they found the hook lashed to a short wooden handle, the instrument he used to gaff the salmon. He gripped the handle firmly and struck his adversary in the thigh. The man swore and released his grip.

Henry was so badly wounded that he was no longer useful to the kidnappers. The man with the gun walked over his limp body to help subdue the redheaded Swede. He reloaded his gun and pointed it downward, into the stern of the salmon boat and the back of Olof's head. Olof swung the gaff hook around and knocked the weapon into the river. The wiry man was frantically undoing the half-hitches that secured the longboat to a dock cleat, but the man Olof had wounded was not yet ready to give up the battle. He struggled with Olof for control of the gaff hook.

Whatever drug had been introduced into the whiskey was extremely powerful. The more effort Olof exuded to protect himself, the more potent the poison became as it surged through his veins to immobilize him. During those few split seconds, he was incapable of seeing it coming. The gaff hook tore across his face, ripping his skin wide open like a piece of filleted salmon. He screamed out with such agony that the crimpers thought him dying. They quickly fled for the longboat. He heard the frenzied oars splashing in and out of the water. He also heard Henry's weak voice calling to him from what seemed like another century. "Let them go, Swede Olof ... we'll get them later .... I'm bleeding badly." Olof had to organize what little wits he had left and stop the bleeding from his face. He rolled Henry aboard the salmon boat and took to the oars. The belated arrival of fog was a blessing: the dampness diverted his attention from his own wounds until he had gotten Henry to shore.

∞

It was of little solace, but Ingrid was assured by the stranger that both Olof and Henry were fortunate to be alive. She eyed the speaker tentatively through the mesh of the screen door, wondering why he had come to offer up such consolation. "I'm a representative of the Columbia River Fishermen's Beneficial Aid Society," he explained. Graciously, Ingrid allowed him entrance. She left him alone in the sitting area and excused herself to the kitchen to prepare tea. Though the man was properly attired to visit in the afternoon, it was apparent he felt uncomfortable with the circumstances. He hemmed and hawed until consuming several of Ingrid's cookies, then daubed his moustache with the corner of his napkin in a self-conscious gesture.

"Ahem!" he began. "We at the Beneficial Aid Society, of which your husband had the forethought to become a member, find this matter ... extraordinary. We're not entirely certain the benefits were meant to cover such an incident. In fact, if your husband, Olof Andersson, were to die, heaven forbid, he might not qualify for burial expenses. It is sad, but true, that your husband was not acting as a gill-netter when the trouble befell him."

"Oh, mercy!" Molly blurted out from the settee. "When's a gillnetter not a gillnetter? He's white and works for a cannery, doesn't he?"

Ingrid, the one who should have considered the news shocking, did not. She reached for the serving platter during Molly's interruption and offered their guest another cookie. Not one iota of this grisly affair made any sense to her. "You're taking this quite well," he commented. Ingrid nodded her head in agreement.

"I think you oughta show the bum the door," Molly said decidedly as she flashed looks of annoyance in Ingrid's direction.

"I think I'd better be going," their visitor announced quickly. He took his hat from the end table as Ingrid rose from her seat. "Nice talking to you, ladies," he stammered.

"Don't let the door hit you on the way out!" Molly yelled in his wake. "Of all the gall! So it didn't have anything to do with the gillnetters, hmm. Hope the ebb tide carries you out to sea!"

Ingrid's calm was abandoning her. What had Olof done to himself? His beautiful face had been butchered, yet the rest of the world continued to argue over the importance of the event. Ingrid could see the results, but why couldn't they? Whenever she tended to her husband's minor shoulder wound, a small area grazed by a bullet, she feared she would make too much of the depth of the stitches on his face and the unnatural skin tone surrounding them, and she would scream. Her eyes could follow the damp cloth as she patted the wound extending from his earlobe to the corner of his lip, affording what comfort she could; but her words of solace were hollow. She seemed to see two people looking up at her: Olof her lover, and Olof the gillnetter. She loathed the latter ... the one who would make her no promises. "I think I'll go look in on Henry," Ingrid said to Molly. With quick steps, she headed down the hall to concern herself with the man on whom she placed the preponderance of guilt.

Henry's face was drawn and tired, but at least it was intact. From his waist to his armpits, however, he was wrapped in bandages. A bullet had shattered several ribs and nicked a corner of his lung. The doctor had claimed that he had never seen two men lose so much blood and survive. He'd also said something about them being such good friends that the tall one (referring to Olof), had refused to have his wound tended to until he was certain his partner would live. What the doctor had explained as a selfless and almost heroic act, Ingrid could not fathom. She saw things differently.

She sat in the chair next to Henry's bed and held his hand. She was well aware that the onset of infection could kill him. Henry's eyes were open and focused on the ceiling. "Do you want me to send a letter to your parents?" she asked him. "I can find someone to write it in Finnish."

"No," he answered, "later. How's Swede Olof?"

Ingrid bit her tongue. Tears were beginning to course down her cheeks. "He's all right," she responded. "Resting."

"His face?"

"Not so good."

Though Henry's hand had an unnatural feel about it, powerless to perform the work for which it was designed, it bent around her fingertips and squeezed down ever so gently. Ingrid was more confused than ever. The blame belonged somehow with that accursed Columbia River, she thought, and the way it influenced their lives. She remained on the outside, looking in.

∞

At times Ingrid could detect the subtle difference in Olof's way of thinking; at other times it was so well masked behind his facial disfigurement that she looked away. She knew he was plotting revenge. At night, when she lay next to him, she dared glimpse the deep scar on the left side of this face, believing that if such a grotesque mark had been left on her own face, she would surely consider suicide, or escape to the furthest recesses of the earth to live in isolation. She had to remind herself constantly it was not she who had been brutalized, yet as a witness to the fitful dreams haunting her husband's sleep, she would often pull the pillow over her face and cry out her frustrations. Regardless of his gruesome visage, he remained virile and expectant. She was caught in the middle.

Henry's convalescence was a different matter. His breathing was slow and labored, and at times it seemed he might not make it. A simple cough could send him into convulsions. During the first two weeks, sitting up in bed was more than he could manage. But Olof began making trips to the cannery, and Henry was determined to follow. Soon he began dressing and going for short walks. Thereafter he spent the afternoons at the cannery, mending the nets and performing other, less-arduous tasks. It was obvious something was driving him to heal his own body.

When Olof and Henry finally returned to the drift, Ingrid could detect a nervous edge about them both. She knew their skittish behavior had nothing to do with fishing, but rather the reassertion of their masculinity. The whiskey scow had been removed from its moorage at Desdemona Sands, and purportedly Olof was not optimistic about locating its whereabouts. Unfortunately, neither he nor Henry could clearly recall the faces of the crimpers due to the effects of the drugs. They had to rely on bits of memories, like a strong odor of cologne and general body types. Olof revealed little else in Ingrid's presence, but she had the distinct impression he must have a clue as to where the crimpers might be otherwise he would have let the intrigue die. She waited and worried. It wasn't her place to proselytize the Lord's messages of forgiveness, so vigilance appeared to be her only recourse when it came to matters left unsettled.

One particular night, Ingrid was walking down to the docks to see if the fishing boats were coming in. The intrigue was still foreign to her, yet she had come to realize that the finality of death was not so fearsome as living passively in fear. She followed the rutted riverside trail down to the cannery, finding nothing pernicious about the soft halo forming around the sunset. It was an unsettled feeling in her stomach prompting her to hurry. She recognized Olof by his height. Two other boats were following his, remaining in an unusually tight formation as they headed downriver. Ingrid swallowed deeply. The law of the land and the sea were applied quite differently, but she had to believe that in either court, justice would prevail. As for Olof's ability to dispense justice, she did not know. It depended on who was in control: the youngster who had awkwardly presented her flowers while the other boys stood around jeering, or the Columbia River gillnetter who had been beaten and battered. Olof had always been different from his peers, making inroads where others dared not go. As a child, his height and unusual red hair had separated him from the crowd, making him self-reliant, a trait he had turned to his advantage as he had reached manhood. He had never outgrown his earnestness, his courage. This Ingrid had to remember.

Four other fishermen had volunteered to go along. Any more would have given the attempt unwanted publicity. They were armed. The three boats docked at Swilltown, Astoria's red-light district, and there the vigilantes separated into two groups, one headed by Olof and the other by Henry. Henry's was the first to enter the Dockside Tavern. He hung back as one of his two partners approached the bar to order drinks. The night was young, and the establishment was not crowded. The volunteer vigilantes had no intentions of starting a gunfight. The deal was straightforward: they would help Olof and Henry escort the guilty to the waterfront, and from there they would head out for the evening drift, free of complicity.

The tavern was well-lit and congenial, the exact opposite of the ambience aboard the whiskey scow. Henry thoroughly studied the faces of both the bartender and patrons, and saw no one who stirred his memories. He moved to the far corner of the room and selected a table next to a side-street entrance. One of his fellow patriots was handing him a beer when the door opened, and two men walked directly in off the alley and passed behind him. He got a whiff of cologne which triggered faint memories of a suit jacket and the way in which the wearer stroked the lapels. The man who passed behind him was followed closely by a larger fellow, either a bodyguard or flunky.

Whatever his title, he was poorly compensated for his talents because his dress was shabby. "Go and see if you can find out the name of the man wearing the suit," Henry whispered to one of his companions. "If by any slim chance it's Danny, go outside and tell Olof to meet us at the side entrance."

Thomas Bergman, the fisherman who volunteered, had the personality to meet the challenge. He walked right up to the man wearing the suit and slapped him on the back. "Donald, isn't it? Donald Irvington from San Francisco!"

The man recoiled from the sudden jolt. "Danny!" he blurted out. "It's Danny Bell, and I wouldn't know you if your face was on a wanted poster!" Laughter broke out among a few of the patrons.

Henry heard every word and was satisfied. He watched as Thomas finished acting out his role. The gill-netter backed his way toward the front door, bobbing his head up and down like a man accustomed to making such blunders. The door closed behind him as Henry kicked over the table and shattered a beer stein. Danny Bell was quick to approach the two rowdy drunkards, with his bodyguard one step behind. Everything was going as planned. Henry flashed a gun in Danny's face at the same instant his companion shoved a steel barrel between the ribs of the brawny fellow. The door to the alley opened and there stood Olof. He was now menacing, with a visage to dissuade the fiercest at heart. No struggle ensued when Olof motioned the perplexed hostages into the alley. Although only two of the four assailants were available, these were the ones who had done the damage to his face. Olof prodded the captives down the rungs of the ladder and into the boat with the gaff hook. There he bound them hand and foot and stuffed rags in their mouths, while Henry kept a gun on them. "It's sweet revenge," Henry commented, but for Olof this moment afforded little payment in kind. "Let's just get it over with," he grumbled.

The old sailing ship was low to the water, loaded with canned salmon. No one appeared to be on deck. A ladder was hung over the side. Another ship was at anchor no more than fifty yards away, and Olof watched it more carefully than he did the ship they were about to board. Crimping was illegal, and two gillnetters caught in such a sordid affair would not warrant compassion from a judge and jury, no matter what the circumstances. Timing was everything and, according to the moon's position, Olof guessed they were within fifteen minutes of consummating the deal. Henry quietly brought the boat around to meet the ladder. The air was still and sounds carried. Olof untied the ropes securing Danny Bell's ankles and lifted him onto his feet. The wrist restraints would also have to be removed before he could climb the ladder, but less than a stone's throw away Olof noticed a salmon boat drifting past. His adrenaline began to flow. He kept his eyes on the shadowy configuration of the boat for a few seconds, enough time to allow his upright hostage to jump overboard. He started to dive in after him, but Henry grabbed his shirt sleeve to restrain him. "Don't do it!" Henry said sternly, but Olof's emotions remained out of control. As Danny's upper body resurfaced, Olof leaned down, and with the agility of one accustomed to handling two hundred fathoms of gillnet while dislodging forty-pound salmon, he pushed the man under the water's surface and held him there. It was gratifying, but not gratifying enough. Henry stood silently by, watching and wondering.

In the meanwhile, a mysterious figure had appeared on the deck above them; and he, like Henry, held a gun in his hands. Olof let out an audible sigh of relief. He'd come right up to the moment and had willingly balked. He couldn't kill either man. He dragged Danny from the water and urged him up the rope ladder. The man who had wielded the gaff hook, and scored his face for life, followed.

∞

Ingrid began walking, abandoning the open moorage area for the secluded pathway abutting the sloping hillside. A calm-inducing darkness had settled in among the spruce trees on her right, and to her left, the inky-black river lapped quietly; but along the river few rested, and Ingrid's footsteps were not about to disrupt a world at sleep.

The stench of rotten fish carcasses was overwhelming. The catch of chinook salmon was good that year, and what could not be processed was collecting in pockets along the river's edge. Silhouetted against the last shards of a golden sunset, the canneries seemed regal; but man's industry was often a dirty business. Ingrid had become accustomed to the smell of salmon flesh...earthy when fresh, putrid when spoiled. She observed the first cannery in bewilderment, for it seemed to disregard the tenacity of the men aboard the small fishing boats. Day after day and night after night, Olof faced the treachery of so many unknowns. It seemed wasteful to disregard his efforts in such a careless manner, but he, too, was part of the puzzle. Men could be driven to do strange things when such abundance was there for the taking.

Ingrid wrapped her arms around her chest and recalled a Swedish lullaby, something to test her memory of simpler times. Trusting herself to recall that which was, including Olof's once-Christlike visage, gained her the courage to move forward, one step at a time.

Having passed the walkway leading out to the first cannery, she stopped singing and slowed her pace. She peered into the darkness ahead and the shadows surrounding the next stretch of open riverbank. Something moved. She concentrated on a spot where the moonlight came streaking across the water, crossed the path with lessened intensity, and dead-ended abruptly in a thicket of willows. This particular segment of the landscape seemed so correctly defined as to waylay her fears. Even so, she glanced up the hillside and located the slabwood road beginning next to a cloistered village, known as the Shanties, where the Chinese can makers and fish gutters were housed. From there eastward, the planked route cut a wide swath through the low-growing willows paralleling the river. Having an alternative route was reassuring. If she should find herself in peril, she could abandon her riverside walk and make her way to the boardinghouse via that semi-inhabited route. But she studied the riverside pathway with renewed determination and saw nothing to dissuade her. It wasn't far to the next cannery. Besides, the Chinese laborers were at work from dusk to dawn, traversing the area constantly without fear of sudden movements. Their high-pitched voices carried across the river from the innards of the canneries, conversing as they did most often, with a great deal of enthusiasm. More than likely the fish-gutting crew had caught up with the day's catch and would soon come flooding from the canneries' doors. She wasn't alone.

Halfway between the two canneries, she saw it again. What looked like a dog moved along the water's edge, while investigating the fish carcasses. She had no reservations about walking right past it. The Chinese laborers were streaming out of the cannery behind her, involved in conversations as they headed for their quaint village. Ingrid felt foolish. She resumed the lullaby to renew her confidence and practiced the tonal quality of the lusher rhymes to occupy her mind. The animal started backing away as she came up to it. It growled. She halted dead in her tracks, but her voice continued to drift ahead of her. "Rida, rida, ranka," she sang softly, "Hasten heter Blanka."

The moonlight reflected off the cougar's eyes. The head of the huge cat seemed soft and pettable, but its eyes were deadly. Ingrid stopped singing; childish verses were powerless over such a beast. She began talking to the cat, negotiating with it. "You think you're omnipotent here, don't you? Like the wild winds, strong currents and irascible men. But I'm no threat to you. I'm just a woman, trying to make her way home."

With one shoulder leading the other, the cat was poised to strike. The moonlight rippled down its back while the animal remained as still as stone. It was truly a magnificent thing to consider, so perfectly built that Ingrid could find no fault with it. She stopped her aimless banter. In the blink of an eye the cougar shot past her, and she turned in time to view the melée and hear the screams. The cat lunged at one of the Chinese workers and took him down. Ingrid watched in horror as the fish-gutting knives were raised, and the cougar was hacked to pieces. Then there was a strange wailing noise that sent Ingrid reeling. Again, somebody else might have died in her place.

Ingrid collected her thoughts before entering the boardinghouse. Molly's raucous laughter did not bode well for a meaningful conversation. For several minutes Ingrid stood on the porch and looked through a window, observing the boardinghouse matron cheating herself at solitaire. Ingrid wanted Molly to shed some light on what had just occurred, but she was not at all certain how to phrase her request. Eventually Ingrid gathered her courage and approached the table where Molly was seated. "I think the

Chinese workers have suffered a misfortune," she said frankly. "I think we should send for the sheriff and the doctor."

Without looking up from her cards, Molly made her reply. "Let them do for themselves. A little opium cures most of their ills." She quickly swept the cards from the table and shuffled them repeatedly.

Ingrid could hardly blame Molly for dismissing her request so easily. She frequently failed to make her point. "A large cat," she stammered, "a large cat of some kind came out of the dark and maybe killed one of them."

"A cougar or a mountain lion is what you mean," Molly replied. "But it don't make no difference. The Chinamen heal themselves with Mongolian witchery. Is the cougar still wandering the riverbanks?"

Ingrid shook her head "No."

Molly failed to look up. She observed the rows of cards on the table and began counting out the rest of the deck by threes and checking the uppermost card against the rows. It was as if the incident was of no import whatsoever.

"No," Ingrid said, hoping her voice would arouse Molly's interest. "They killed the cat with knives."

"That's good," Molly replied. "Then there's no need to bother the sheriff. Unlikely he could track down a cat at night, anyway. A cougar just comes by once in awhile, looking for a free meal of salmon guts ... nature's way of cleaning up the waterfront. A Chinaman got unlucky, is all. Don't worry your pretty little head about it. Better to worry about your husband. He's the one who's got a hankering for blood."

Ingrid withdrew from the conversation and quietly headed for her room. If she allowed them to, Molly's suppositions could erode what little faith she had managed to retain. She would never pretend to totally understand the man who blended so naturally with the harshness of this raucous society, but neither would she reduce him in stature to a wild animal, capable of cold-blooded murder.

Early August, 1876

Once Olof and Henry got wind of what all the ruckus was about, they decided not to join the crowd forming at the cannery manager's door. "It isn't worth the time or trouble," Henry commented. Olof was in complete agreement: "Even if the Chinamen are dark-skinned heathens, they don't know anything about fishing. When they fail to bring in any salmon, all their demands will be forgotten." Following this casual exchange of opinions, they went directly to their rack and loaded the net aboard the boat. In light of their abbreviated fishing season, their own success or failure was a far more pressing matter.

The salmon boats were in tent formation as they waited for the tide to turn. The sprits had been turned into ridgepoles and the sails draped over them, in the forward part of the boats, to provide shelter from the weather. Someone aboard one of the nearby boats was playing on a fiddle, while someone else hummed softly to the tune. Both Olof and Henry were nodding off, although Olof continued to struggle against the soothing sounds because it was his watch. They were north-northwest of Desdemona Sands, well inside the mouth of the river. The river was silky and unusually placid. Under the moonlight it looked as solid as a dance floor, waiting for the lights to be raised and the dancers paired. Olof replaced his chaw of tobacco with a piece of horehound candy, hoping his tastebuds would prevail in his war against sleep. Then he heard the strangest sounds, much like somebody clapping out of time to the fiddler's tune. It was such a nonsensical idea that it got his attention. He looked for the source of the riddle aboard the boats in the vicinity but saw nothing unusual except for the fiddler's sprite-like image, perched in the bow of a boat. He settled back and stared at the star-filled sky. It was almost as beautiful and compelling as his sweet Ingrid. He placed a hand against his scar and it felt hot to the touch, searing into his being as surely as if the devil had branded him. It was Ingrid's fidelity that kept him going; she was capable of recognizing the unaltered man within.

The fiddle and accompanying voice fell silent. There was movement aboard that particular boat, as there was aboard many of the others. The tide was turning, and the entire fleet was about to slip upriver with the current. Olof stretched. It was time to dismantle their shelter and get to the business of catching fish. He was just becoming focused when the sounds returned. This time they were accompanied by human moans. Olof reached inside the tent and shook Henry by the shoulder.

Henry crawled out on his hands and knees. He was groggy. "Is it time?" he mumbled.

"Listen," Olof said, "stay very still, and maybe you'll hear it."

The clear night air was bound to give preference to the garbled conversations of the fishermen grouped nearby; nevertheless, Henry succeeded in separating out the eerie disturbance. "What the heck is that?" he asked. "Sounds like an animal being whacked over the head and then gasping for air before it drowns."

"It's a ways off," Olof replied, "more toward the Washington shore. But the night's so quiet and sound carries so far, it could be miles off. It could even be coming from land."

"Perhaps it's coming from the quarantine ship," Henry replied. "Maybe some poor soul has fallen overboard and doesn't have the reserves to save himself."

This time there was a shrill cry. In the foreground the boat pullers were taking directives from their captains to position their boats in drift formation, but Olof maintained his composure and got a fix on the sound's origination. It was emanating from an area even further north-northwest, at a fishing ground situated between Washington State and Sand Island, a drift staked out by another cannery. "It sounds like someone's in trouble," Olof grunted, "but it probably isn't smart to make it our problem when we've got an empty fishlocker to fill."

Again, there was a disquieting moan. It sounded pitiful. Olof was inclined to overlook it, but Henry was not. He laid to the oars and headed toward Sand Island. Olof didn't dispute his boat puller's decision. They were likely sharing the same thoughts, suspecting the existence of more crimpers, who continued to practice their trade in a blood-thirsty fashion.

They rowed less than a quarter of a mile before coming upon the first salmon boat, drifting along without a soul aboard. The oars resembled arms disjointed at the shoulders, dragging stiffly through the water. Olof pulled the boat alongside and got a rope tied to its bow. They towed it toward Sand Island. Another boat was adrift in the immediate vicinity and a third appeared to have been beached. The masts and sails of each boat had been removed and discarded, including the one turned upside down and dragged up on the sand. There were no personal items to be found in any of them, not even the core of a half-eaten apple had been tossed aside for the sea gulls to pluck clean. Olof lit the lantern and inspected the boat on the beach. It confirmed what he and Henry had suspected: all three boats displayed the name of their cannery.

"The tide is wrong to think we'll retrieve any bodies on the island," Henry said solemnly. "They'll be drifting upriver with the current."

"There won't be any bodies to find," Olof corrected his partner. "Whoever did this used the sails to wrap up the victims before they weighted them down and threw them into deep water. They wouldn't be foolish enough to salvage any of the gear; it's all been rented from the cannery and could be identified."

Henry removed his watch cap and scratched his head. There was not any sign of activity on the river; not even a lonely gillnetter was trying his luck on this normally productive drift. The moonlight wove itself among the small stands of willows on the island, but there was no movement, no clue as to where one might turn to find those guilty of such a crime. Olof, however, could not refrain from expressing what was heavy on his mind. "Somebody really had it in for those Chinamen," he surmised.

Henry reached a little further for the obvious conclusion. "And it's all going to come back at us gillnetters. Here's clear proof of some real unscrupulous characters working this river, fishing our drifts as we speak and expecting to break bread with us at the supper table. Whoever did this had a lot of help, and much of that help had to come from our own ranks."

Olof spat in the sand and stomped on the spot with such force as to leave a two-inch-deep impression.

∞

The word finally came to her, the very one she'd read in the newspaper: murder. Molly sat across the dinner table and chuckled at the whole messy affair, but Ingrid could not. Although the names of the fishermen who had returned the boats were not mentioned, the article, too, held them culpable. There were at least forty fishermen gathered around the table in the dining hall to participate in Saturday dinner, and in most cases their behavior was too perplexing to be able to appraise the group as a whole. To Molly Bochau's dismay, five languages were being spoken as the platters of fried sturgeon and boiled potatoes went from hand to hand. In Ingrid's mind, nothing was ever as cut-and-dried as was reported in *The Daily Astorian.* She posed a question to her husband, intent on clearing his good name. "Why did it say that angry fishermen murdered some Mongolians? You and Henry found the boats and didn't have any idea what happened to the fishermen aboard, let alone that they were Mongolians ... and murdered. You should stop by the newspaper office and have the matter cleared up. If the men who disappeared were dark-skinned, I would imagine they were Chinese, from the Shanties. Their families will have no idea what happened to them unless someone gets to the bottom of it."

In the company of the other fishermen, Olof's manners tended to mimic theirs. He wiped his mouth with the back of his hand before answering. Ingrid grimaced slightly but forgave this social infraction in light of the situation. At least he was groomed better than most. Olof cleared his throat, viewing this as being neither the time nor the place to answer such a question. "Later," he answered cryptically.

Thomas Bergman, seated on Ingrid's right, had a question of his own, one shared by many. "Why in the hell did you return those boats, anyway?" he asked heatedly. "It would have been better for us all if you'd burned them on the beach, and left no one the wiser that anything had happened to them dang Chinamen." Thomas concluded his speech in deference to Ingrid: "Excuse me, ma'am. Didn't mean to interrupt."

Ingrid blushed, not in response to the acknowledgment, but from what she had inadvertently begun. Casual conversations had stopped, replaced with disgruntled looks being directed at both her husband and Henry, seated on Olof's left. "Yeah," another fisherman joined in. "Explain why any right-minded gillnetter would think it necessary to return those boats to the cannery. The canner didn't give a hoot when it came to renting out his equipment to Mongolians, so why didn't you force a little humble pie down his throat and let him choke on the loss?"

"Because the canner will simply pass the cost of the boats on to the rest of us," Olof answered calmly, "and that would be one thousand, two hundred dollars taken from our pockets." Henry's head turned, as did many others. Ingrid was startled by this unusual display of diplomacy on her husband's behalf. His comment, nevertheless, seemed to have the desired effect. Each and every fisherman was soon refocused on the generous meal. The war was fought and won in mere minutes. "I still don't understand why it always has to be the gillnetters getting the blame," Ingrid stammered. The room drew in upon her. Bread returned to plates, and all paused for Olof's response. According to those involved in the crime, his wife was poking around in dangerous places not intended for a woman, not even a beautiful one.

Henry leaned over and whispered in Olof's ear. Olof stiffened, hearing Henry's best guess as to where the trouble might come from. "The fellow who called them Mongolians," Henry offered quickly, "he's probably the one to watch out for." Ingrid observed the private exchange in dismay. "I didn't say YOU were involved," she offered apologetically. Laughter erupted. Again Ingrid blushed, but this time she'd been humiliated and shamed. She left the table abruptly, distressed by Olof's apparent refusal to differentiate himself from the others.

Even with a baby growing inside her, Ingrid was determined to do her part. Olof, like most of the boarders, had gone elsewhere seeking employment while Astoria rested beneath a light blanket of snow. He was somewhere upriver with Henry, felling trees, while she was faithfully living up to the small sign in the window: "Sewing 5 cents a rip; 10 cents a button; wash taken 10 cents a tub." Business wasn't booming, but it afforded her enough extra income to open a savings account at the bank. Having her own resources afforded her the luxury of seeing a future with options. Privately, she thought about taking her baby home to Sweden, prior to Olof's return in the spring. Her fealty to a man disfigured by such a combative nature did not bode well for its upbringing. Also, there was the river to take into consideration. Not only was it dangerous and destructive, but it seemed to demand those very same qualities from the men who strove to bring it under control. In America, appearances and approbations were both deceiving. There were no proven allegiances to rely upon when making such a grave decision, and her mother's philosophy was inadequate to bring clarity to her thoughts. "There's no such thing as being one's own person ... there are only people ... duty bound to serve family and country."

Chapter Three

~ ~ ~ ~ ~ ~ ~ ~ ~ ~ ~ ~ ~ ~ ~ ~ ~ ~ ~ ~

1877

Ingrid watched her husband out of the corner of her eye. Their supper guests had come and gone, and even though Olof and Andrew Van Dusen, a local merchant, had shared congenial witticisms at the table, something was amiss. Olof was restless, an indication his mind and mood were changeable. He pumped back and forth in the rocking chair and hummed to himself, oblivious to the world around him. Ingrid could not help but surmise that Olof's restiveness resulted from an earlier comment made by Amy Van Dusen, Andrew's wife. Amy had said matter-of-factly that she felt comfortable being in the company of Swedes because they were a simple and hard-working, God-fearing people. Now, just as then, Ingrid considered the comment unbecoming and assumed her husband had been equally astounded. There were good people and bad people, but no simple people ... even God's idiots, by nature, nurtured insights about the world. Ingrid had never purposely represented herself as being an old-world fixture, and for a number of reasons, she had come to revere God's presence no less than that of the Columbia River's, particularly in light of the odd array of people it attracted and the way in which it presided over all their lives. Perhaps the simplicity she had been associated with came from tolerating such unfounded comments. "A penny for your thoughts," Ingrid said courageously. Olof blotted out the communication, rising instead from the rocker and walking directly to the front door. "I have some business to attend to," he said curtly. Ingrid put down her knitting and watched her enigmatic husband disappear into the night. Again, she and her unborn were left to contemplate where they fit into this alien environment. She had made her choice and would endure the consequences, but her child would not have to suffer such complacency, for he or she would be born American.

The fire hall was only a few blocks away from their new home. The old hand-pumper fire engine had been pulled out onto the street and left there with a large sign stating that it had been condemned by the city and was for sale to the highest bidder. Henry was waiting in the shadows alongside the building, inspecting the new fire engine that had displaced the old. The large doors to the building were wide open, yet the chairless room was incapable of accommodating all the gillnetters who had come to the meeting. Many of the attendees wandered around outside, smoking cigarettes and whiling away the time. Olof started wedging himself into the building, and Henry fell in step. Many of the fishermen were familiar to them both and they exchanged nods, while others were fresh off the sailing ships and steamers. Nonetheless, this gathering was imperative to new and old alike because it was in direct response to a meeting of the canners, convened two months earlier during the off-season. Things needed resolving before they got out of hand. In eleven years' time, twenty-eight canneries had been added to the first built upriver at Eagle Cliff, Washington, and of these, the majority were situated along the banks of the lower river. The protection and propagation of salmon was in question. The dedicated gillnetters needed cohesion to retard rampant growth before it consumed both the fish and their livelihoods.

Olof assumed it would be evident, even to those who had no heritage linking them to the fishing industry, that it was incumbent upon all to help curb this insane growth. Most of the men were immigrants like himself, coming from countries with tired resources, places similar to Sweden, where hopes had been stifled by repressive governments and overpopulation. In America there was a freshness worth preserving; in this room there was cause enough to bring the gillnetters to their senses. The Columbia River was a dream come true, even for those who had never fished the Baltic in stormy weather and exchanged a day's toil for a half-bucket of herring.

At eight o'clock sharp, the meeting came to order. Henry nudged his captain in the arm as they stood side by side against the shiplap wall. "Vote in the Dane for chairman," he suggested, "because he speaks American and sticks to his own drift." Olof scrutinized the fisherman from a distance and saw nothing unworthy about Henry's candidate, a local resident who fished for J.O. Hanthorn, a reputable canner. The voice vote was taken and the Dane lost, defeated by a Finn, who quickly moved to the front of the room, accompanied by both cheers and guffaws. The newly elected leader was followed closely on the heels by a cocky fellow, his boat puller, Olof supposed. Olof took the loss in stride: in America such appointments were not made by the Crown and therefore represented the will of the people, regardless. While Olof remained unmoved by the outcome of the vote, Henry folded his hands across his chest and mumbled something unintelligible. He knew what was about to occur.

The first few sentences came out of the chairman's mouth, and many of those in the fire hall began milling around, talking among themselves. The speaker's voice was clear and strong, but the words were delivered in Finnish. "Oiy," Olof grumbled. (He had missed Henry's meaning altogether when he had mentioned that the Dane spoke American.) There were those who began extricating themselves from the crowd in disgust; a dozen or more exited through the wide-open portals to be joined by those who had been excluded by the lack of room in the building and were ready to leave, given the slightest provocation. Already the solidarity of the gillnetters was threatened. A fair-haired Norwegian tried halting the exodus with a few words of wisdom spoken in a very loud voice: "I thought we were here to head off the wars on the river!" More comments ensued, some in Swedish, Danish, and American ... but many more in Finnish, because the Finnish-speaking population had been delivered a victory of sorts. It was old-world politics, raising its ugly head. From the side of the room, Olof observed the chaos as it reached a fevered pitch. One participant, nevertheless, stood out from the others as he hovered around the newly elected chairman and appeared to show a certain disdain for the crowd's behavior. He stood about six feet tall and was clean shaven. He wore a light-blue, collarless shirt and sleeves rolled up to his elbows. His trousers were dark brown and had a slight sheen, a perfect match for the hair slicked down to his head. Olof supposed the chairman's advisor and boat puller was about his age, but he was too pretty in the face for Olof's approval. A man with a perfect complexion bothered him. Olof stepped away from the wall and let his opinion be known. "Let's get down to the business of fishing!" he shouted in American.

It took a minute or more for the crowd to come to order, but they did. Olof was undeniably a man's man, deserving of their attention. His added height and unusual red hair and beard made an impression, but the scar, the scar on his face, lent him credibility. If they hadn't seen him before, they had heard rumors about the man who had had the courage to take it upon himself to rid the river of some crimpers. And his boat puller, Henry, was a Finn who had willingly thrown in his lot with this brazen Swede. Whatever Olof Andersson had to say, the assembly was willing to hear. "There are two things we need to clear up tonight," Olof said with conviction. "We need to raise the price of salmon to the canners … and we need to see to it that all gillnetters stick to their designated drifts."

Olof made his brief speech and looked in the direction of the chairman. Having outlined the business at hand, he expected the chairman to deal with it. The chairman, a man named Pekka Rytkonen, was in conference with his boat puller, Olavi Pustinen. Both men appeared to be hemming and hawing over Olof's suggestion. Again the crowd became restless. Another speaker in the back of the room voiced his opinion: "Why should we raise the price of fish to the canners when they'll only refuse our catch? And why shouldn't we lay out our nets wherever the fish are? The river's big enough for all of us and more!"

There was thundering applause. Olof appeared to be outnumbered and, except for Henry's support, lonely in his desire to direct the future. Pekka Rytkonen, a middle-aged individual with a receding hairline, was preoccupied with reading the crowd's reaction, but Olavi Pustinen was staring at Olof, sizing him up. Henry poked Olof in the ribs. "Looks like we're in the minority," he cautioned, but Olof wasn't so certain. Olavi's interest in him gave him renewed courage.

There were many things to consider before Olof threw himself wholeheartedly into this dispute. Each cannery along the river had to be well-represented by men such as the outspoken Norwegian to have any impact on the others. Too, it required the skilled, like himself and Henry, to outweigh the influence of the transients, those men who would gladly devalue the fish for short-term gains and would go from drift to drift, encouraging lawlessness on the river.

The canners could always depend on an ample supply of these undisciplined laborers to muddy the waters, but could they always rely on the abundance of fish? This was the one point on which everyone should agree, that the salmon would someday be in jeopardy. Ingrid, though reticent to state her opinions, had once mentioned that there would be no civility on the river until a well-represented population of resident gillnetters could create stability within the industry. But his sweet Ingrid's insights were always compromised by limitations. Astoria was growing from within, as was she, and their child was not to be born into turmoil. Amy Van Dusen's words only reaffirmed such female logic, and in recalling their guest's assertion that he was by nature a God-fearing man, Olof had failed to draw the same conclusion. He couldn't afford to use fear as a motivating factor. Olof had a family to provide for, and a way of life he intended to preserve. With or without the substantive support of the other fishermen, he bolted for the front of the room.

Henry was slow to follow. On the river he and the scar-faced Swede enjoyed an indivisible relationship, but on land there were obstacles to surmount. Perhaps Olof could ignore the Finnish jeers being hurled on them both, but they summoned Henry's ethnicity, bringing it to the forefront. For the moment the group's consternation was derived more from his participation, than from that of the headstrong Swede's. They wondered where his allegiances would lie. If the majority of Finnish gillnetters were opposed to making changes on the river, would he, as a Finn, be a traitor to their cause? Henry had not foreseen such dynamics coming into play. He heard both derision and encouragement, neither of which gave him a clue as to where this stand of Olof's would eventually lead.

The fire in Olof's eyes was enough to back down Pekka Rytkonen, who relinquished the floor to the intense Swede. Olavi Pustinen was another matter. His face was stern and unmoved, and as Olof came to the forefront, he drew within an arm's length of him. Henry took an equidistant stand on the opposite side of the speaker, and the room soon quieted.

"In less than a week we'll be on the river," Olof began, "and a few things need to be straightened out before then. The canners have talked about how many fish we're catching, and about how many they're throwing away. Some of them figure, if it keeps going on like this, somebody will have to plant fish to keep their industry running. But I don't figure it's just their industry; I figure it's as much ours as theirs, and we should do something about the problem before the salmon are gone."

Rather than directing a rebuttal at the speaker, Olavi quickly unleashed his cynicism upon the crowd in Finnish. "Do you think Swede Olof here has the answer?"

Boos ensued, raising Olof's ire to a higher level. He glanced at Henry, knowing his boat puller would have to come into play. Even though it was a fishermen's issue at stake, it was being misconstrued by Olavi Pustinen to appear otherwise. Olof would have to rely on his own resources to overcome this hurdle, but at the moment Henry was staring off into space, himself disillusioned. Confounded by this sudden turn of events, Olof was obliged to hear his adversary's arguments. Temporarily, Olavi had the floor.

"First of all," Olavi pronounced with smug certainty, "there is nothing to be gained by asking more from the canners. As long as there are fish in the river, and there will be salmon in the river for years to come, a price hike to the canners will simply reduce our incomes. They don't care about us; they simply care about amassing money. Most of them have winter homes in California, and endeavor to send their sons to college so they may never need know what honest work is all about. If Swede Olof here thinks that we'll win by setting ourselves up to take a loss at the hands of the rich, then he doesn't have any idea what America is all about. It's the same the world over: each man for himself!"

The room erupted in cheers and Olavi stepped aside, distancing himself from Olof. But Olof was not ready for defeat. The politics at play were echoes of the past, an old game meant to pit the rich against the poor and thereby imbue the issues with emotional chicanery. He drew himself up to his full 6 foot 5 inch stature and shouted over the riotous crowd: "We're missing the point! Who cares about how much money the canners make as long as they leave enough salmon in the river for us to gillnet forever!" Then his voice dropped off, and he said something to Henry. Henry's voice cracked, trying to rise above the din, but he repeated Olof's message in Finnish. Olof then repeated it in Swedish. As quickly as it had begun, the cheering subsided. Again, the brazen Swede and his Finnish boat puller stood united, though outnumbered, but this time they had earned the majority's appreciative attention.

"We'll ask a few cents more per salmon and still make the same amount of money. The canners'll have to stop throwing away fish to make up the difference. And for those of you who keep switching drifts, there'll be a heavy price to pay. A good fisherman should be able to lay out his net most anywhere on the river and keep his family fed."

Pekka Rytkonen raised the obvious question. "What'll we do if the canners aren't in agreement?"

"Then we don't fish!" Olof retorted tersely.

Olof and Henry left the meeting together, but at the road leading to the boardinghouse, Henry pulled his watch cap over his ears and they parted ways in silence. This night, their partnership had nearly foundered. Olof glanced over his shoulder and dismissed the notion that he saw Olavi Pustinen hurrying down a shadowy side street to catch up with Henry. Perhaps Olof was still obsessing over this man who could raise his ire. One out of a hundred people struck him in this fashion, but those who would serve the self-serving, just like Olavi Pustinen had been doing, were usually up to no good. Someday they would meet on the river, and then Olof would have the satisfaction of spitting upwind from the man and seeing what effect it had on a flawless complexion. A little chaw, known as Scandinavian dynamite, was all he would waste on an opportunist such as Olavi Pustinen.

∞

The strike was so short in duration that it failed to make the newspaper. At best, it was an embarrassing rumor never coming to fruition. A few boats hesitated, but they gradually filed out onto the drifts, realizing the futility in making a stand against the larger group of migratory fishermen. Ingrid could sense the disappointment in her husband's lethargic movements, but silently she was relieved because the controversial "emigrant" had been defeated. It was her turn to come to the forefront and rearrange their lives. Even Amy Van Dusen had jokingly referred to her belly as being as large as the governor's mansion and containing the same amount of sway, but only Ingrid could verify the implications in Amy's statement. The Andersson children were soon born, first the boy and then the girl.

The fraternal twins were quite different. Little Henry was strong and healthy, while Hanna Jane had to fight for her life … at least that was what the white-haired doctor had intimated to Olof in private. The last to be born weighed only four pounds, and her cries were fitful, inadequate to expand her lungs and bring color to her cheeks. Ingrid was weak following the prolonged deliveries, but Olof was impoverished by worry. He cradled Hanna in his arms and walked her around the living room, hoping she would see the concern on his face and react accordingly; but her eyes wandered only briefly before shutting, as if she preferred sleep over the struggle that was life. Little Henry eagerly took nourishment from his mother's breast, yet Hanna would refuse. Olof peeked into the bedroom and saw Ingrid's tear-stained face, buried among the pillows. Little Henry was safely cradled in the small crib against the wall, as Amy sat quietly in the rocking chair, watching over them both. Olof picked up his daughter and left the house quietly, stepping into the spring sunshine with his baby girl in his arms.

"What the heck do you think I know about raising babies?" Molly stammered.

Olof just stood there in the boardinghouse kitchen, protecting the tiny bundle in his arms and looking forlorn. "The doctor says she might not make it, and Amy Van Dusen says to rely on the Lord. I figured you'd have a better answer. This young one is sweet and takes after her mother, whereas Little Henry looks like me and is as strong as a mule."

"Little Henry?" Molly queried in amazement.

"Hanna Jane, here, came along second. She's half the size of her brother but doesn't have half the spunk. Regardless, I don't think her mother wants to give her up to the Lord just yet … at least, I wouldn't suppose as much."

It was unlike Olof to speak of the Lord, let alone confess his inability to solve a problem. Molly folded back the blanket gently and understood the cause of the gill-netter's plight. The child was serenely calm, as if the life given her would be taken back shortly. "Will she draw milk from Ingrid?" Molly asked.

"No," Olof replied, "not a drop."

"I said I don't know much about this sort of thing," Molly said nervously, "but years ago I remember a frail one, such as yours, taking a liking to goat's milk. I don't know what the difference is, but it worked in that one instance."

"Anything," Olof replied, "anything's worth a try." He pulled a chair toward him with his foot and sat down. He rocked Hanna gently in his arms and watched Molly as she went about making her brew and heating it on the wood stove. She had gotten a little broader in the beam with another fishing season under way, but her severe hairdo was unchanged, and she clomped around the kitchen like one who was in charge. "A pinch of sugar couldn't hurt," she muttered, "because a pinch of sugar is what Mr. Bochau used to recommend to cure a horse gone off its feed. But then again, he fattened up the chicks on chopped boiled eggs with an eye to the future. Boiled eggs and sugar were two of his favorites, so he'd eat half of whatever food he thought might perk up the stock."

"Then your husband was a farmer?" Olof asked. Molly could spin a fair tale, and at the moment she could say most anything and Olof would believe her. The little girl in his arms had shut her eyes again, and it seemed her angelic pose was permanent.

"No, he was a fur trapper," Molly replied. "He rode a horse and roasted fowl. He was a man of few implements. He liked to wander as far north as Canada and as far east as the Rockies. In between times, he'd come home to see how the chickens were doing. I guess he never thought much about raising children because he was always off wandering."

Molly's voice sounded as matter-of-fact as usual, but it became more directed as she turned to the table and placed the kettle in front of Olof. "Now we've got to see how we're going to get this concoction down that little one's neck," she said. "Try dipping a finger in the milk, and see if she'll suckle it off your finger. We'll take it one step at a time, and hope Hanna Jane is a fighter like her pa."

Hanna Jane rested that night in Ingrid's arms with Olof watching them both from the doorway. Little Henry slept soundly in the crib.

A week later Olof entered the office of *The Daily Astorian* on an errand. It was unfamiliar turf, yet he recognized the man behind the counter from a brief interview he had given concerning the disappearance of the Mongolians. Olof had long since forgotten about the incident, but the man, hiding behind a visor and bushy black beard, was still in evidence. When their eyes met the reporter recoiled slightly — a reflex to which Olof had become accustomed and would use to his own advantage. "I'd like to have the announcement of my children's births printed," Olof said rapidly, intent on keeping the focus upon the business at hand. "It happened about a week or so ago."

The clerk-reporter fumbled around for some papers before spreading them out on the counter. "Exactly when?" he asked. Olof had to think a moment. The interim days and nights were a blur. Between fishing and the feedings of goat's milk, followed by Little Henry's desire to be lifted in and out of his mother's arms, Olof had lost count. "Make it last Monday," he replied. "Ingrid won't care, just as long as everybody knows they were born American."

"Ingrid's the mother?" "Yes." "They?" the clerk queried. "Two," Olof answered, "a boy and a girl." "Do you have the birth certificates?" No. Olof had forgotten to bring along those precious papers guarded so judiciously by Ingrid. He shook his head. "But the boy is called Little Henry, and we call the girl, Hanna Jane." "Last name?" "Olofson and Olofsdotter." "Your name is…?" "Olof Andersson." "That isn't possible, sir, in America your children would be given your family name. Little Henry Anderson and Hanna Jane Anderson." Olof was well aware of American conventions as explained to him by Ingrid, but for the chance of seeing his children's names tied indelibly to him, it was worth playing the fool. As long as they were mentioned in the newspaper, Ingrid would concur with this minor infraction. "Which is it?" the clerk asked. "Is your last name Anderson, or Olofson?" Olof grimaced and his voice became stony as he exaggerated the pronunciation of the double s's: "Andersson. But the children should be named after me. Olofson and Olofsdotter. That's the way it's done in the Old Country." "Where do you live, Mr. Anderson?" Olof gritted his teeth before replying. "Across from the Clatsop Mill." "What's the street address?" "We're two houses from the corner." "How long have you lived there?" "Not yet a year." "What's your occupation?" "Fisherman." "Ah! That explains it." "Explains what?" "Why, you're unschooled in certain practices." Olof laughed, having been given an excuse for trying to promote a white lie. "I just wanted to see Hanna Jane Olofsdotter and Little Henry Olofson in print," he explained forthrightly, "can't blame a man for trying."

The reporter took a second piece of paper and slipped it over the first. "Maybe we can make a deal, Olof Andersson" he replied, and this time his lips replicated the "sh" sound associated with the double s's. Again the two men eyed each other. The reporter offered his hand over the counter in a gesture of friendship, and Olof took it. "Name's John Lord, and I believe we've met in the past. I'd like to get the opinion of a gillnetter as to the truth of two items I'm getting ready to print." Olof nodded his head in agreement, seeing as how the request might result in his having his own way.

"Are you aware that an average of five men per week drown in the Columbia?" John Lord said tersely. "What's happening out on that river?"

Olof wetted his lips before answering. "Many of the fishermen aren't real fishermen, and they don't know what they're doing when they get into rough water with two hundred fathoms of net taking control of their boats."

"I've heard there is too much whiskey out on the river," John countered. "The moonshiners in the mountains have smiles on their faces and money jingling in their pockets … if you get my meaning." He massaged his beard and waited for Olof's reply.

Olof wasn't about to fall into the reporter's trap. "You take greenhorns and put them out on the Columbia, and you've got drownings," Olof replied easily. "The whiskey just makes it worse."

The interviewer tensed up. "How about this?" he asked haltingly, as if Olof's credibility hung on the outcome. "Some gillnetters claim to have tried fishing for salmon in the Pacific Ocean. They say they caught porpoises as large as good-sized hogs and sturgeon almost equal to buffalo in weight, but no salmon. Is this possible?"

Now Olof found himself massaging his beard. "Foolish but possible," he replied, "if the ocean was calm and the currents not too strong. But it would cost 'em a few hundred dollars in nets, so I don't suppose anyone would be that stupid. No, I'm not certain I'd believe that one." Olof sounded lighthearted, pleased to have his opinions heard.

John Lord removed his visor and laid it on the counter. "You're wrong about that fishing expedition into the Columbia," he said gruffly, "just like you could be wrong about a lot of things. When we met before I didn't realize you were the man who escorted Danny Bell and his henchmen out of town, and although you did Astoria a great service," he cleared his throat, " you realize I didn't dare print that story, just as I avoided mentioning your name in connection with the death of those Mongolians, only because there wasn't any proof of complicity. This town doesn't need any more troublemakers, but now that you've got children, I'd assume you'd make every effort to keep your name out of the obituaries."

Olof offered no rebuttal to this man who was so naive as to believe the Columbia River merely an extension of the land. John Lord was good with words but knew little about true fishermen. The real gillnetters were a minority, a breed unto themselves and greatly underestimated by those who judged them as a whole. In America everyone was expected to perform equally, but for those who were weaned aboard their fathers' fishing boats — braving the icy-cold wind of the Baltic Sea as cresting waves baptized them — few survived equality. Olof kept his wits about him and left the building before responding by spitting clear across the street, into an advertisement for ice cream that was painted on the side of the Delmonico Restaurant.

Summer, 1878

"We should call them Bill and Coo," Ingrid whispered in her husband's ear. The reference to the newlyweds meant nothing to Olof, but he nodded his head in agreement rather than showing his displeasure with Ingrid's prating. "Henry is happy with her, and that's all that matters to me," he grumbled.

Ingrid, too, was getting flustered by it all. This event was foreign to her, both ill-conceived and poorly executed. "But at least you can eavesdrop on their Finnish," Ingrid replied in exasperation, "while for me it's like being given the cold shoulder. Perhaps you haven't noticed, but neither Lottie nor her family has given us the time of day since we've been here. They should at least make the effort to include us in the conversation, no matter how awkward. Even Henry seems to be ignoring us."

Ingrid's observations were accurate. Since she and Olof had climbed the steep stairs and entered the home of the bride's parents, their active participation in the wedding day had come to an abrupt end, replaced instead by a view of the river and an assortment of cakes and cookies to pacify them. Lottie's family, emigrants first from Finland and then the nearby state of Idaho and the mining concerns therein, had been avoiding the Anderssons, in spite of the fact that they were the closest thing to family Henry could supply for the hurried occasion. Except, of course, for Molly Bochau, who had gotten all gussied up and attended the nuptials, only to refuse the invitation to partake in the reception. "Where is Molly when we need her?" Ingrid complained. "Whatever happened to 'Only American spoken here?' "

Olof's thoughts had wandered elsewhere. He supposed Henry's in-laws were unnerved by his scar and preferred to keep their distance. Lottie would never give him the time of day, even when she had been inclined to visit his boat as it came and went from the cannery. The oddest part of it all, however, was Henry's reluctance to speak of Lottie when they had set sail and had ample time to share confidences. Expediency had taken precedence over any casual conversations, as they would rush to get to the head of the drift. It was a proven fact Henry liked to talk about the people he loved, but perhaps in this instance it was too personal. Henry seemed convinced by the young woman's attentions, and for that reason alone, Olof could find little fault with the urgency of this marriage. Why one person was attracted to another he could not say, but he believed Henry's dedication to Lottie was genuine, because Henry was genuine.

Ingrid could not read her husband's thoughts as he gazed upon the Columbia, but she assumed they were thinking along similar lines. For Henry's sake it was incumbent upon them both to make the effort. She had to wonder what made her so judgmental when she, too, had suffered the scrutiny of others. "I'd like to get to know Lottie," Ingrid proposed. "Since you and Henry are like brothers, I think I'll invite her to lunch and work out our differences ... should there be any. Once she's met Henry's namesake, I'm certain we'll become dear friends." She paused to think about the children she adored and how they absorbed her time, an hour or two of which could have been devoted to establishing a friendship with Henry's chosen. "I'm at fault here ... I really didn't make the effort," she said apologetically.

The idea of a female friend whose husband was a gill-netter was appealing. If she and Lottie could overcome the language barrier, there would be much satisfaction gained from their friendship.

∞

The first words out of Lottie's mouth took Ingrid completely by surprise. They were delivered in crisp American: "May I come in?"

Ingrid opened the door even further and allowed the petite brunette to enter.

"Where is the little boy named after Henry? I'm so eager to meet him."

Ingrid wasn't certain she had heard the request correctly, nor was she convinced this could be the same peasant girl who had tittered during her own nuptials and had clung to Henry like a wet rag. In her hurriedly stitched wedding gown, Lottie had appeared both shapeless and guileless, but those first impressions were wrong. She was far more sophisticated than Ingrid had believed. "Little

Henry and Hanna Jane are both napping," Ingrid answered quickly, "but we'll wake them later, after lunch."

"I don't eat much," Lottie replied. "I've never taken a liking to hard bread, cheese and salted herring."

Ingrid overlooked her guest's comment concerning the traditional Swedish fare. She might also say the wrong thing as she searched for some common ground on which to establish a rapport. She led Lottie into the kitchen. Seeing the fruit basket on the drainboard gave her renewed courage. "Then you'll be pleasantly surprised because I've prepared something much more American," she said with confidence. "I must admit I'm greatly relieved to find you speak American. At the wedding reception, I jumped to wrong conclusions. Language can be a big barrier, and I was hoping we'd become dear friends because the number of gillnetters' wives are few and far between. But I suppose you've already noticed that. Most of the women here are either wed to merchants or ... well, you know, they service the single men."

Lottie offered nothing in response. She settled herself at the table in the seat offered her. Ingrid busied herself by presenting the food and observing Henry's chosen with greater objectivity. Lottie, though small in stature, had naturally curly hair that looked very fashionable, piled loosely on the crown of her head and held there by combs. The flowery pattern in her dress material highlighted a diminutive figure. Her brown eyes were always busy, searching the interior of the room for more information; yet her mouth was molded by a lower lip that tended to push upward and outward to suggest a semblance of doubt. Ingrid recognized in Lottie a developed and complex personality. Ingrid seated herself and offered a platter of fresh fruits, just off the ships and meant for Lottie's enjoyment. They were expensive and unusual, a treat intended to inspire congenial conversation. "Banana?" she asked. "Or, perhaps a plum or a peach?"

Lottie observed the yellow fruit with dismay. She had never seen a banana.

Ingrid insisted: "Take the banana. It is sweet and easy to become accustomed to. Please!"

Lottie took the banana and immediately bit into it. Her teeth tugged on the peel and Ingrid's bewilderment turned into friendly laughter. Lottie dropped the banana on her plate, and her face turned red. Her anger was uncontrollable, and in her native tongue, it spewed forth like a geyser. Ingrid dropped the platter and added to the confusion. Between the two of them, they had woken the babies. Little Henry's cries became more shrill as Lottie continued ranting. There seemed no end to the unintelligible outpouring.

Ingrid tried shushing her guest. "Please lower your voice! I didn't mean to offend you," she pleaded, "but waking the children will buy you no favors!"

Lottie was shocked. Apparently criticism was something foreign to her upbringing. She began pouting like a child, and Ingrid excused herself. She left her guest to herself and scurried off to mother the twins.

Lottie's humiliating experience was transitory. Alone, she looked around the kitchen and saw nothing extraordinary, except, of course, for the fruit. "My husband is quite the storyteller," she muttered, "but I don't see any wealth here, amassed by a gillnetter." She was not certain what she had expected, but this was far more enlightening than listening to rumors. "Sweet Ingrid isn't so sweet," Lottie mused. "She's just another immigrant, trying to pretend that she's American." She ran her hands across the tablecloth made of durable cotton. It was cotton rather than linen, a far cry from what she had been led to believe, making it even more apparent how far afield she and Henry were in setting their goals. If this was what he had hoped to gain for them in the future, Lottie wanted no part of it. These were people as poor as she, but representing themselves as being better. Her parents had taught her about the encroachment of one culture upon another and the ensuing emptiness. "There isn't even a remnant of Sweden here," she remarked critically.

"What was that?" Ingrid asked. She had entered the room unnoticed.

"I'm surprised there is nothing Swedish in your house," Lottie responded enigmatically.

"Any remembrances went down with the ship," Ingrid replied with an edge to her voice. "I wish I had things from my homeland to display, but Mother Nature had other ideas."

"I've also noticed how you use the word 'American' to mean 'English.' America is the country, whereas the chosen language is English. I speak Finnish and English, neither of which is American."

A chill ran up Ingrid's spine. Three years ago she might have quietly conceded, but not now. "'American' is the language of both the land and the people," Ingrid said haltingly. "This isn't England with English traditions. 'American' is more ... it includes my thoughts ... as well as yours." Ingrid sat down at the table, prepared to begin anew.

"See, you've done it again!" Lottie exploded. "You can't pretend such differences don't exist! As a Swede and a Finn I assure you we share little in common, but pretending to become American by speaking English is distasteful."

Lottie's voice again reached a level capable of disturbing the twins, but Ingrid did not care. She had never heard such ill-founded nonsense in her life. She glowered across the table, hoping to exorcise the demon gnawing at Lottie's innards. Lottie began buttering a biscuit. She had regained her composure as quickly as Ingrid was about to lose it. She took a bite and returned the food to her plate. "They're good. Did you bake them?" Ingrid was unnerved by her guest's changed tone. It was impossible to know if Lottie was touched in the head, or disposed toward ethnic divisiveness. Ingrid's words were breathy: "You said something about my Swedish keepsakes, and I was wondering why?"

"Because too many people disregard their heritage in favor of convenience. If you're not rich, you should at least be somebody and cling to something worthwhile. Swede Olof has Henry fooled into thinking that he's working for a good fisherman, while I can look around your house and see the truth for myself. Most people don't understand the subtle differences, but a pauper should be his own pauper, and a prince should be his own prince. The days of servitude are over ... yet they continue. Your husband should find a boat puller who at least speaks the same language. Much as you and I, we can exchange words but not ideas, because you're speaking American and I'm speaking English. Do you understand, Ingrid?"

Ingrid understood all too well. When she had sat at the boardinghouse table one memorable Sunday afternoon, and wandered into the world of the gillnetters by mistake, she had found herself overlooking the obvious and mistrusting her instincts — but not this time. Lottie was a confused young woman, filled to the brim with indecision and looking every which way for an avenue of escape. Ingrid had been there herself, but Olof had pulled her through. In a way, Ingrid's heart should reach out to her, but Lottie had a nasty edge to her. The comment about trading Ingrid's Swedish heritage for convenience stung her. No, they would not be dear friends because friendships seldom arose from insults. Ingrid hoped to bring the luncheon to a rapid conclusion: "Would you like to see the children before you leave?"

Lottie seemed appeased by the invitation. She even smiled, thinking she had made some needed inroads.

May 17, 1879

For the new bride, Lottie Hihnala, marriage was a sham. She could see through it as clearly as she saw through Astoria's veil, a city purported to be the Venice of the North, delving into the far reaches of the Columbia, built on piles. The description of Astoria, with all the glamour implied, was a farcical notion, much like Henry's dreams to succeed in a place that stunk of rotting fish. The river's unabated lapping did not help matters much, and having a tavern across the street and a Chinese wash-house next door added to Lottie's disillusionment. She could hear gibberish coming from all directions, and most often the frequent storms, lashing against the timber-framed underpinnings, were welcomed distractions. She relied wholly on the savings amassing in Henry's tin box to compensate her for tolerating such surroundings. Henry had promised her a lot, and she expected those promises to come to fruition.

She had fallen fast asleep, but was awakened when the door hinges squeaked and Henry's boots struck the floor. "I thought you said you weren't going to get involved," Lottie grumbled.

Though the room was small and cramped, Henry made his way around the bed with the agility of a cat. "I certainly did, but on second thought, I went back on my word."

His reply was cocky and incoherent, leading Lottie to her own conclusions. "You've been drinking. Go sleep it off on the couch."

Henry was too upbeat to allow Lottie's grumblings to bother him. "No, I haven't been drinking. I was at Engine House No. 1, and this time there's a real fishermen's union about to come into being, with laws, by-laws and a constitution. It'll mean more money for us, sweet Lottie, and when my family arrives, we can live in a great big house with a Chinese handmaiden to serve us tea. Ma and Pa Hihnala will have the best of everything, and the brothers will get off to a good start. And, as for us, only blue skies and nets full of salmon." Henry started to crawl into bed, but Lottie repelled him with her feet, sending him crashing into the wall. "What'd I do wrong this time?" he snarled.

"You called me 'sweet Lottie,'" she snapped. "Don't ever confuse me with Swede Olof's bitch, and don't lie to me about sneaking off to attend any fishermen's meetings. You're still only a boat puller and not a captain. It's time you woke up and smelled the stench that comes with being second best."

Henry had heard Lottie's condemnation of his fishing partnership for as many nights as they had slept together, but dragging Ingrid's name into the fray was something new. "I don't know why you're suddenly so sour on Ingrid!" Henry retorted. "To my knowledge, she's never said a bad word about you."

Lottie sat up in bed and pulled the covers around her neck. The room was pitch dark and reeked of damp must, like a cave in which wild animals performed their breeding rituals. The heavy scent of the river seeped into every nook and cranny, so that even in sleep, one's dreams were driven by primal urges. A young woman might be misled by strong arms embracing her ... even those of her husband. Lottie wanted certainty, more than sensuality. "Ingrid is a good-looking woman," she said to Henry. "I suppose you've noticed that."

Henry could not see his wife's face, but the recurring jealousy was there, and this time it revealed itself in total disregard of his fealty. "She's Olof's ... and a man doesn't look at another man's wife!" he exclaimed adamantly.

"Would you? Would you look at her if she wasn't?"

Henry groaned. Night after night it went on like this, with Lottie creating improbable situations to test him. What if he wasn't a boat puller? What if his family never made it to Astoria? What if Olof died, and Ingrid were free to wed? What if Olof died ...? But Lottie had outdone herself this evening. He struggled around in the darkness until he found his boots. "I'm going for that drink in Swilltown," he announced in rankled disgust.

July 4, 1879

Ingrid left her umbrella open so it might dry out on the porch, but the wind threatened to blow it down the street as soon as her back was turned. She pumped it, hoping to shed most of the wetness, and carried it into the house. The weather did not bode well for all the activities planned. Nevertheless, she and an ardent few had decorated the fire engine and hose carriage with flowers, employing the winsome artistry of optimists. Astoria was crammed full of people who had come from as far away as Tillamook County to participate in the speeches, parade and competitions, thus the event had impetus, regardless of the winter-like rain. According to *The Daily Astorian,* "Salmon City" was going to host the most entertaining day of the year. All discouragements were to be set aside; even the members of the Columbia River Fishermen's Protective Union were to march in the parade and, weather permitting, participate in an extraordinary sail contest of their fishing boats. The prizes for the competition were also of good humor, an indication that the gillnetters could be brought among the fold and accept some gentle ribbing.

Olof had read the list several times and wondered if they were of John Lord's doing: a roasted sturgeon, a hat from the wreck of the *Great Republic,* three lots on Sand Island (a fishing ground near the mouth of the river to be represented by a mythical governor), and a land claim in Alaska. The newspaper was clearly making an effort to promote the day of national independence with a truce in mind, and Olof had every intention of taking it to a higher level. He and Henry could easily out-sail the best of the Butterfly Fleet, and on this day of celebration Olof was of a mind to prove his point. It was time Astorians began to recognize his permanence in their midst.

As for Ingrid, she was anxious to learn how Olof had fulfilled her request to show off their American-born twins. It was a proud day for them both.

When she first saw it, Olof was rolling it across the floor with a watchful eye, appraising it carefully. Then he left it in the middle of the living room for Ingrid to puzzle over. He soon reappeared, carrying Hanna Jane while Little Henry toddled along, clinging to his father's pant leg. He set Hanna in the left side of the box and coaxed Little Henry to sit in the right compartment. Next he took the long handle and steered the contraption around the room on its wooden wheels. "It's made from a fish-box," Olof announced with pride. "There won't be anyone else in the parade with a baby carriage such as this."

Ingrid didn't know what to say. Olof was right about the uniqueness of his invention, but the oddity of it was disconcerting. A large wooden box, used for packing salmon, wasn't exactly what she had had in mind when she had set him the chore of bringing the twins to the parade. Maybe a red wagon with blue and white streamers? Or a trip to Carl Adler's Variety Store, to check out the ad in the newspaper announcing their procurement of a fine lot of baby carriages to be sold at bottom prices. But this? "Oh, my," Ingrid said in dismay. "They could fall out on the steepness of the hills." But she could see that Olof's ego was somehow tied to his creation. He was almost giddy, pushing the fish-box around and around.

Olof stopped pushing and observed Little Henry, extricating himself. Little Henry tended to be skeptical like his mother, whereas Hanna Jane, the apple of her father's eye, remained in the box, hoping for another ride around the room. "A fathom of rope'll do it," Olof protested. "Whatever you think, Olof," Ingrid replied distractedly, "because it might not matter anyway." Outside the window a wet and disagreeable gully-washer had opened up, and there was a goodly possibility that much of their planning would be for naught.

By word of mouth, news of the changes spread. There were cancellations and postponements, each of which seemed more disappointing than the last. Ingrid had already begun retreating back to her house, the weather being too inclement to risk the possibility of the children falling ill. Still, she'd gotten a good look at the decorated storefronts and the fancy horse carriages bedecked with garlands and flowers, and at the moment of her departure had reconciled herself to the fact that the reading of the Declaration had fallen from the schedule.

The oilskin outerwear kept Olof dry, but standing around on the corner, waiting for Henry to join him, was discouraging. As Ingrid and the fish-box carriage disappeared from sight, he had the feeling something was amiss. Coincidentally, the Fourth of July was Henry's birthday, and regardless of the weather, the fishing partners had sworn to make the most of it. Olof was dismayed by Henry's tardiness. They had made big plans, inclusive of winning the sail race.

At one o'clock sharp, the grand marshal, in a wagon led by a fine team of horses, started the parade. In spite of the steady drizzle, many spectators lined the street, waving their flags and encouraging the soggy procession to move ahead. Next to come was Lambert's Brass Band, followed by the Liberty Car carrying the Goddess of Liberty and thirty-eight misses, their flirtatious smiles hidden beneath umbrellas. Then the Ancient Order of Hibernians fell into line and braved the rain with their flags flying, but still no Henry. Olof could not imagine why they had missed each other and started heading in the direction of Henry's apartment. In front of the Dockside Tavern he found his question answered.

The night aboard the whiskey scow being the exception, to Olof's knowledge, this was the worst condition Henry had ever been in. Had he not wrapped himself around a hitching post, he might have been trampled by the unusual number of horses and carriages passing by. "Hitting the whiskey a little early?" Olof asked. Henry's eyes rolled around in his head like two marbles. Olof raised him off his knees and tried to get him to stand erect. "Where's your hat?" he asked. Henry's hair was dripping wet, rivulets cascading down the indentations aside his nose. He smelled so strongly of whiskey he could very well embarrass himself by spilling his guts on the street. "I think we oughta take a slow walk along the river," Olof suggested. "A little untainted air in the lungs couldn't hurt."

Henry promptly shoved Olof aside. "It's my birthday, and I'm going to celebrate until I drop!" he retorted in slurred speech. "So ... where's the parade?"

In truth, Olof had never given much credence to marching in a parade. It was only the race inspiring his interest. Yet, in light of Henry's condition, all bets needed to be called off. "Forget the parade," Olof advised calmly. "Better to head home and let Lottie brew you a stiff cup of coffee."

The thought stung Henry to the core. " ... And we're going to win the salmon boat race later!" Henry said defiantly. "But first we've got to march down the street like we don't give a damn! It's my birthday, Swede Olof. Can't deny a man a little fun on his birthday."

Henry's voice was sing-songish, playful and immature, and his appearance was ragged, disheveled and unkempt; yet he staggered off in the direction of the music being played by the brass band, and Olof saw no other option than to keep track of his best friend. Truthfully, Henry would not be the only one touched by the bottle this day, and perhaps a briskly paced march would burn off the alcohol, leaving no one the wiser. At least that was what Olof had in mind when he grimaced ever so slightly and rushed down the rain-slickened street to catch up with his fishing partner.

The Alert Hook and Ladder Company, then Rescue Engine Company No. 2 — a steamer drawn by appaloosas — parted the respectable gathering of about fifty gillnetters

who were waiting their turn to march. Someone had made a
long banner, and the first six fishermen lined up behind it
and started down the street following the fire equipment.
Olof had trouble keeping Henry under control as he veered
into the crowd. "You drunken fisherman," a woman said in
disgust. She folded her umbrella and held it out like a
sword, poking and prodding at Henry to keep him at bay.
Olof steered Henry back into the middle of the other
marchers, knocking some aside in the process. Henry pulled
a whiskey bottle from inside his clothing and offered it to
those he had offended. "Take a swig for my birthday!" he
shouted out. "Me and America have our birthdays
together!" Olof took the bottle from his friend and
pretended to partake in the offer. As he did so, Henry
staggered off in the direction of a flag, stretched across the
entrance to a general store. The crowd began booing and
hissing, upset because Henry had his hand to his heart and
was giving his own rendition of the Declaration of
Independence. A bullish figure of a man stepped forward
and pushed Henry into the street where he fell, bringing an
end to his drunken wandering.

Olof still had the bottle in his hand when he rushed
over to assist him. The sorrowful look on Henry's face was
heartrending. Olof could not immediately dispose of the
bottle, but the celebration was over for the two of them.
"I'm going to take you home now," he said definitively.

The marchers had left them in their wake as Astoria
Engine Company No. 1, with its equipment bedecked in the
flowers Ingrid had tied so carefully to its carriage, saw the
opportunity in the moment. Many of the parade watchers
clapped their approval as the force of the water from its
hoses sent Olof and Henry reeling around like clowns, but
Ingrid, who had settled the twins with Molly Bochau so that

she might enjoy a rare moment, felt nothing but contempt for the city's population. She put her hands over her eyes to hide her shame and disappointment.

Chapter Four

~ ~ ~ ~ ~ ~ ~ ~ ~ ~ ~ ~ ~ ~ ~ ~ ~ ~ ~ ~

March 1880

America was purported to be the land of opportunity for those immigrants who were willing to work every waking hour and place the responsibility for success upon themselves. Nothing was guaranteed, except that growth was inevitable and change was part of the process.

Olof, thirty-one years old, was also beginning to see that making life affordable was both a lonely and pragmatic business. He could not depend on others to provide him with opportunities — he had to make them for himself; and without looking ahead, each day's gain could be tomorrow's losses. Life as a gillnetter was inherently unpredictable. The long winter months spent off the river were painfully repressive, providing Olof with long hours of reflection that increased his determination to make fishing work for him and his family. He was, after all, free to make his own destiny, which included the Columbia, because he was a fisherman.

Olof's off-season work at the sawmill was a purposeful part of the plan, meant to enhance his own ability to change. From dawn to dusk, he worked alongside Henry, hand-winching lumber aboard the sailing ships bound for San Francisco. The repetitious nature of the work dulled the senses, but nonetheless Olof's financial resources grew and his spirits rose as spring began making an early overture. The sky overhead was cumbered with fist-sized birds, flitting in and out through the open apertures in the milling shed, having reclaimed the abandoned nests built high in the rafters. Even Henry craned his neck upward on occasion, to witness nature's renewal.

Now there was always a note of resignation in Henry's voice. The stakes were escalating and Lottie was becoming more demanding. Olof would grow irritated at his friend's extreme caution in even simple matters. "It sounds like a good idea," Henry might reply, "but even with the bridge in place over Scow Bay, it's too far. We'd both be away from home for days at a time." Here Henry would pause mid-sentence, presuming Olof would have the sensibility to fill in the remainder without saying it aloud. "And Lottie wouldn't approve of my fishing for the Scandinavian Packing Company, because she rejects anything connected with my past — you in particular. Can't you see how such a proposal will work in her favor, driving a deeper wedge in our friendship?"

But no, Olof could not read Henry's mind any longer; marriage and booze had created an impenetrable barrier. Olof reserved his thoughts on the Scandinavian Packing Company while he ate his lunch and watched the swallows in their work. "We used to be like that," Olof commented, but purposely his words were too hushed to hear. Henry was seated to his left, occupying the same bench just inside the milling shed; but his lunch remained untouched on his lap, his eyes riveted on a pile of uncut logs. It was not unusual for Henry to drift off in such a manner. Olof could not retrieve his friend when he turned inward like this, and he didn't try. He kept his own focus, intent on doing the best for the both of them.

Word on the streets was that the fishermen would be asking sixty cents a fish during the upcoming salmon season, and that the canners were already taking an opposing stand. Resentment over the first failed strike, followed by his public humiliation at the hands of the Astoria Fire Department, had greatly altered Olof's philosophy concerning such matters. A family man could not afford to vacillate and allow the currents of public opinion to pull him under. Regardless of the old-world quality of the Scandinavian Packing Company, it afforded a plausible option for both Henry and himself. It was an association owned and run by the fishermen. If a strike should ensue, it was doubtful such an enterprise would participate — the result of the action being counterproductive. The obvious drawback, as Henry had just stated, was in the cannery's location. It was east of Astoria, located across Scow Bay in a small but growing hamlet called Uppertown. Even Olof had reservations about going to such lengths to disassociate himself from the migratory misfits, but if the majority of fishermen continued to fit this bill, then it was time to grow in a different direction.

Of the gillnetters, fewer than 10 percent were married or hailed from the towns that gave them temporary employment. The Scandinavian Packing Company was trying to alter those statistics and create a population of permanent residents who had a direct stake in the industry and the local economy. Olof needed to get this across to Henry ... before Lottie, or whiskey, thwarted his intentions. For reasons unknown to Olof, Lottie didn't much like him or his family; but as for the booze, its detrimental effects were in constant evidence. Regardless, Olof and Henry were gillnetters, and such influences counted for naught on cold, sober nights drifting the river. If Henry and Olof had one thing in common, it was that they took things at face value; and on the river Henry was Olof's mainstay.

Olof finished his cheese sandwich, wadded up the brown paper wrapper, and let it drop on the two-inch-thick cushion of wood shavings covering the floor. He glanced at Henry, who was warming his hands around a cup of coffee while inspecting the rambling interior of the sawmill. Olof needed to draw his boat puller back into the present, before his listlessness proved to be dangerous on the river. From time to time this errant thought had crossed Olof's mind, but it was not within him to say as much. Trust was the foundation of their partnership, and now it was time to trust Henry with the dream that had guided Olof through the winter. "I've been thinking about buying a salmon boat," Olof said candidly.

For the first time in months, Henry perked up. He cracked a childish grin, an indication they continued to think along similar lines. Owning one's salmon boat was nearly unheard of ... but it boded well for their team. He said nothing in response, but his eyes welled up with tears. He was a desperate man, grasping at straws. There were times like this when Henry did not know whether to laugh or to cry. He had misplaced his genuineness somewhere in the shuffle.

∞

The dingy winter days and nights had dragged on and on, and the wind and rain had combined to sour everyone's spirits. For uninterrupted weeks, the river and sky had blended together bleakly, causing the sun and moon to alternate unnoticed. Lottie was prone to moods of despair. Henry had hopes that with the spring she would rise above it all. He laid out Olof's ideas for her consideration, and then they sat staring at each other across the supper table while she turned them over and over in her mind.

Lottie was pretty: pert and petite, and girlish. But underneath there was a driven personality, unusual for a woman. She was opinionated, giving no one the benefit of the doubt and winning her arguments by indefatigable determination. She, too, wore on Henry; but he was more accepting of her wayward tongue, even after a backbreaking day at the sawmill. She was his Finnish lifeline to the past, an umbilical cord extending all the way to the Old World. More often than not, he simply shut out her words and listened to the Finnish accent, recalling where he had come from and feeling vindicated for any shortcomings beyond his ability to correct. He pretended and she performed, both coping with the lack of intimacy between them.

"Generosity begins at home," Lottie quipped, "so I'd like to know what's in it for Swede Olof, and how it's going to benefit us. I can understand why your captain would prefer being included among the Scandinavians, seeing as how his name, Olof, means heir of his forefathers, while as for you ... the world has worshiped kings named Henry. I once tried explaining this to Ingrid," Lottie continued, her voice tinged with cynicism and ridicule, "but it fell on deaf ears. You can't have it both ways. You can't expect to be somebody by sufficing as a nobody. Success in America is for those who willingly extricate themselves from the old norms and try doing things differently. Money is nothing to scoff at, and if you dug a smidgen deeper, dear, you might discover someone who is desirous of achieving kingly status. Gillnetting is a pastime for paupers, and you could have stayed in Finland and been a pauper."

Henry reached for a cigarette and lit it. There was a compliment buried somewhere in his wife's logic, but he had never thought of himself as a pretender to a throne, only an unpretentious fisherman. Yet it was Lottie's way to catch him off guard, allowing him to fantasize for brief moments until the wasted minutes had taken him far afield. He watched her divide what was left on her plate into two distinct portions: a forkful of mashed potatoes, and a forkful of canned beef. If her actions were symbolic of the rift between them, he ignored them, wishful that this discussion would not go asunder. He had expected the issue of the Scandinavian Packing Company to go awry. Still, the move for independence on behalf of Olof and himself should warrant credibility, being out of the ordinary, something Lottie could sink her teeth into. Henry inhaled deeply and watched the ensuing smoke dissipate in the air. Lottie forked the meat atop the potatoes. She was about to lift the combination up to her mouth, but halted mid-air and returned the food to her plate. If her sudden reversal in plans meant anything, he would soon find out. She could be a dozen different fictional characters, playing whichever role suited her at the time.

Henry took a deep drag on the cigarette before making his rebuttal, aware his fishing career was again on the line. Night after night their discussions revolved around his goals, and night after night Henry found himself making more concessions while Lottie shoved her food around her plate.

Wasn't it enough that he had already tabled the idea of bringing his family to America until he had built a house? Even in Lottie's estimation, he was gradually ensuring their future.

It was up to Henry to plead his case with more credibility, so he chose his words carefully. "Olof will be liable, indebted both to the salmon boat and the packing company. I see it as a gesture of friendship, and akin to looking a gift horse in the mouth to think otherwise. He's offered to go half and half on the catch, and I couldn't do any better if I were captain of my own boat."

Lottie stirred in her chair before pressing her back against the three wooden slats and settling her forearms on the table. For an instant their eyes met and locked, but nothing transpired in the connection. "You really don't have any long-term goals, do you?" she asked bluntly.

Other than bringing his family to America, no, Henry really didn't have anything driving him. Prior to his marriage he had thought of himself as being successful, having sailed halfway around the world to put down roots on a foreign soil. Then Lottie stepped into the picture. She was a lovely young woman, and he was grateful for their marriage. On the other hand, she aspired to things beyond his ability to deliver and never gave him a moment's peace, knowing as much. There were women in the city of Astoria recognized for their comings and goings — the envy of most — but the canning industry gave its favors to the few, not to the many.

Henry snubbed out his cigarette on the edge of his plate. "It must be hard for you to understand," he said frankly to his wife, "but it all takes time and money, and earning money is what Olof has in mind. It makes no difference who we fish for, as long as we're free from strikes and can operate independently."

Lottie's mind was racing. Henry's facial expression was both firm and reflective, as if he had conveniently bought and paid for her opinions, and she should say "thank you" before being swept off into the bedroom. But not in America. The whores who lived a few streets away had more freedom than she, but she wielded more power. She could control Henry, mold him and manipulate him. Her voice became lustful. "Dear husband, there is no difference between a princess and a peasant girl, other than determination. I do intend to rise above the ranks, with or without your assistance. As for Olof and his brood, they are peasant stock and will surely grind their fingers to the bone, getting nowhere. Leave the fishing to the gillnetters, and set your goals a little higher. Someday you'll get it through your thick head you're capable of more."

Henry remained seated, poring over the empty admonitions that had rained from Lottie's mouth. Lottie, on the other hand, leapt from her chair and went storming into the bedroom, slamming the door behind her.

In the privacy of the unlit room, Lottie flung herself on the bed and pounded her fists into the pillows until her wrists went limp. She had made the biggest mistake in her life and did not know how to deal with it, regardless of her ability to improvise. She had almost told her husband the truth tonight, yet for all of Henry's understanding, he would not tolerate it. Not only did she not love him, she loathed him, and every ounce of her being wanted to be free of him. Yet he was too loyal, too old-worldish to see that changes needed to be made. What was unheard of in the Old Country was transpiring inside her. She did not feel committed to her husband, nor did she feel safe in his arms or settled by his presence. She wanted to be rid of his insufferable forbearance, because she was tired of experiencing the guilt. She had made a horrendous error in listening to her parents; marriages of convenience did not evolve into more over time. What they did evolve into was a mistrust for everything and everyone in their vicinity, and a lustful need for someone else to come into the picture. An image of Olof Andersson popped into Lottie's mind, and she bit down on a pillow. Even he inspired movements within her body that Henry could not. Henry was playing a game of denial with her he could not win, and she intended to keep chipping away at his self-worth until he saw fit to free her of her obligation. Unless, of course, Henry should reverse his fortunes, and then the war between them could end in a simple truce. But that was an unlikely pipe dream, for even in America, women were towed behind their husbands' carriages like plows, tilling the soil for the express purpose of planting seeds. Lottie cringed thinking about the predictable roles in a woman's life, and what lay ahead of her in order to change them.

∽

Hanna Jane was the sunshine of Olof's life, and Little Henry the inspiration. Both children had Ingrid's deep-blue eyes; but Hanna Jane's hair was a neutral brown while Little Henry's was a tangled mass of fiery-red curls. Hanna Jane was not as spunky as Henry, but her docile attitude made her even more appealing. She held a smile long after her delicate fingers found something delightful to investigate, and she was accepting of everything, even her father's awesome stature and visage. Little Henry, on the other hand, poked and prodded at everything, questioning what he did not understand and taking a belligerent stance when answers would not suffice. He would point at Olof's face, wondering why the two sides were different, knowing that his father would tell the story again, the one about the evil crimpers who tried to sell men into bondage. The children played well together, although Hanna Jane fatigued quickly, and it was not unusual to find her curled up asleep in the fish-box while Little Henry was enlisted to assist Ingrid in the kitchen. Everyone indulged Hanna Jane's frailty, because she was not supposed to be alive, let alone wide-eyed and cheerful. Even Little Henry was aware of his sister's uniqueness. He would keep a close eye on her when teams of horses went rushing up the street, although his feet wanted to race against the other youngsters who were free to follow.

Every moment Olof was able to spend with his children was an enlightening experience. He could recognize those traits that he and Ingrid engendered; and every night when Ingrid swept them off to bed, his heirs gave him a great deal of satisfaction and reason to advance himself.

Following his discussion with Henry about buying a salmon boat, Olof slept only in spurts that night, his mind trading visions of the river with images of his children at play. The upcoming meeting of the fishermen was imminent, and time was wasting. Dawn had yet to crack on a warm but drizzly March morning, yet what he had to say could wait no longer. "I think I'm going to buy a salmon boat," he said to Ingrid as they crawled out of bed. She stopped short of slipping on her robe or allowing her bare feet to touch the cold floor. She pulled the bedcoverings over her lap instead, waiting for Olof to light the kerosene lamp. "What?" she replied drowsily. "Did you say something about buying a salmon boat? We can't afford a salmon boat." She spoke in jest, as if the idea was intended to be nonsensical, meant to send them back beneath the covers where Olof might be allowed to pursue his teasing. Yet Olof lit the lamp, and Ingrid could see the seriousness in his facial expression. She had also tripped upon the announcement of the meeting in the newspaper, but had disregarded it, wishful that this fishing season would go smoother than most. She placed her feet on the cold floor and stood upright, pulling her blonde hair back from her face to ask the critical question: "How much?"

"Nearly all of our savings," Olof replied, "but that would include a net."

Ingrid understood she was free to say no there and then, and that would be the end of it. "Is Henry going to be fishing with you this year?" she queried. Olof nodded his head in the affirmative.

Ingrid's face showed no sign of acceptance or rejection, but she had to think beyond her immediate reaction, which was no. Whenever Henry Hihnala's name came into the picture, her wariness surfaced. She had ample reason not to trust him, or his wife. Recollections of the parade would never leave her, and as for Lottie, she remained an unknown, lurking in the shadows like a mountain lion, waiting to pounce. But aboard a salmon boat, a different set of guidelines came into play, and the rules and rewards were quite different. It was not for Ingrid to make judgments in this instance. Her life was not at stake, only their savings. In effect, Olof wanted her trust, not her gut reaction. "Is it that important to you?" she asked, her voice quivering.

Rather than answering, Olof turned to the business of pulling his trousers over his long underwear. She supposed that her question was superfluous, the implication of its importance having already been established. On the other hand, she had no reason to apologize for her redundancy, because it was not her place to lend endorsement to matters beyond her comprehension. She would never understand what it was about gillnetting that inspired her husband to lend his heart and soul to the Butterfly Fleet. He exacted beauty where she saw only brutality, and he found courage from those things causing her fear. He could lend his bravery to any other occupation and find success, but because of the wonderment bestowed upon her by her children, she was willing to accept the inexplicable, and not be the one who would destroy another's dreams. "Go ahead," she replied softly as she pulled on her robe, "go ahead and buy your salmon boat."

∞

It would have been so easy if Henry had agreed to fish for the Scandinavian Packing Company, except it wasn't the case, and Olof was looking at many more nights of dream-interrupted sleep, anticipating the next step in the evolution of the gillnetters' union. His idealism favored a strike, while his faith was strained, weakened by past experiences and instances of hopes torn asunder. Too, he found himself in the precarious position of owning a salmon boat, a liability sitting idle while payments for moorage and net-racking privileges came due. Nothing about a strike boded well for his financial security, but he could not turn a deaf ear on his industry. Any way he looked at it, he was surely damned.

Spring, in its early arrival, afforded a molten blue sky overhead for Olof's walk to Foster's Exchange Hall. As agreed, Henry was there waiting, hands in his pants pockets and looking surprisingly sober. It was an obligation Olof wanted to make brief. He found standing room among those gathered just inside the doors, his intent being there to observe, rather than becoming the focus of dissension. Both he and Henry scanned those in attendance, casually matching names with faces. Many who had marched in the Fourth of July parade were present, and kitty-corner across the room, pressed amongst the crowd, was Olavi Pustinen, his arms folded across his chest. The mood of the gathering was entirely different from the last strike meeting. It was serious, somber and businesslike, and as the chairman worked his way through the crowd to reach the front of the room, everyone fell silent. He went directly to the heart of the matter, opening the meeting with statistics concerning the profit levels of the canners. His words were clear and convincing, leading one to believe that at either fifty cents a fish, or sixty cents a fish, the canners could continue to do a good business. No one interrupted the speaker's train of thought, and no one disputed his research. Even Olavi Pustinen appeared supportive, listening attentively. "They're coming around to your way of thinking," Henry whispered over his shoulder to Olof. "It appears the canners could cut down on the waste and still pay a fair wage."

Olof saw the whole thing from a different perspective and was not convinced. He did not respond to Henry's comment. Instead, he tried to grapple with all the misgivings running through his mind. The long-term problem, which never got sufficient debate, was the abundance of canners and gillnetters, and not the distribution of profits. Neither side of the argument would admit to the raping of the river, until the river was destitute. Then they would all pack up and move on, woefully sorry their sons could not partake in the river's former bounty. It was a tired lesson — passed down from the Old Countries.

Olof removed his hat and scratched his head. Something else needed saying, but a speech from his heart would fall on deaf ears. His concern for the future of the mighty Columbia would draw riotous laughter, and he would be seen as self-serving. Olavi would repeat himself, shouting above the crowd that there is enough for everyone — and everyone for himself!

Olof's hand settled on the back of his neck and felt the perspiration. There was only a handful of fishermen such as himself, men who had actually invested in the river's future by buying a salmon boat. If a strike were to ensue, it would have to have meaningful consequences or, as it would in Olof's case, result in the loss of hard-earned gains. More than ever, Olof needed convincing. He glanced at his boat puller, and for an instant wondered as to the depth of Henry's commitment. Talk was cheap, compared with the worth of their partnership.

"It all sounds well and good," Olof blurted out from the back of the room, "but who exactly does this organization represent? The problems in the past have come from those who weren't really gillnetters ... men just passing through and looking for a quick buck. I don't intend to put my livelihood on the line, unless everyone else is willing to do the same. Seems there are those among us who don't see fishing as a long-term occupation, only a means to an end. Let's weed them out, before we go looking for concessions from the canners."

Henry took a giant step sideways. Olof had outdone himself this time, saying things others dared not utter, setting the room afire, bringing many angry eyes to focus upon the Swedish-Finnish partnership. But Olof had succeeded in proving his point by flushing out those who fit his profile, and they were there among the crowd, lobbing angry threats, denying the truth. It had been a goodly while, but Henry started rolling up his shirt sleeves in preparation for an all-out fray. But curiously, Olavi Pustinen drew the crowd's ire upon himself. "Seems Swede Olof has forgotten his own history," he responded with a smirk. "It wasn't so long ago he promoted such a strike, and now he wants to cower behind its failure. We're all here together, aren't we?" Olavi chided. "And who's to say which one of us isn't a real gillnetter?"

The crowd burst out in appreciative applause, while Olof's face turned crimson. Again, he was lonely in his observations, while Olavi, like his supporters, refused to cite himself as being part of the problem. Greed and short-sightedness were not attributes limited solely to the canners; abundance could create avarice in anyone. Olof grimaced at the realization, but the members of the union would hold their course as long as men such as Olavi would tell them they had rights based on the endless bounty of the Columbia. Olof could not promise otherwise and held his tongue, supposing the momentum of the meeting too strong to suppress. Like the others, he watched Olavi Pustinen make his way through the crowd and take a position at the front of the room. Olof had seen it before. This time, however, Olof was not going to contradict him. He had lost this battle before it had ever begun.

Olavi addressed the crowd, but his words were directed at Olof. His voice was cryptic and his message quite clear. "The chairman has a resolution for us all to sign, professing our dedication as both gillnetters and strikers. I'm certain Swede Olof will be the first to sign. Once he was our inspiration, eventually leading us to this point of no return. So wish us all luck and hope the canners will meet our demands."

The clapping was thunderous, and Olof knew he had been beaten by a skilled adversary. Olavi was obviously a man with hidden aspirations. Olof had previously assumed

Olavi to be a boat puller, but now that belief was being refuted as he watched Olavi add his name to a list of strikers. He was obviously the captain of a salmon boat, but which cannery he hailed from Olof did not know. Like the other migratory fishermen, he showed up for the season and then conveniently disappeared — at least, so Olof thought.

∞

Ingrid had seen that same desolate look on Olof's face before, coming on the heels of a failed strike. She watched him push Hanna Jane around the room in the fish-box, but it was evident from his listless efforts that something was wrong. Aware that their savings were nearly depleted Ingrid had enough information to digest at the moment; the rest of the story could come with time. She held her tongue, knowing that Hanna Jane's adoration for her father was the best medicine to cure his affliction; but as for her, old feelings of betrayal began resurfacing. She was disheartened by Olof's inability to disclose the truth. At times like this, she wanted to grab him by the shoulders and shake the gillnetter out of him. If she were to be part of this river life, she needed to be trusted with its secrets.

For her part, Lottie stared at Henry with such cold indifference that chills ran up and down his spine. It was wishful thinking to believe that a simple "I told you so" would suffice. Her eyes darted around the sparsely furnished room while her meal sat untouched on her plate. This could be the straw to break the camel's back, Henry thought to himself, but he lowered his eyes to his food and began sopping up the gravy with a slice of bread. The silence was deafening, worse in many respects to the outbursts.

∞

Two weeks later, John Lord was seated at his desk, looking through the window, keeping an eagle eye on the two-block-long parade of fishermen marching by. He made careful note of the signs they carried, including "60 Cents or NO Fish," and "Hold the Fort, Our Day is Near." He was always skeptical when the fishermen came together in large groups, but the music and banners seemed so non-threatening as to allow him to turn to other matters — specifically, a recent county census. He scanned it several times, deriving a certain amount of satisfaction in seeing the possibility of a story there, a verification of the unusual nature of Astoria during the fishing season. The total number of people accounted for was slightly more than seven thousand; and of that number, over two thousand were Chinese, 80 percent of whom were employed by the canners. Thirteen hundred fishermen had been tallied, 91 percent of whom were single, and 86 percent of whom boarded at the local rooming houses. There weren't any surprises here, including the fact that only 13 percent of the fishermen could claim U.S. citizenship, and only 1 percent were native Oregonians. To say it simply, Astoria was in a state of flux, growing through a period of unaccountability while reaching maturation.

John Lord was candidly unsympathetic toward the striking gillnetters. The census provided the basis for his wariness, by highlighting their migratory status. On the other hand, he found it difficult to align himself with the canners, knowing their profit levels were well above of those of the average businessman, and their risk-return factor was far less than that of the gillnetters. Putting together an objective news article concerning the striking fishermen was a difficult venture, particularly in light of the Chinese population, drawn to Astoria because of what the canners called "their indispensible industry." At some point, this phrase needed further edification. The Chinese had been displaced from the railroads following the driving of the Golden Spike, and then been wooed north by the canners to provide cheap labor. In many respects, the lot of the Chinese fish gutters could be cast alongside that of the gillnetters, both of them providing the labor required to fill the tins for export.

But it was difficult for an East Coast prodigy such as John Lord to find fault with those who exemplified success and could deem themselves to be the Empire Builders of the Pacific Northwest. The men who had fathered the canning industry were transplants from the East, and there was fraternity among them, based on a similarity in education and upbringing. Beyond this commonality in backgrounds, the early cannery entrepreneurs had to be admired for their knowledge of commerce and trade, and the way in which they had applied it to the natural resources along the lower Columbia River.

John Lord put down the census papers and peered out from beneath his visor, returning his attention to the parade, wondering if Olof Andersson would be there among the striking fishermen. Perhaps gillnetters who had established residency, men such as Olof Andersson, would someday represent the majority in their cause. The number of transients from California was being challenged by the influx of immigrants coming directly from Scandinavia, Finland and Russia. Still, it was premature to believe this strike would have any impact, regardless of the ethnic homogeny. Even if the scarfaced Swede was a factor, 86 percent of the gillnetters were uprooted wanderers, giving the canners the better odds.

With all the facts before him, and a parade passing by, John Lord rose from his chair and began pacing the small cubicle in front of his desk. The last thing Astoria needed was bad publicity, and his story would certainly be seen as such, and probably be reprinted in newspapers all over the country. Cities were hungry for growth, seeking a permanent population base from which to nurture pros- perity, not disparity. A story of the canners versus the transient gillnetters would not draw the type of citizenry Astoria needed. Quite the opposite, it would open the door for more drifters, and more upheavals. Women would be dissuaded from settling here, and John Lord, being single, needed to think twice before he seeded his own fate. He trudged over to the stove to pour himself a cup of coffee. "The truth isn't always prudent," he muttered to himself, "but then again, truth is a process, not a point in time."

∝∞

By April 24, one month into the strike, the difference between fifty cents a fish and sixty cents a fish was seen as less significant. Olof had guessed such would be the case, and he approached the meeting hall, fuming. He met Henry in the brisk evening air, and the two men covered the remaining thirty yards of sloping terrain together. The packed roadbed beneath their feet was slickened following an afternoon rain, yet their footsteps were sure, like those of soldiers, marching into war. "How are you going to vote?" Henry grumbled, whiskey heavy on his breath. "To knock 'em off the river," Olof answered tersely. Henry nodded in reply, agreeable to bringing this awkward strike to a head, regardless of the means.

Not all the gillnetters had seen fit to live up to their end of the bargain, and of those who had, many were getting uneasy. Each day, a few more gillnetters were returning to the river, strengthening the probability of war among the fishermen and keeping the canners away from the bargaining table. In effect, it was a waiting game. Olof had thought it through a million times in his mind, and he was prepared to turn the tide on the migratory majority.

Olof readdressed all the issues in his mind, prior to his speech. The pressure upon him to return to work was tremendous, yet forfeiting one-quarter of the fishing season was ample reason to solve the problem once and for all. It continued to be a long-term issue, and those who had started the dispute would see the fire in his green eyes if they proposed reneging. His intention was to force the issue, and to make very certain something came of his lost income. He covered the half-block distance assertively and started up the stairs with Henry two steps behind. Already the hazy collection of smoke seeping out from the building's interior was evident in the air.

He brushed up against another gillnetter who was making a fast exit. Their eyes met for only a second, but it was Olavi Pustinen, going the opposite direction. Always, Olof's instincts were the same. He did not trust the man, and having brushed up against him, Olof stopped dead in his tracks. He watched as Olavi continued in his flight, while Henry walked around him and disappeared in the crowd.

"There are too few to maintain a strike," the chairman repeated himself.

From head to toe, Olof was the color of rage. He refused to allow the attendees to depart the room, blocking the doorway with his body. He raised his fists in the air and clenched them firmly to resemble two rocks, ready to hurl at his enemies. "So what was it all for?" he shouted over the crowd. "Somebody explain to me, why in damnation did I give up one month of fishing for this sorry lot?"

Henry surveyed the crowd, noting a preponderance of empathetic expressions. Many were also devastated by this unconscionable turn of events. There was ample cause for Olof's hostility. Without total commitment at the outset of a strike, why divert one's energy to a lost cause? A hand went up in the crowd, and a shaky voice aired his own frustration. "So what do you propose we do? Kill the scabs?"

The anonymous questioner prompted a few guffaws and snickers, but most of the attendees were sobered by the seriousness of their plight and were anxious for Olof's response. He had thought about this long and hard, preparing for the inevitability of this moment. If the canners could stand on the sidelines, confident of the gillnetters' tendency to subvert themselves, there would always be dissension on the river. What Olof was about to propose was both innovative and risky, and not old-world politics revisited. He took a long glance around the room, and noted that there was more elbow room than usual. Finally, he was addressing the cream of the crop, those with long-term visions of the river. He was among his peers and took a deep breath before proposing such a radical idea.

But someone else had other ideas, and the floor trembled beneath Olof's feet as glass shards showered the room like buckets of ice pellets, flung from the heavens. Others in the room felt their footing temporarily impaired while a bomb blast disrupted what was to have been Olof's moment of revelation. Many went tearing out of the room, shoving Olof aside in the process. Others walked out slowly, crunching through the glass fragments strewn across the floor. In less than a minute, the hall had been emptied of its occupants, with the exception of Olof, who remained behind, unwilling to turn and run. He reached down and plucked a glass shard embedded in his pant leg and dropped it. It made a tinkling sound when added to the refuse pile on the floor, too delicate to discern above his labored breathing. In the wink of an eye the strike had been success-fully busted, and Olof could only stand there and contem-plate the depth of his despair.

He gazed upward, focusing on the six ceiling lamps and their unnatural gyrations. They were swinging ever so slightly, enough to remind him of what had just occurred. He took a large step forward, testing the integrity of his own equilibrium. Cautiously he crunched his way through the shards, headed for one of the gaping apertures where windowpanes had once provided a barrier. Dusk was heavy upon the city, and shapes and forms were more meaningful than their definitive parts, but there was sufficient light to see men wandering around a curious hole in the back alley. Olof retraced his steps, now certain his suspicions had merit.

Henry was waiting outside, conversing with Olavi Pustinen on the dirt walkway. To their right, a dozen gill-netters were milling around on a small patch of calf-high grasses going to seed. Olof halted on the porch before making his descent. He could not believe his good luck. The culprit was there in their midst, sharing idle chitchat with Henry. His shirt sleeves were rolled up to his elbows, and his polished trousers were familiar. Olof took the series of steps in one leap and lunged into Olavi with the full force of his upper body. The object of Olof's ire careened into the gathering of gillnetters on the grassy area, falling to his knees while sending the others scurrying. Olof looked the Finnish fisherman in the face and saw it wasn't Olavi Pustinen.

He was speechless, but Henry wasn't. "What the hell do you think you're doing?" Henry gasped. "Beatin' up on some Finn 'cause somebody interrupted some righteous speech about the sanctity of your river? I suppose you figure we should take it in the jaw because you own a salmon boat, and the rest of us don't count for naught! I've had it with you, Swede Olof," Henry growled, "you and your puritanical notions. You're one sorry excuse for a fishing partner!" Henry roared. "Even been skunked!"

Olof ignored Henry's condemnations, and he extended a hand toward the man whom he had sent flying to the ground. He bent from the waist and braced himself, meaning to return the fisherman to his footing; but the man brushed aside the open palm, as well as the words of apology that were too late in coming. "Sorry," Olof said in a throaty voice, "I thought you were somebody else."

"Always the impulsive Swede!" Henry exploded.

"I can't talk to you when you're drunk," Olof said and started walking away.

Henry grabbed him by the shoulder and swung him around. In his left hand, Henry had a whiskey bottle clenched by the neck. "You sound like my wife!" he hissed before raising the bottle and imbibing a mouthful.

Olof shook his head like an annoyed animal, ridding itself of flies. Dusk was almost a thing of the past, and night would soon engender more unknowns as he headed for the drifts to lay out his net. "Are you fishing with me tonight?" Olof asked sternly.

"You're not getting off that easy!" Henry announced in a strident voice.

Olof stood as still as stone, while a horse-drawn carriage traversed the street behind him. Henry's threat went in one ear and out the other, the clopping of hooves upstaging the moment when the bottle struck him firmly in the chest. Whiskey sloshed over his clothing, and Henry appeared ready to strike him again.

"What the hell!" Olof shouted and raised an arm to protect his face from a second blow.

Henry tossed the bottle aside and began rolling up his sleeves. In Olof's estimation, Henry was too drunk to throw a good punch. "What's this all about?" he said with lessened hostility. "What's got your goat?"

Henry peered up at his friend with a boyish grin on his face. "You tell me!" he quipped. "Why in the hell did you knock down my friend over there?"

Olof glanced over his shoulder and made brief eye contact with the fisherman he sent flying. "I thought he was Olavi Pustinen," Olof replied, "the man who set off the bomb."

"But you don't know that," Henry replied. His voice was sing-songish, a telltale sign the whiskey had control of his reasoning. "You don't know that Olavi Pustinen lit off a bomb; you just guessed as much because you don't like him. You don't like us Finns much, do you Swede Olof? Otherwise, why would they call you Swede Olof, the heir of your forefathers? Or is that just conceit on your part, something to make us think you're a good fisherman, when you're just a reject from your homeland like the rest of us. But you pretend to be better than the rest of us, owning your salmon boat and protecting the river from the likes of me. I'd be cap'n of my own boat if it weren't for you. Did you know that, Swede Olof?"

"Better head home and sleep it off," Olof replied in a surly voice. "The booze has got ahold of your brain."

"Not so fast!" Henry answered quickly. "I've got more to say to the likes of you."

Olof started walking off. He glanced over his shoulder at the small crowd of curious onlookers disbanding. They, too, were moving toward the river.

Henry did not know where to go. The bomb blast meant nothing in comparison with the first explosion he had witnessed that day. Earlier that afternoon, when news of the possible dissolution of the strike had hit the streets of Astoria, Lottie had been there, waiting for him. He would never forget the setting. She was sitting at their table, her back pressed into the chair slats with her hands folded neatly before her, never batting an eye as the truth spilled from her lips. Henry had gotten up and walked across the room, asking only for additional time. Lottie had bit her lower lip before hiding away in the bedroom; as she had already admitted to herself, Olof Andersson could awaken feelings in her that Henry could not.

Henry came at Olof from behind, sending him sprawling to the ground with a forceful shove and a well-placed kick to the lower legs. For a moment Olof was aware of a dull pain in his chin, then he felt the full weight of Henry upon him, and knees digging into his lower back. He was momentarily pinned, and Henry used the element of surprise to land a fist in the side of his head. Olof got his bearings quickly, and with his arms and legs pushed into the ground and succeeded in getting Henry off his back. But Henry was quick to re-engage, and landed another forceful punch in Olof's upper arm. Olof was mad, but not mad enough to take the open shot at Henry's rib cage. Instead he tried moving away from his assailant, grappling to stand erect. Henry continued coming at him, pulling at his legs as he tried to rise. Then Henry lunged forward and grabbed a handful of Olof's shoulder-length hair and yanked on it, giving Olof's neck a nasty snap. Olof could feel pain surging from his right shoulder blade into his inner ear, reminiscent of that instant when the gaff hook had met up with his flesh, and he knew he had been injured for life. For a moment, he thought he would pass out, but Henry was about to land his full weight on his upper body, and he realized he had to fight back. Henry was more than drunk, he was half out of his mind. Olof made a fist with his left hand and swung wildly, hoping to wing his best friend and bring him to his senses. His desperate maneuver only managed to turn him around and earn an extra second to get to his knees. Henry was still there, trying to kick him in the face.

"Damn you!" Olof yelled, and caught a leg as it came toward him. He twisted the leg, and Henry fell backward, the air knocked out of him. Olof was slow to gain his footing, but Henry was even slower. With incredulity, Olof stared down at his partner, sprawled on the grass.

Henry looked up at him, wearing that boyish grin as he sat upright. "I suppose you'll be looking for another boat puller now," he exclaimed in gasps.

Darkness was nearly upon them. Neither of them could afford what was happening between them, and Olof had to think seriously before responding to Henry's question. He was faithfully linked to Henry, for on the river they were kindred souls.

"It's up to you," Olof replied, extending a hand to lift Henry from the matted grass. "I figure the river will cure whatever is ailing you. If not, we'll let it go at that."

From Henry's perspective, nothing had been settled. "I could say I'm sorry," he replied, "but you are a hard-headed Swede and prone to snap judgments. Life isn't as simple as you make it, believe me. Not everything is always going to go your way."

Olof walked off slowly with drooped shoulders, confused and bewildered by the complexity of the evening's events. Henry lagged two steps behind, grieving over losses Olof could only suppose.

Chapter Five

~ ~ ~ ~ ~ ~ ~ ~ ~ ~ ~ ~ ~ ~ ~ ~ ~ ~ ~ ~

May 3, 1880

Olof never freely discussed the poverty associated with his childhood. Like most of his fellow emigres, those memories were kept buried deep in the soul, a place where people and events — the good and the glum — were confined in their infancy, a safe distance from a grown man's emotions. There were times, when picking up a net full of fish, he would experience flashbacks and comparisons would come readily to mind. Foremost would be the remembrance of his mother's jubilant expression, a sigh of relief following the presentation of two salmon, caught by his father following a lengthy fishing expedition off the coast of Poland. Why this vision repeated itself at the height of his own jubilation he could not say, but at that moment when he understood his good fortune, the world would seem unbalanced, giving little credence to the suffering of his past. It was a lesson in appreciation he intended to impart gradually to his children, but meanwhile, his old-world remembrances were a burden because the bravery behind those distant faces was inexorably linked to feelings of despair. Although his mother had cheerily exchanged their good fortune for a block of cheese, the sale of the fish would buy his father only a few days' reprieve, a brief interim wherein Olof could memorize the tired expression of a grave fisherman who spoke about the lack of firewood, and the need to return to the Baltic before the onset of winter encrusted it with ice. Such was Olof's childhood, a lesson in harsh reality concerning a man's obligation to provide for his family. Thus, there was no turning back when he set out on an all-night fishing vigil, because there was no excuse for failure on the Columbia, a river teeming with salmon.

Ingrid's memories of her childhood were her guide-posts, and she relied on them to give her sustenance in her new life. She exacted the good from the bad and edited out those stark moments of poverty and peril, as if they had never influenced the course of her maturation. In Olof's absence, she'd take her children on her lap and explore the wonders of her upbringing, of the birth and death of those she had come to love, as well as the clarity of the rules by which she had lived. It was her way of keeping community alive in a world filled with strangers. "Hanna Jane," she would say to her daughter, "is a name that came from two brave young girls I knew, one Swedish and one English." And, as if further elucidating would bring her a modicum of comfort, she would add: "Hanna is your aunt, and Jane is a fond memory."

Little Henry, always indignant when his mother's tone of voice became insipid with sentimentality, would remove himself from Ingrid's arms and face her head on. "Jane drowned," he would add defiantly, so his little sister would be sure to know the truth, "and Papa said the other one is likely to starve for food. Ain't no fish in Sweden!" Henry would chirrup, his arms stiff at his sides and his blue eyes clear and focused. "That's why it's better here!"

"You have much to learn about the ways of the world, young man," Ingrid would counter. "Your father could as easily be a farmer as a fisherman. It's only the bedevilment of men that binds them to that river, and the bedevilment of young boys that makes them repeat words without knowing their meaning. Your grandmother should be here to give you a good talking-to about family and duty. Your father is simply doing what his father taught him to do, and thereby fulfilling his duty."

Henry, like his father, would then fall silent and turn his back on the intimate family gathering of females. On the porch, beyond the rigors of his mother's tutelage, he could see the sails of the Butterfly Fleet spread across the Columbia's surface, and his heart would yearn to be one with manhood and explore the freedom he associated with the river.

On Monday, May 3, Olof and Henry had drifted with the ebb tide and sailed home on the flood. Evening would soon be upon them, but their twenty-four-hour clock was still ticking, and the river was filled with fish. They rapidly went through the routine of unloading their net. Olof spat in the river, disgusted at the river's untimely placement of a snag in the path of his first drift. Henry quickly pounded nails in the polished poles and draped a six-foot-long portion of diamond webbing over them, exposing the ruined area of net so the patching could commence. Neither of the Swedish-Finnish partnership lifted his head to observe the remainder of their cannery's fleet, rapidly off-loading salmon in preparation for the next drift. When the river was willing to deal in silver currency, it was each man for himself, and with one-fourth of the season lost to the strike, that silver currency heightened the competition.

"You're going out again?" Ingrid asked with an edge to her voice. "At least take along some sandwiches to keep up your strength. I'll rush home and make some."

Olof refused to look up from his net mending to give Ingrid the courtesy of a reply. The canneries were running full tilt, his net had a gaping hole in it, and a run of fish was moving upriver. Time was chasing him, and he intended to outrun it.

"What about you, Henry?" Ingrid asked. "Wouldn't you appreciate a little food in the stomach?"

Henry kept tension on the net while Olof continued to patch the hole with the wooden needle wrapped in twine; still, the offer sounded enticing. "I never turn down food," he replied.

"Then I'd be glad to return home and make something tasty," Ingrid replied in a huff.

"There's no time!" Olof exclaimed, exasperated. "Henry can go hungry along with the rest of us."

Ingrid released her grip on Little Henry and Hanna Jane alike. She placed her hands on her hips in a rather assertive manner. "Well, I never!" she replied, now peeved. Her enigmatic husband failed to respond as the wind pressed her skirt into her legs, and her blonde hair rose and fell in waves against her back. The few salmon boats moored alongside the net racks were tugging at the pulleys in rhythmic refrains, and Ingrid, as always, felt sorrowfully misplaced amidst these strange orchestrations. "Come, children," she said to her son in particular, "it seems we're unnecessary here." Little Henry turned a deaf ear on his mother, determined to observe the men at their anxious work. His heart was racing along with theirs, sharing their urgency to return to the river. "But I want to stay and watch," he pleaded as a heavy hand fell on his shoulder. "It's too dangerous," Ingrid said with resolve, and Little Henry looked up at his mother with the eyes of one who had just been told a lie.

Out on the Columbia, the wind was building as night was falling. In their desire to make up for lost time and income, much of the gillnetting fleet had already gathered beyond the river's mouth, hoping to be the first on the flood to net into a big run. Olof and Henry lagged woefully far behind. "Doesn't smell right," Olof commented as they tacked into the wind. "Nothing's ever right," Henry answered flatly.

Olof, ignorant of the implications in Henry's statement, overlooked it. "The air is heavy with the sea," Olof continued, his voice solemn and unusually throaty. "We could be at the mouth of the river for the weight of it."

"But we're not," Henry remarked sarcastically, then quickly changed his tune. "There are other things to worry about," he offered matter-of-factly, "things that have nothing whatsoever to do with the weight of the air, or the feel of the river."

"What might they be?" Olof inquired, but his question was meant to be rhetorical. He was perplexed by the way in which the landscape was merging into the river, and his points of reference were playing flirtatious games with his sense of reckoning.

Henry, given the opportunity to speak his mind, didn't know where to start or, if he dared begin, where the truth would eventually lead him. Then, like Olof, he looked overhead, trying to glean some truth from the depths of the starless sky. "It seems Lottie never wanted to marry me," he finally admitted. "It was a marriage of convenience, something her parents arranged to catch themselves a full-blooded Finnish son-in-law."

Henry's admittance caught Olof completely by surprise. He had supposed something like this had been the case, but the truth was far worse aired than the supposition kept secret. "Oh," he said to himself, his reply too muted for Henry to hear. He did not wish to say anything to make matters worse, nor did he want Henry to reveal anything he would later regret. "Women come and go," Olof finally said, but the lack of conviction in his voice betrayed him.

Henry could excuse Olof for tactfully avoiding the issue. In cases of the heart, neither he nor Olof had experienced such treachery. "Should I divorce her?" Henry asked, his voice almost gleeful, as if there was some daring in doing such a thing. "Or should I give up fishing, and try a new start elsewhere? Perhaps I could return to Finland, and explain the plight of my unloving wife." Henry's voice trailed off at the end. He had run out of options.

"Give it time," Olof replied, although the advice was meant for himself as much as for Henry. Time had always worked in Olof's favor. Given time, Ingrid had come to her senses; in time, Hanna Jane had survived her frail beginnings; and, in time, Olof would improve the politics on the Columbia. "When is your family coming from Finland?" Olof asked. His inquiry was heartfelt, meant to set Henry back on an old track and going somewhere with a definitive outcome in mind.

The question had the opposite effect, however, stirring up old memories of more hopes gone awry. Henry reared up from his seat near the bow of the boat and started to rush at

Olof in the stern, but stopped short of acting on his emotions, because Olof was correct in this instance, and his frustration misdirected. "I believe they'll arrive on the same day Lottie decides she loves me," Henry offered jokingly. "I couldn't have them both; now it appears I won't have either."

At the moment, Olof's thoughts were focused on the business of fishing. He was oblivious to Henry's sudden approach and rapid rejoinder because something was different about their progression downriver, and even more so than Henry's plight, it made him uneasy. Mother Nature was giving him something new to ponder. His usual navigational aids — the inky mountain outlines set against the loosely woven fabric of night — weren't in concert with his reckoning. A gusty southwest wind continued to move them north-northwest much quicker than expected. Olof made a snap decision. "Let's lay out the net here and now," he said. "We'll never make it to the river's mouth to join the others."

Olof's salmon boat had cost him four hundred dollars in cash, and the net another three hundred dollars, two hundred of that on loan from the cannery. Although these fiscal responsibilities weighed heavily on his mind, Olof had deceived himself into believing he could control his own fate, while Henry was wise to the pitfalls concerning self-determination. Still, he and Henry worked well together within the open, twenty-two-foot fishing vessel, and on nights like this, when the elements were changeable, the river was ultimately in control of them both.

∽

Ingrid entered the living room and held the door open, waiting for Little Henry's tardy steps to catch up with hers. Hanna Jane moved slowly to the sofa, where she curled up with a blanket. "Hurry up," Ingrid chided her son, "the wind is taking all the warmth out of the house." Little Henry brushed by his mother, but his eyes were downcast because he did not share his mother's urgency to arrive home. His lower body was dangling from his shoulders, and his legs were gimpy, affecting movements similar to those of a stringed puppet responding to the whims of another. He went to the sofa and plopped down next to his sister, exuding a long sigh of disapproval. "Don't act like this!" Ingrid scolded him. "Ah, Ma!" Little Henry groaned. "I just wanted to watch Papa do the net." "It's nothing for little boys to concern themselves with," Ingrid replied sharply.

Later that night, Ingrid rolled over in bed and lit the kerosene lamp on the bedstand. Even with the lamplight dispelling the notion of any ghosts lurking in the corners, the wind gusts rattled the windows, and Ingrid felt the grip of fear upon her. She could hear the sheeting rain beating against the glass and the howling wind in the attic above. She knew she was wide awake and conscious, yet the vision of Olof's outspread arms was before her, and an old terror returned. She quickly slipped into her robe and was out of bed. She peered into the neighboring bedroom, allowing the kerosene lamp to cast its light on her twins. Little Henry was curled up and sound asleep, but strange noises were coming from Hanna Jane, as if she were having trouble breathing. Ingrid moved quickly to her daughter's side and gently laid a hand upon her forehead. Hanna Jane turned away from her mother's touch and resumed a fetal position on her other side. Her raspy breathing stopped, and Ingrid gently tucked the blankets around her.

Lottie was aware of the storm the moment it struck the Astoria waterfront. From the raised porch of her parents' home, following a sumptuous meal in honor of her mother's birthday, she had escaped into the darkness, inviting the wind-driven rain to drench her from head to foot. She looked not at the river, however, but at the rivulets of water rushing down the dirt road in front of the house, until she was satisfied that the storm was of its own making.

The storm came upon Olof and Henry unexpectedly. The river's surface formed in deep troughs, and the sheeting rain slid into them broadside. Olof immediately began picking up the net as Henry laid to the oars. The men knew what had to be done. They worked in silence, because the river was wild and rolling, and the pouring rain had created an impenetrable shield between them.

At any time, the Columbia could foil the best-laid plans. When Lewis and Clark first ventured a guess that they had reached the mouth of the Columbia, they were more than twenty miles short of their destination. From the northern banks of the Columbia they saw nothing but furious waters and rainstorms, and in their exhausted states assumed this was it: the Pacific Ocean. The river, fifteen miles wide at this point, was far from exposing the true nature of its power, however. Seven days later their canoes finally brought them near the mouth of the river, but upon seeing the Pacific Ocean Captain Clark thought it quite the opposite because it roared like rolling thunder. On November 28, Clark wrote in his journal about the wind shifting to the southwest and an accompanying hard rain that beat down upon their lodge without mercy, destroying their stores and further dampening their spirits. Now, seventy-five years later, Olof and Henry were again witnessing the Columbia's changeable temperament.

Olof continued hauling in the net, sometimes throwing a fish in the locker, but more often than not flinging the salmon overboard. The catch no longer mattered to him, because he was losing ground to the river and fearful of the situation worsening. His precarious position, standing in the stern of the boat as it dove into the swells, spoke of reckless heroism, but riding this storm out was inconceivable, and he hastened to bring this nightmare to an end. All he wished for was firm ground beneath his feet, and the net and boat intact for another day. As he imagined himself coming through this storm unscathed, his muscles tensed up, a natural reaction to doubt. Somewhere in that happy ending, Olof was accountable for more than just himself and the equipment. Henry, too, relied upon him to make the right decisions.

Henry's mind was awash in recriminations. He worked the oars by rote, barely considering Olof's perilous position at the stern. As the boat rode the backside of a wave into a trough, he braced himself, and as it pitched upward, he reassured himself that Olof was still there, fighting the odds. Beyond the boat there was nothing but water and more water, darkness and more darkness, rain and more rain; but inside the boat there was ample time to drown in dismal recollections.

Henry considered bailing, but bailing would take him away from the oars. In Lottie's eyes, being a boat puller was no great achievement, he mused, but if she could be witness to this scene, she would have to respect his dedication. But then again Lottie would not understand any of it, Henry corrected himself, because she had never loved him, and love was what drove a man to succeed where others might not. Henry was still lost in his thoughts when Olof laid into the second set of oars.

The salmon boat was holding its own. It was an open, carvel-built craft, sharp forward and aft, the ends being shaped nearly alike. It had a shallow keel and a centerboard, which allowed the boat to pass over the river's numerous sand bars. To compensate for a low freeboard, it had narrow side decks and a three-inch-high coaming running around the inner edge of the decking. The interior of the boat was divided into net room, standing space, fish lockers, and fo'c'sle. The height amidships, from the gunwale to the keel, was two-and-half feet, and the height at the ends was three feet. It was designed for stability in choppy water, running either stern or bow first, and getting the net in and out with ease. But it was never designed to outwit ten-foot swells.

Olof was angry. His oilskin outerwear kept his body comfortable, but his eyes were strained, trying to see beyond the boat's perimeter. He called back to Henry: "Can you make out Chinook?"

Henry's rambling thoughts focused upon Olof's request; perhaps he could make a difference in this one instance. Over his right shoulder he sought the town of Chinook along the Washington riverbank, but he could not see beyond the towering swells and confirm they were even in concert with the landed world. For all Henry knew, they could be inside Sand Island and crossing Baker Bay, or approaching the Middle Sands where the Pacific meets the Columbia, or worse, slipping toward Cape Disappointment and the infamous North Breakers. He threw what was left of his spent energies into the oars.

Olof was not often afraid. Now, in controlling his fear, he centered his energy flow on avoiding what would bring it edification: hitting a sand bar. There, the pounding waves would rapidly disintegrate the salmon boat, and the storm would surely sweep the gillnetters out to sea. He kept his ears attuned to any change in the monotonous droning of the rain and the repetitive lashing of the swells against the boat. He continued to fight the odds, intent on keeping fear from disabling him.

In the years to come, Olof would never be able to tolerate the memory of what followed, starting when the river rushed in upon him, and ending with the horror of seeing Henry disappear overboard. Olof found himself alone, clinging to the boat for dear life. As the boat was torn from his grasp, his feet came in contact with the riverbed. Though exhausted and disoriented, he ran through water up to his armpits, searching, calling, trying to beat back the breakers, yet there was no sign of his friend.

Unlike Molly Bochau, Ingrid put little credence in what was printed in *The Daily Astorian.* One month earlier, her skepticism had again been validated via a reprint from *The Oregonian,* a newspaper from the upriver city of Portland. This particular story concerned a meeting of the Portland Board of Trade. According to the Board, there was too much being made of the Columbia River bar, and that "Again, no accident [on the bar] had been reported which, so far as testimony goes, might not easily have been averted by prudence, skill, and tug boats of sufficient power." For days, the story had grated on Ingrid's nerves, dredging up old memories and making her more mistrustful of new world expediency. Then, on May 5, two days after the storm, she was seated on the living room sofa with Hanna Jane's head in her lap, reading the newspaper column concerning the storm.

"Why are you crying, Ma?" Little Henry asked.

"Because it's so hard to know what to believe," Ingrid answered frankly. "They've found abandoned boats littering the Washington shore, and ... bodies floating in the river. Four boats showed up in Baker Bay without men or gear, and at Scarboro Hill the same number of boats were discovered swamped, without men in them."

"But none of them was Papa," Little Henry said angrily, his blue eyes flashing and his body rigid. Ingrid reached out to place a hand on his shoulder, but he moved beyond her reach, keeping his eyes glued to her tear-stained face while trying to fathom her complaint.

"I sure wish I had my *Bibeln*," Ingrid admitted sorrowfully.

"What for?" Little Henry shouted. "Pa ain't dead! He don't need no prayers!"

"I wanted to take you home to Sweden before you were born," Ingrid responded. "I've always known this time would come, and I didn't want you to be part of the pain."

Little Henry stood his ground, staring at his mother incredulously. He wanted to flee the house and go find his father, but that could wait a minute longer. He grabbed the newspaper from Ingrid's hands and stomped on it.

Ingrid's voice was cool and unshaken. She ran her hands over Hanna Jane's feverish brow as she spoke. "You can wad it up and throw it in the wood stove, for all I care," she said. "It isn't what's written in the newspaper that matters. What matters is that your father has been missing for two days, and that's a reality we must learn to accept."

Henry was both hurt and confused. What Sweden had to do with his father's disappearance was beyond his realm of understanding. Why the newspaper inspired such a dour attitude in his mother was another mystery. He turned toward the front door to make his escape, but there was a knocking.

"Get that on your way out," Ingrid snapped, her voice frigid.

Little Henry jerked the door open, his heart racing. "Pa?" faded from his lips the moment he saw the expression on Amy Van Dusen's face, also cool and contemplative, just like his mother's. He and the visitor brushed by each other. Little Henry's mind was set on pitching camp at the cannery, regardless.

Before dawn, Olof had scoured the immediate beach area a half-dozen times. His footsteps were becoming laborious from traversing the silty terrain, and his hands ached as a result of probing through the piles of fallen trees and rocks in the vicinity. He was soaked to the skin and weary from his distress. He intended to find Henry Hihnala alive. As the sunlight began to flow down the river from the east, he could understand the limited scope of his earlier endeavors. He was in a small cove, no more than fifty yards wide, contained on either end by rocky outcroppings, collectors of many years of storm-tossed refuse. His salmon boat appeared as if it had been lifted by a gentle hand and dropped amidst a growth of shoulder-high willows, set back two feet from the high-water line. Had it struck either outcropping, it would have been part and parcel of the river's tribute; but it was upright and, miraculously, with the plank-on-frame hull intact. Olof could scarcely believe his good fortune. He ran his hands along the washboards, caressing the wood, relieved that he still had something with which to work.

Captain W. P. Whitcomb, of the steamer *General Canby,* was in the pilot house, keeping an eye out for more fatalities. Since early morning, he and his three-man crew had retrieved two bodies from the river and spotted numerous boats without men or gear aboard. In continuing his perusal of Baker Bay, he was convinced he would only find more of the same death and destruction. Still, it was his duty, as a volunteer member of the Fort Canby Lifesaving Station, to make the attempt. Seeing Olof Andersson, standing inside the stranded salmon boat and bailing out water, brought him a glimmer of hope. "Land ho!" one of the deck hands called out in a jaunty manner.

Olof looked up from his work as the steamer came into full view. He was tempted to wave his arms with childish abandon, but he was not a child anymore, and his hands returned to their work. Captain Whitcomb, a man of some repute along the lower river, studied the stranded gill-netter briefly before working the steamer against the current to close on the shore. His first impression of the redheaded, scar-faced gillnetter, who gave no indication of being over-whelmed by his predicament, was of someone beholden to no one. Too, the salmon boat wasn't painted in the usual cannery colors. Taken together, Captain Whitcomb saw Olof's plight as being that of a more personal nature. He wasn't one of the sorry statistics. The steamer ever so gently dislodged the salmon boat from its willowy dry dock, and the deckhands drew on the towline until both boats were side by side, bow first into the current. "Come aboard and dry out, and we'll take your boat in tow," one of the deckhands offered nervously, but Olof cranked his head upward toward the pilot house in order to see the captain who had extended him this courtesy. For several minutes they studied each other, then Olof untied the towline and set himself free. "Thanks!" Olof called out, and Captain Whitcomb's ruddy lips parted ever so slightly to mouth the words: "If I were you, I'd consider myself damn lucky." Olof merely resumed the task of finding his friend.

The return of the ebb tide would take Olof as far as he dared go: Chinook, the Chinook River, Wallicut, Ilwaco, Fort Canby, and then Cape Disappointment. Past Cape Disappointment loomed the Pacific Ocean, the line of demarcation between hope and desperation. He took the only oar left at his disposal and started paddling, easing his way along the shallows of Baker Bay, hopeful of locating Henry before his journey's end. In his mind's eye Olof pictured Henry, seated on a log, hunched down and out of the wind, a knitted cap pulled over his ears.

Beyond the westernmost outcropping of rocks, Olof came upon Chinook, the town that had eluded him the night before. Readily he saw a beached cannery boat and a net on the sands. There were a dozen local residents inspecting the wreckage, but Henry was not among them. "Were there any survivors? Olof called out. "None!" came a reply, and Olof continued on, seeking a more acceptable answer.

A quarter-mile further on, Olof's oar came in contact with a submerged object. The interaction jolted him, drawing his concentration off the shoreline. The storm-swollen river was murky and thick, rich with the brownness of stirred-in soil, yet he saw what he saw, and his lower jaw dropped open. His arms were shaking uncontrollably as he rested the oar across his lap to keep from losing it overboard. The salmon boat beneath his had no color to differentiate it from the river, but it was very real, and not a shadowy reflection of the craft above. It drifted along for several yards underwater, sending chills up and down Olof's spine. The experience was akin to walking through a cemetery and being able to view the corpses through the solid earth. "The dead should rest in peace," Olof grumbled, and the current finally moved him beyond the eerie vision.

Olof was not one to give his physical welfare much consideration, but the sky was bleeding whatever warmth it could out of the sun, and it felt good when the priceless outpouring touched his face. He peeled off his oilskin outerwear and let the golden rays penetrate his shirt and trousers. His skin was beginning to tingle, going through a process of rejuvenation. His stomach growled, yearning for Ingrid's cooking. For the first time since the storm had caught him off-guard, he was beginning to come to grips with his situation.

He had never been alone in a salmon boat before. Henry had always been there at arm's length, dissipating the monotony of their drifts with his harmonica playing and storytelling. Olof had never experienced the kind of loneliness unfamiliarity could bring, nor had to rely on the river's continuous lapping to keep him company. With the exception of what he was doing at the moment, there was no relief in sight. His odyssey along the Washington shoreline was part of the healing process, a means by which he could assure himself there was no returning to what was.

At Wallicut, a salmon boat from the Aberdeen Packing Company had gathered quite a crowd. Putting ashore near the gathering looked risky, with exposed mud flats and the shallow mouth of the Wallicut River making it a less-than-desirous stopping point. He called out again, "Are there any survivors?" One rather squatty-looking fellow shrugged his shoulders, and Olof continued paddling.

With Ilwaco in sight but the tide turning, Olof was slowing down. His singular oar would take him no farther against the flood. Without a sail to take advantage of the late-afternoon winds, he was completely beholden to the river and all the quirks that made it so unpredictable. He started thinking about his family, and how Ingrid was coping with his disappearance. He was miles away from home, a distant place on the horizon, recognizable only by the outline of mountains that appeared as misty apparitions, about to succumb to a late-afternoon drizzle. Short of his journey's end Olof gave into the flood tide and began drifting upriver, the ocean breezes at his back, taking him slowly homeward. There was no cause for jubilation, yet the memory of his mother's welcoming face occurred to him briefly, until it was supplanted by the grave visage of his ever-wearied father, someone with whom he could share the reality of the moment. He, like his father, was bound to drift with the currents, wondering where the morrow would take him, struggling to control his losses against the elements.

∞

Amy Van Dusen followed her own rules of protocol: she would never eat food at a wake or accept refreshments from someone less fortunate. She waved Ingrid's offer of cookies aside and remained standing until Ingrid insisted she take a seat. "It isn't as bad as it sounds," she opened the conversation, "because our Lord is far more forgiving than He is vindictive."

Ingrid didn't know what Amy's visit was all about, but she assumed it had to do with the storm and Olof. Ingrid watched as her visitor's eyes immediately settled upon the crumpled newspaper, lying in the middle of the floor. Rather than offer an explanation, Ingrid continued to rock Hanna Jane in her arms and let Amy do the figuring, giving free rein to the woman who prided herself on insightfulness.

Amy, predictably fastidious, removed the hatpin from her broad-brimmed bonnet, secured it through the grosgrain ribbon, and carefully set aside the whole affair before making her pronouncement. She pointed at the newspaper as she spoke. "I suppose that was what Little Henry's rush was all about," she said.

Ingrid had no reason to deny it. "Yes," she replied calmly. "Olof has yet to return, and Little Henry has greater faith in his father than many."

Amy's eyes darted between the newspaper and Ingrid. She could tell Ingrid had been crying, but having read the paper herself, she knew Olof's name had not been mentioned. She set her jaw slightly askew on her face and assumed the demeanor of one given to contemplative moods.

Ingrid was far more uncomfortable with the unsaid than the spoken. "I have no idea whether Olof made it or not," she offered propitiously. "Are you certain you won't have a cookie?" she added.

Amy turned to face Ingrid squarely. She wanted to get her suspicions off her chest. "Many people believe that not so many gillnetters died, as ran away," she admitted frankly. "Gillnetters and boat pullers don't make much money, and following the strike and the storm, they just left their boats beached and went looking for greener pastures."

Ingrid started laughing.

Amy blushed, confused by Ingrid's reaction. "What's so funny?" she asked querulously. "Many of the boat pullers, in particular, are just farmers' sons. What do they want with that kind of hardship? As for the captains, you've said yourself they're mostly transients, men without families. Why should they risk their lives for some smelly salmon?"

Ingrid could not contain herself. She was on the verge of uncontrollable hysteria when Little Henry rushed in the door, Olof only a few steps behind.

Amy immediately rose from the sofa and took her hat in her hands. The greeting was awkward. "Nice to see you, Olof," she stammered. She was mortified, and quickly escaped the house without making her proper farewell to Ingrid.

Ingrid's laughter was slow in subsiding. She wiped her face with the back of her hand, but only looked up at Olof occasionally, as if his presence was nothing out of the ordinary. It was a curious sight for Olof, who had expected slightly more. He was tired and hungry. Worse, his heart had already been broken. He walked into the bedroom to change his clothes and prepare for the difficult task ahead.

∽

Lottie opened the door and returned to the table, leaving her guests to do for themselves. Olof was properly groomed for visiting, and Ingrid was dressed in church-going clothes. Lottie immediately put the pieces together and wished them gone. "You may come in if it pleases you," she said begrudgingly.

Olof took his hat from his head and held it in his hands. He felt more comfortable near the doorway, but he approached the table, nevertheless. "I don't know what happened to Henry," Olof said outright. "I can only assume he drowned."

It was an awkward moment for Lottie, because such an announcement would normally have brought forth tears. She would have been expected to cry and bemoan her fate, and allow the bearers of bad tidings to comfort her; but it wasn't in her to continue the role playing.

"Thank you for bringing me the news," she replied.

Olof was aghast. "Don't you want to know what happened?" he exclaimed.

"Not really," Lottie answered, returning Olof's direct eye contact. "If Henry is dead, may his soul find peace in heaven."

Ingrid turned, ready to leave. She placed her hand on the doorknob, unaware Olof was standing his ground, replaying the last conversation he had with Henry in his mind, trying to sort truth from fiction. Giving Lottie the benefit of the doubt, he made a giant leap of faith. "I suppose you'll be sending money to Finland, to bring Henry's family to America. It was what he wanted."

Lottie's stare was harsh. Olof, in his naiveté, had expected something different. He had expected Henry's wife to rise to the occasion as her husband would have, but he was beginning to see who Lottie was, and why Henry had given himself to drink and despair. It was too little too late, but Olof refused to let the point drop. He looked around the rather bleak surroundings and added things up. As long as he could remember, he and Henry had been earning wages, and through all those years, Henry had been setting his aside, waiting for the right moment to spend them. Those off-season jobs felling timber and loading ships had amounted to something. Even with his wife and children to provide for, Olof had managed to buy a salmon boat. Now Lottie was sitting on a small windfall, and she did not have the courtesy to shed a tear over the man who had left her such a legacy.

"You will be sending a letter to his parents," Olof said firmly.

"And say what?" Lottie retorted. "That their son may or may not have drowned?"

Ingrid closed her ears to the conversation, feeling somehow a traitor, more in accord with Lottie's perspective than Olof's. She stood aside, her hands gently clasped together, pressing the folds of her skirt to her stomach. She observed the indifference in Lottie's eyes, empathizing with her. Prior to Olof's return from the river, she had experienced the same resentment, the same lack of tolerance for being the one to accept the bad news, and then bear the responsibility for moving on. It was stressful, listening to Olof as he tried to extort payment for the dead. Years earlier, when Ingrid had been in the same position, her pleas had fallen on deaf ears. "Get on with your life," Olof had advised her, and now he was getting a taste of his own medicine. Ingrid knew exactly what she would do if she were in Lottie's place. She'd slap Olof across the face to get his attention, then ask him forthright, what gave him the right to put all their lives in jeopardy? Ingrid looked down and observed her hands. They were clenched tightly, her knuckles white knobs. The idea of drowning brought out the worst in her. She was sad for Henry, Olof and Lottie alike, but ultimately she was afraid for herself. Everything concerning the Columbia River exacted a higher price than she was willing to pay.

∞

Olof held Hanna Jane firmly in his arms, although the time had come to put her down. Her goodness could not outstay the coldness overtaking her body, and her eyes were losing their luster and wonderment. Gently he touched her eyelids and the clarity behind her deep-blue eyes disappeared. How long Olof had been standing there with his body frozen in time he could not recall, but Ingrid's wailing seemed to have gone on forever. Little Henry had stepped outside on the porch. He, too, was trying to distance himself from his mother's grief. It had all happened so suddenly.

Little Henry watched a sea gull circling overhead. In so many ways it was like him, apart from the others, exploring what it meant to be alone. Little Henry was incapable of understanding the finality of what had just happened, nor did he wish to. As the sea gull would eventually tire of its isolation and return to the river where it belonged, so would Hanna Jane rejoin her brother, he thought, and all would be as it was. Little Henry's sister remained an extension of himself, the more accepting of the pair, the angelic half. Hanna Jane faithfully represented the good in them both, while Little Henry was free to test the boundaries of his childhood and be the precocious son who said things beyond his age. Little Henry knew he excelled because of Hanna Jane, and Hanna Jane was angelic because of him. Everyone said they complemented each other, he protecting her from the horses stampeding down the street, she coming between him and their mother's condemnations. They had been so closely atuned to one another that Little Henry could not recall even one instance when they were at odds. Hanna Jane had simply vanished, and without her he had no idea how to react. He was the strong one, and determined, now, to wait for her return.

Little Henry felt the strength of his father's hand upon his shoulder. They stepped off the porch together, Little Henry following Olof's lead. Little Henry could tell there was a purposefulness in his father's elongated stride. "Where we goin', Pa?" Little Henry asked. "To make a casket and stop by the stone cutters," Olof replied.

The Clatsop Mill was located kitty-corner across the street, and Olof passed through the front office and was well into the heart of the operation before Little Henry could catch his breath. Olof immediately veered off into a corner of the drying shed, where he started through a pile of planks. He turned the planks over rapidly, returning most to the pile. Little Henry was so absorbed with his father's inspection of the lumber that he failed to notice they had been joined.

"Another casket?" the interloper asked in a heavy brogue.

"My daughter's," Olof answered without looking up.

"Seems you've got a run of bad luck going," the ruddy-faced stranger replied. "First your boat puller, and now a youngun'."

"I'll leave a half-dollar on my way out," Olof said.

Little Henry listened to the conversation with curiosity. What these two men had to say to each other was straightforward, unlike the rambling verbiage shared by the womenfolk who came to visit his home. There was less anxiety and no emotional outpouring. Little Henry immediately took a liking to this man. He was almost huggable, wide around the belly and obviously disdainful of dress codes. His red suspenders had been worn nearly through, and his flannel shirt was half in and half out of his trousers. He was non-threatening and undemanding, apparently an old acquaintance of his father's from the previous winter.

"Most of these boards are full of knots," Olof said in disgust.

The spectator didn't seem to take the remark personally. "The good stuff got shipped out," he replied. "This your son here?" he turned to Little Henry. "A chip off the old block, I'd say, with the red hair and all. You gonna turn him into a gillnetter?"

Little Henry blushed with embarrassment, and the speaker returned his attention to Olof. "What did the daughter die of?"

"Diphtheria."

∞

The road leading to the cemetery was nothing more than a wide swath cut through the trees and underbrush. Much had been made of getting it properly groomed, but the grooming was occurring through usage, rather than political jousting. Many families had lost children to the epidemic; just as many children had bequeathed fathers to the storm. The newly dug graves were very much in evidence, with their recent bouquets of cut flowers protruding from the ground. Little Henry saw the small casket his father had made standing next to a rectangular hole in the ground. Molly Bochau was placing flowers on it. Little Henry looked away, far more intrigued by the broad expanses of water flaring out from the base of the high promontory, running away in every direction. He felt like he was standing on top of the world, rising above the tallest tree. The air smelled sweet and pure; he felt that everything was safe and secure.

"Come along, Little Henry," Ingrid said.

Little Henry watched as a small gathering of people came together around the casket. They were all so quiet and solemn, each of them moving slowly, hesitant to get near the hole. His mother's hand felt sweaty, but he knew he dared not break the clasp. He allowed her to lead him toward the casket, a strange box that was to be his sister's resting place.

The crowd became so quiet that Little Henry could hear robins singing. Then the man in the black robe opened a book and started reading. As he read, Ingrid released her grip on him: she was crying. Little Henry, wedged between his parents, looked to his father for some understanding. Olof was staring at the casket, lost in his own thoughts. "Shall we pray?" the minister asked. Little Henry watched

as people folded their hands and lowered their heads. He
tried to follow suit, but he could not seem to take his eyes
off the box.

"The Lord is my shepherd," reverberated across the
hillside as the voices came together, his mother echoing the
solemn passage in Swedish, while his father's contribution
was too muted to be audible. Then the crowd parted slightly,
and Molly Bochau came forth. She was dressed in black
from head to toe, and her voice was thundering. She kept
her focus on Olof as she told a strange tale about Hanna
Jane drinking goat's milk. Little Henry was pleased with the
story and the chuckles it evoked from many in the crowd.
When her voice fell silent, it was Ingrid's turn. Ever so
softly she repeated a Swedish nursery rhyme Henry had
heard a million times. "Rida, rida ranka," her voice wafted
out over the hillside, "Hasten heter blanka, Vart ska vi rida?
Rida sta och fria...."

Memories started flooding in on the young boy, and
the security of the high promontory seemed to vanish. He
had moved off into another time and place, and there was
Hanna Jane, staring at him with delight. His mother was
bouncing him on her knee, rushing him forward on the
horse Blanka, getting him ready to woo the Maiden
Margareta. Hanna Jane was clapping her hands frantically,
urging him to get there on time. The pitch of his mother's
voice was getting higher, knowing the suitor was just about
to reach his fair maiden. Then Little Henry leapt off his
mother's knee and and tried to shake the tears of delight
from Hanna's face. Little Henry recalled it all too vividly,
and he reached out for his mother and shed his tears in her
skirt folds.

The final leg of the funeral parade seemed inter-
minably long. The buckboard jostled down the hillside

behind three other carriages. Olof sat beside Ingrid, while Little Henry rode in the back, switching his attention between the scenery and the horses. The casket, in its absence, was a stark reminder of the finality of death. Ingrid said not a word; she seemed lost to her family. Olof let her off at the doorstep of their home and went to return the buckboard to the livery stable. He, too, was unable to accept Hanna Jane's death. She had been the sunshine of his life, as much as Henry had been the rain and the wind.

Little Henry disappeared into his bedroom to change his clothes, but the tone of his mother's voice stayed with him, making him cringe.

"What do you mean you're going to fish for the Scandinavian Packing Company?" Ingrid shouted. "Hasn't any of this meant anything to you? Don't you realize how close you came to drowning?" Ingrid's voice was strained to the point of breaking. "How dare you bring this up now! Your daughter is barely cold in her grave, and you're thinking about gillnetting. I swear I'll return to Sweden if you go back to that river! I swear I'll do what I should have done in the beginning, and take my children home with me!" Ingrid's eyes were awash in tears. "But I've lost one of my children, haven't I?" she added dejectedly.

Olof was also emotionally spent, but excuses would not buy him time. "A man's got to earn a living, regardless," he said softly. "In spite of all that's happened, we've got to build back what we've lost. The fish are still running, and I'm beholden to the bank for a net and the replacement of my gear. I figure.... "

Ingrid cut him short. "You figure what? You figure the Lord is going to be more benevolent with your life than it was with Hanna Jane's and Henry's? Do you really think you can continue to put me through all this? And what about

Little Henry? Do you suppose he's planning on becoming a gillnetter like his papa? Is that what you had in mind?"

Olof studied his beautiful wife, but his answers were slow in coming. Beneath those deep-blue eyes was something frightful, similar to the hull of a sunken salmon boat, peering back at him through murky waters. Both were cold and unforgiving revelations, and both were determined to drag him down. He tried to give Ingrid's words an opportunity to settle in before he said anything else. She had just stepped back in time, becoming that cold, indifferent stranger who had arrived in America, expecting promises. In a way, Olof felt insulted. If Ingrid preferred returning to the poverty of her past, rather than trusting in him to make a better future, then so be it.

"You can do what you want with your life," Olof said solemnly, "but Little Henry should be allowed to make such choices for himself. I still think America has much to offer … but everything comes at a price."

Ingrid watched her husband disappear through the doorway. His words were echoes of her own, yet they sounded unfamiliar, coming from him.

Chapter Six

~ ~ ~ ~ ~ ~ ~ ~ ~ ~ ~ ~ ~ ~ ~ ~ ~ ~ ~ ~

July 2, 1883

The tall oblong-shaped vase containing daisies was only a diversion, like the small cups and saucers that had been their sailing partners. They had been ballast, brought to Astoria in the hold of a sailing ship. The pearly pink swirls on all four sides of the vase were supposed to represent some artist's idea of flowers, but Little Henry knew different, as he compared them with the pure white petals of the real flowers it contained. Yet the oddity and his mother's resourcefulness had held everyone's interest for a few precious seconds, and for that reprieve the youngster was grateful.

"Once you've gotten over the idea that reading is something only women do to while away their time, memorizing your letters will be much easier," Ingrid proposed to the intimate gathering of conversationalists. Nonetheless, pinched uncomfortably in the corner of the sofa, Little Henry was keenly aware the comment was again meant for him. "Going to school will be a wonderful experience, a way of finding something meaningful to do with your life. In the Old Country," Ingrid continued, "the Bible was the means by which most children learned to read. Here in America, however, they make it much easier. There are storybooks to interest young boys."

Little Henry did not believe a word of what his mother was saying, and even if he should, it was of no immediate relevance whatsoever. Attending school in the fall could possibly thwart his future, but whatever was to transpire in the interim took on far greater meaning.

"What your mother is saying is quite true," Amy Van Dusen added. "It's only with education that my husband ventured into merchandising." Mrs. Van Dusen's voice took on a patronizing tone, causing Little Henry to look at her. "You're such a clever boy, young Mr. Andersson, I would expect your future to be equally bright. You can go as far as you want, if only you'll apply yourself."

"Is that all, Ma?" Little Henry whined. The musty odor of women's perfumes clouding the air was becoming as tiresome as the discussion centered around his future. The more his neck itched from the paper collar, the more his desire to head for the waterfront increased. These sedentary sessions devoted to proper behavior cut into his freedom. "There might be ships coming today," he said casually.

"Is your husband expecting a shipment from San Francisco?" Mrs. Holmes spoke up, addressing Mrs. Van Dusen, the merchant's wife. Little Henry eyed Mrs. Holmes with particular interest. She was a large woman, visually capable of keeping him contained. The folds of skin beneath her chin could not be ignored, in spite of the damming restraints of a fastidiously tied bow clasping her matronly bonnet to her head. She, of all the visitors, could inflict real pain. Mrs. Holmes was the schoolmarm, and he was supposed to be on his best behavior in her presence.

"Not that I'm aware of, Mary," Mrs. Van Dusen said in response.

Little Henry glanced around the room, seeking a sympathetic face. Some of the women at this afternoon social he knew to have children. He wondered if they, too, made attendance at such gatherings obligatory. Somehow he doubted it, being the only child thusly detained. Mrs. Felton's boys were free to chase hoops down the street and holler at the sailors coming into port. It was only he, Little Henry, who had to sit so properly and listen to female chatter.

"Pa said I could go down to the waterfront whenever I wanted!" Little Henry exploded.

Predictably, the one to foil his escape was Mary Holmes, the formidable schoolmarm. "Well, I never!" she gasped. "In the classroom, such outbursts won't be tolerated! Children are to be seen and not heard," she continued, "and that's a rule I expect you to observe."

Little Henry's lower jaw slid sideways. "Yes, ma'am."

Ingrid set down her teacup and stared at him relentlessly. Her hair was drawn back severely from her face and restricted to her neck by a tightly wound bun. Her blue eyes were cold and purposeful. "Go to your room," she said, her disappointment in Little Henry's deportment quite evident.

"Maybe you shouldn't be so hard on him," Mrs. Felton intervened. "As you well know, Ingrid, boys will be boys."

Little Henry took his mother's silence as a cue to head for the bedroom. There he removed his church clothing and lay on his bed, thinking about his father and wondering when the gillnetter would save him from undergoing such scrutiny. Little Henry felt unfairly singled out. With Hanna Jane gone, and Olof on the river for days at a time, the sole focus of his mother's attentiveness had fallen upon him. Truthfully, Little Henry was less apt to find his father seated in the living room than he was to catch a reassuring glimpse of him sailing across the water, the image he had had in mind when he had spoken of the sailing ships. There was something encouraging about watching the Butterfly Fleet, expectant of recognizing that renegade salmon boat, the one belonging to Olof, the man whom Little Henry had come to idolize.

Ingrid's teachings about duty to family and country, as well as being one's own person, were difficult for a six-year-old boy to follow. More often than not, these rules met resistance in their application, and Little Henry could show ample proof of that. A young boy with flaming-red hair and natural curls did not find friendships easily made. His peers were discerning of differences, regardless of the freedom that America provided, and Little Henry's unique hair color was ample reason to place him at odds. His glib tongue also put him at a disadvantage because, like his father, he was not one to take insults lightly. Although his mother assured him he was American, he felt no obligation to that assignation whatsoever. It made him different from his parents. As far as the disparity between his parents went, Little Henry was ignorant of anything out of the ordinary. His father was a dedicated gillnetter gone for days at a time, and his mother was a woman, given to baseless notions with no bearing on him whatsoever.

Tom and Howie Felton were crouched in the shade of a spruce tree, keeping an eye on their mother's whereabouts through the Andersson's living room window. She had said something about an afternoon social, but they needed assurance of its duration. Like most of the other boys in town, they had plans of their own to make the best use of such a hot summer day. Tom, the older of the two, took Howie by the shoulder and started dragging him away. Howie, seven years old, tripped and careened into the window with a thud. Mrs. Felton, a very unpretentious woman, observed their plight with a certain amount of sympathy. "Well, they've certainly embarrassed themselves this time," she shared with the other women. She rose from her seat and motioned to her sons to meet her at the door.

Tom, ten years old, stood front and center. "Why are you peering through the Anderssons' window?" she asked him.

"Me and Howie was wonderin' if we could go swimmin' down at the log boom. It's awful hot, Ma." Tom's story was half true; the rest of it he intended to keep secret. He looked down at Howie sternly, making certain his younger brother would refrain from adding anything extraneous.

"Why don't you take Little Henry with you?" Mrs. Felton replied. It wasn't a question; it was an order. She glanced over her shoulder at Ingrid, okaying the idea with her hostess. "Boys will be boys," she added as an afterthought, not forgetting how Ingrid had just laid down the law with her son.

Ingrid was aware that the consensus of opinion was rapidly turning in Little Henry's favor. After all, it was a hot day. Drops of perspiration were beginning to bead up on Mary Holmes's forehead just below the brim of her bonnet. Ingrid's feet were swelling uncomfortably in the confinement of her high-top shoes, and Mrs. Felton's cheeks were flushing as the warm air wafted in off the street and struck her in the face. "I suppose Little Henry can go," Ingrid announced begrudgingly.

Astoria was a city of such incongruities, it was bound to arouse a young boy's curiosity. It was both colorful and crowded, most of it changeable from one block to the next. There were buildings with steeples and others with cupolas, some with peaked roofs and others with ornate dormers, some built over the river and others footed on land. Taverns were plentiful, and the comings and goings of their odd array of customers were in complete contrast to the activities of the dandies, well-dressed visitors patronizing the smattering of hotels. On one corner there was the Astoria Soda Works; on another, the brewery. Some of the mercantiles offered both river and street accesses, making it possible to stand at the candy counter and wave to the passengers lining the side of a passing sternwheeler. There was the shooting gallery, the China wash houses, a blacksmith shop, a choice of eateries and, of course, the brothels, canneries and sawmills. On a hot day such as this, the log boom located just south of the Clatsop Mill seemed the most desirous. There the boys gathered along the riverbank and swam in the Columbia.

Little Henry was keenly aware that the invitation extended him by the Felton brothers had been made under duress. Still, he would have taken his freedom at any price. He lagged a respectful distance behind and watched the older of the two brothers, Tom, who was doing the same — trying to size up the unwanted tagalong. It was nothing new to be observed in such a cautious manner. Friendships were not arranged by mothers. Instead, they evolved through sheer fortitude. Beyond the sanctity of his own bedroom, Little Henry was on his own.

There were more than a dozen youngsters already gathered on the riverbank, making use of the protected waters created by the log boom. It, like a bent arm reaching across the river's surface, held the choppy waters at bay, creating a quiet pool apart from the river's domain. Little Henry's pace slackened to a crawl, seeing what awaited him. The older boys were having a heyday, pushing the younger ones in the water and forcing them to cry uncle before releasing them. It was easy to predict his fate. He made up his mind to slip away and find a better method of keeping cool.

"Your father is a gillnetter, isn't he?" Tom said unexpectedly. Little Henry, whose body and mind were both turning in a different direction, had to stop and allow the Felton brothers to catch up with him.

"Yeah," Little Henry answered honestly, although he was somewhat suspicious of the question. "Yeah, he is."

"Then he smokes and drinks," Tom Felton replied matter-of-factly.

"He chaws," Little Henry corrected him sternly. "Spits Scandinavian dynamite."

Tom looked Little Henry up and down, wondering if there weren't some redeeming qualities in this youngster who had been given into his care. "Hmm," he replied, the squarish lines in his broad face falling into place, while the cowlick centered directly above his left eye tufted upward, doing its own thing. Tom, like his younger sibling, Howie, had the ability to hide behind an emotionless face, to form his opinions without blinking his dark brown eyes or twitching his pencil-thin lips. He stood a full head taller than either Little Henry or Howie, yet he was at that scrawny stage of development, and with only overalls to hide the growth process, the narrowness of his shoulders and the weakness in his chest were quite evident. In spite of his added height, he seemed to lack the constitution to pose a threat. He finally broke the silence, airing one more important question. "So, why do they call you Little Henry? It's kind of a stupid name, isn't it?"

Little Henry's expression changed. His eyes narrowed as his lower jaw slid sideways. He knew an insult when he heard one and, like his father, he wasn't one to take any guff. "Not as stupid as yours," he snarled.

Tom took a giant step backward. "So, you think you're a real spitball, don't you, Little Henry?" he retorted snidely, because Little Henry's hands were already fisted, and his red hair was a faithful addition to the appearance of his fury.

"I was named after my pa's boat puller!" Little Henry exclaimed. "And my pa says he was the best on the river!"

Tom Felton's face again fell into an emotionless state. If it weren't for Howie, the standoff could have ended in disaster. "I thought we was gonna have a smoke!" Howie blurted out, the secret finally exposed. He took a handful of the straps on his older brother's overalls and gave a good yank. "Let's go before Ma gets out of the social," he protested nervously.

Tom took a few obliging steps in the direction Howie was leading him, yet he stopped briefly and made quite an unexpected offer over his shoulder. "If you can keep your mouth shut, Little Henry, you can come with us."

Little Henry looked at Tom's backside with mistrust. The shouts of other boys being tossed in the river were sufficient warning. "No thanks," he said quietly, and trotted off.

Little Henry was accustomed to being alone. Without Hanna Jane's company, he had learned to find his way to favorite haunts, investigating the status of those enterprises which interested him most. His first stop was always at the old cannery, the one which his father had worked for before Henry Hihnala's death. Although Olof would not be there, it felt comfortable to wander among the net racks and watch the sea gulls go into a frenzy as the fishermen unloaded their salmon. If no boats were being unloaded, Little Henry could walk out as far as the receiving dock and observe the river, aspiring to catch a glimpse of his father on his upriver trip to the Scandinavian Packing Company. Little Henry did not understand any of the rationale behind his father's move to such an estranged part of the waterfront, but just a glimpse of the salmon boats gave him a sense of identity, coming and going on their ritualistic expeditions.

From the cannery, Little Henry might turn to the city streets for enlightenment. These were the sights and sounds that brought his mother the most joy, including the glittering accouterments of a hotel lobby, as well as the colorful display of fashionable hats in the milliner's window. If the day was excessively hot, a door might be propped open and he would gaze with amazement at the organ inside the steepled church, the one not far from the three-story bank building.

Time permitting, he could wander out to where the buildings fronted the river and walk the plank-on-pile streets, imagining the distance between himself and the river's surface, rather than showing too much interest in the saloons or the whorehouses on either side. Then, if the gate was unlocked, he could walk beneath the shade of the two-story-high roof that overhung the L-shaped dock belonging to the Oregon Railroad and Navigation Company. If he was extremely lucky, a riverboat would be moored alongside, and he could look in the windows, wondering what it would be like to travel the Columbia in such comfort.

This day, however, was too warm to find solace in wandering. Even the wind off the Columbia was not refreshing, raising the dry earth from the dirt roads and swirling it in the air to constrict his breathing. For two hours, Little Henry sat beneath the overhang shading the O.R.&N. dock, just watching the river, whiling away the time in the proximity of the large coal bunker. There were no boats passing, no sails to pique his interest. The only distraction from this overheated day came from the area of the log boom, and the shouts of boys at play.

Little Henry suddenly grew tired of the heat and spending too much time alone. On his way home, he veered back toward the innards of the Clatsop Mill, tempted to learn the status of the boys at the boom. He wanted to swim, to cool his overheated body in the Columbia. A few of the boys were still there, but most seemed to have gone home. He was at the riverbank before hearing his name called.

The Clatsop Mill found footing on land, then extended over the river's surface on piles. As the gradually sloping ground came in contact with the river, it left a space beneath the mill's flooring, a place where planer shavings and trash collected. Although the shadowing effect of the sun made it difficult to see into the depths of this gap, Little Henry did recognize Tom, motioning to him. It was an intriguing idea, exploring this dark recess on such a hot day. He went willingly, eager to become acquainted with every nook and cranny of his hometown.

When Little Henry stepped out of the direct sunlight, the first thing he saw was Howie, lying flat on his back on a three-foot-high pile of shavings. As his eyes began to adjust to the total dimensions of this shadowy underworld, he saw Tom and four other companions, wandering along the water's edge, barefooted. Little Henry started walking across the uneven ground, sinking ankle deep in some places. The saw from the mill above was loud yet dull, more of a droning sound than an accurate representation of metal ripping through timber. Minute particles of shavings were present in the air, filtering through the gaps in the thick planking above. Little Henry's impressions of this over-looked portion of Astoria's waterfront were favorable. He found a mound of shavings slightly higher than Howie's and lay down. It was comfortable, being out of the sun.

He must have started nodding off. The next few minutes lacked credibility for their dreamlike quality, beginning with the unbelievable scenario of a group of boys being caught red-handed smoking cigarettes. Little Henry never paid the incident any mind because he was just an innocent bystander, half-enjoying their plight as they tossed aside the evidence and went scattering into the sunlight. He remained where he was, hidden in the dark recesses of his newfound world and catching only glimpses of the Felton brothers running away. For a while there were trousers to keep him entertained, the baggy trousers of the accuser still visible between the flooring above, the sloping ground below, and the rows of piles between. But even the mill-worker eventually moved on, leaving Little Henry to lie there and contemplate the onset of mind-numbing terror. He had never even smelled it, but the wind off the river turned the smoke into flames, and they came at him in a blast. He was cornered, with only the river to save him.

∞

Ingrid was first alerted by a shrill whistle at the mill, followed immediately by the deep tone of the fire bell being rung repeatedly in the tower south of City Hall. Upriver another whistle and bell went off in unison, and she ran for the front porch. Heavy black smoke was already rolling over the roof of her house, and flames were shooting into the air: the Clatsop Mill had just exploded in fire. Her first reaction was to seek out Little Henry, but her mind was garbled by all the people rushing up and down the street, the only barrier between her house and the sudden conflagration. Some of her neighbors were fleeing for safety; others were simply caught up in the frenzy, trying to ascertain the seriousness of this development and wondering which way to turn. It was such a hot day, and the roar of the fire in its infancy was already overshadowing the wild clanging of bells in the background. Whatever was to be done, needed to be done quickly.

Ingrid swallowed deeply, hoping to gather her thoughts. The hot air and smoke irritated her lungs, yet she surveyed the fleeing crowds, looking for the youngster with the flaming-red hair. The last time she had seen her son was midafternoon, and he had been headed to the log boom to swim with the Felton boys. She could not believe that he'd still be there, near the heart of the fire, because Little Henry wasn't one to stay settled for any length of time. Again she surveyed the street, but this time she saw a woman running past with a carriage clock in her hand. It was becoming more difficult to remain attentive to any particular person, however, because the wind was agitating the fire, and the rolling smoke was becoming a solid curtain before her eyes. Ingrid ran through the house one last time, calling Little Henry's name. He was nowhere to be found. She returned to the porch. Unlike the woman escaping with a clock, Ingrid had nothing worth saving other than her son. She decided to stand her ground and wait for his return.

Men and boys alike were pulling a fire engine down the street. She could hear them calling to each other, trying to decide which side street would give them access to the river. It was low tide, and the Columbia's depths were far removed from the fire's innards. There was panic in their voices, an uncertainty that made Ingrid angry. For all their good intentions, she doubted their integrity. One of them waved to her, meaning she should follow them. But this house was footed on ground, and Ingrid felt better protecting it from fire, than diving into the unknown. Didn't they realize she was waiting for Little Henry? "No!" she called out firmly. "No! I won't go!"

Ingrid was becoming lightheaded, the heat unbearable. The spruce tree aside the house beckoned to her, as if in its natural form it could provide some contrast to the destruction of her surroundings. She stepped off the porch just as the house exploded in flames behind her. She started running, headed for the road.

The occupants of a hotel were throwing their belongings from the windows. Others, who had escaped the interior, were grabbing up articles from the street and running in the direction of the hillside. Ingrid assumed her son would head for the river, rather than higher ground, because he would be looking for his papa. There were tears of both terror and smoke staining her cheeks, yet Ingrid went on, opposing the foot traffic pushing in the opposite direction.

The workers from the downriver mill went rushing by her, but they were like the wind, going in the wrong direction. They could not help her; she had to help herself. Of all of her son's favorite haunts, he had to be at either one of two: the O.R.&N. docks or the cannery.

It was dangerous where she was going, and Ingrid knew it. The wooden walkways above the river were tinder-dry, fuel for the far-reaching flames. At the entrance to the gun shop she was joined in her panic. Several young men carrying wooden boxes were also going against the flow, headed toward the outer docks. Ingrid stayed behind them, allowing them to make a path through the smoke-filled air. At the Dockside Tavern her progress was blocked by exhausted men rolling barrels across the walkway and dumping them over the edge. Below, the mud flats were littered with kegs and bottles, a last-ditch effort by the proprietor to save his merchandise. There was evidence of optimism amid all this desperation, driven by a sense of dread and remorse.

∞

The fire was highly visible from the wharf areas comprising the Scandinavian Packing Company in Uppertown. There was no cloud in the sky, and the billowing fire immediately caught the attention of those working on their nets. Olof watched it for only a few seconds before he knew full well it was the Clatsop Mill going up in flames. It had to be the sawmill, because nothing else could ignite so quickly. At six o'clock p.m., only seconds after the fire came to his attention, Olof was sailing toward Astoria.

From the river it had been easy to see the path of the fire; it was only the breadth of it that could not be foretold. An hour and a half later, it came as no surprise to Olof when he found his rental house a smoldering ruin. Ingrid's absence, too, was no surprise; she had certainly taken Little Henry to safer surroundings. What did remain along his street was a sickening sight. A few homes and businesses were still aflame, but the members of the bucket brigade had turned their attention to saving St. Mary's Hospital, regardless of the tough choices involved. Olof immediately pitched in, not knowing where he might begin a search for Ingrid and his son.

Fire was almost inevitable for a city built on wooden piles, but the extent of it could never be foreseen, nor its cause. Rumors were spreading among those in the fire brigade about some boys smoking in the vicinity of the mill, but since the mill had been running, there might have been another explanation. But as the citizens of Astoria continued to work into the night, dousing the fires as they arose, it was evident the effects of the fire were far reaching. A dock loaded with canned salmon continued to burn, and as the cans overheated they exploded, popping and banging like gunfire in the distance. It was rumored that men in boats had come into the waterfront area to loot and steal, while on the hillsides where the homeless had deposited their belong-ings, the same was occurring. Against this backdrop of uncertainty and disillusionment, the fabric of the city was beginning to unravel.

Olof could recognize Ingrid from afar. A sigh of relief trembled throughout his exhausted body. He thought nothing of Little Henry not being with her; she had certainly left him in capable hands. He walked down the street cautiously, overstepping the charred debris, much of it still smoldering. He approached her gradually. The loss of their house and worldly goods would take time to accept.

She looked at him with cold indifference, and Olof was puzzled. The embers cast a shifting glow on everything around them. Ingrid said nothing for several seconds but kept her distance, as if the distance between them Olof could no longer bridge. When she did speak, her voice was cruel and without compassion. "I hear the gillnetters are looting the waterfront. Why aren't you with them? You're never here when we need you, anyway."

Olof's mouth dropped open. Ingrid could be caustic, but never this cruel. There was something bothering her not apparent in the mere destruction of the house. Something was missing from this picture, and Olof could only assume she would tell him in good time. He did not respond to her flagrant question but held his tongue. He looked over his shoulder and watched a shadowy figure coming from the southeast perimeter of the mill ruins. It took a few minutes, but the man's outline eventually took on a recognizable form. He was an old acquaintance, Charles Felton, the man who had helped him and Little Henry select the wood for Hanna Jane's casket. He was walking through the debris gingerly, carrying a large bundle in his arms. For a moment Olof wondered what to say to the man, his job gone and this aspect of his life probably ended; for a moment, Olof, too, speculated as to what would happen next, without a roof over his family's head, and no belongings with which to establish another household. He empathized with the hunched-over figure of the man, moving ever so slowly in his direction, with a bundle under his arm.

"Couldn't find a blanket," the man grumbled apologetically. Olof frowned; he did not understand his friend's reference to a blanket. The man removed the bundle from his arm and offered it to Olof.

"Very sorry, ma'am," he said to Ingrid, and then he slipped the bundle into Olof's arms and walked away.

The way in which the top of the bundle cradled in his arms, Olof knew it was a body he was holding. The familiarity told him one more thing, that it was Little Henry. He did not dare look at Ingrid, nor was he capable of pulling aside the odd array of wrappings. He looked up instead, hoping the sky would guide him through the next few seconds. He felt weak-kneed, about to collapse. He was lost on the river, amidst a terrible storm. There was no hope in sight, not even a twinkling light to confirm that he had ever been connected with anything solid.

"I'm going to kill myself," Ingrid said calmly. "There is nothing left to live for. It's all been taken from me, and I wish not to go on."

Olof could hear his words in hers; they were identical, yet said differently. He needed to look at her, and assure her that they could weather this one more storm, but Little Henry's body was dead in his arms, and he could not promise anything. It was incumbent on him to relieve himself of this new burden, before the very core of him collapsed. He could not stand the feeling of weight upon him, so he knelt and laid the body on the road.

"You monster!" Ingrid exploded.

Olof stood up and, without knowing why, slapped her across the face. She never winced from the pain; instead, she stood her ground solidly and stared at him point blank.

At the moment, Ingrid was disappointed but not surprised. His outspread arms had never really been there for her, and neither she nor Olof was capable of walking on water, as in her dream. In the end, however, she had thought she would be the one to strike the final blow, yet that error was only one of many to overlook when searching for the truth.

Olof was two different people, both the man she loved and the gillnetter she despised. Every aspect of their half-hearted love was destructive, ending in the ruination of everyone it had ever embraced. She had nothing more to say to Olof, nothing that could possibly make any difference. It was she who was ultimately responsible for the death of her children, a premise she had to accept. She did not belong in this place called Astoria. The price for her freedom had become far too dear. She could feel herself drowning in her own sorrow as she turned and walked away from it all.

Olof could not leave his son lying there. Even with the city in ruins, there had to be some lumber left somewhere, something worthy of being Little Henry's casket. With Ingrid gone, he dared peel back the wrappings to say goodbye. The tears started to fall freely when he saw the charred remains. His son had not met his death easily, and the realization caused him to release a gut-wrenching cry, heightened in intensity by the chorus of canned salmon exploding in the background. He had to express his agony and expunge the pain from his body before getting on with the business of accepting the blame for his son's death.

All the roads leading up the hillside were blocked. Piles of clothing, sewing machines, lamps, and bedding were strewn everywhere, and the owners were dispersed as well, homeless drifters in their own hometown. The excitement had dissolved into despair, and no one took notice of the scar-faced Swede, carrying his large bundle. The city was sluggish under the weight of the smoke, and everyone was tending to his or her own concerns, protecting their meager belongings.

There were rules concerning the proper dispensation of the dead, but Olof chose to overlook them. He knew exactly where Hanna Jane had been laid to rest, and as the sunrise began to discover his whereabouts on the hillside at the end of Fourteenth Street, he was throwing the last shovelfuls of dirt upon a roughly hewn box. Little Henry had not received the same rituals at his burial as had Hanna Jane, yet it seemed imperative that he be given back to his sister quickly, because she would embrace him without hesitation, regardless of his scarred condition.

When he was finished, Olof leaned on the shovel handle and experienced the same panoramic view of the river that had once garnered his son's interest: the broad expanses of water flaring out from the base of the high promontory, running in every direction. It seemed incumbent upon him to deliver the proper words of farewell, yet the river was far more forceful in its effect. The dawn, shimmering across the pearlescent surface, was sufficient proof that the river was again vibrant and refreshed, adhering to the good Lord's design. And that is how Olof would remember his precious twins, traveling in unison wherever God should take them. Olof's throat thickened as such thoughts came to mind and, much like his son, he preferred to look at the world with amazement, rather than with apprehension. Apprehension had caused him to bury Little Henry so quickly and bring rapid closure to the whole ordeal.

∞

It was another hot, cloudless day in the making, yet Ingrid, aboard the lumber schooner, was not worried about the heat. Soon she would be on her way to San Francisco and then home to Sweden. With the crew going through its preparations to set sail, she could stand aside and observe the citizens of Astoria doing those very things she was avoiding: comparing their losses with their immediate needs. She could not do it again and participate in such futility. What she had lost could not be recrafted by any man's artistry, and her needs were inexplicable, beyond definition. Some of the waterfront continued to smolder, some of it was simply missing, while some of it had escaped the fire entirely. There was no rhyme nor reason to any of it, Ingrid surmised, except that foolish people continued to make it happen, so that others might endure the consequences.

The fire bell in the tower near City Hall started clanging madly, sending chills down Ingrid's spine. She canvassed the horizon for any sign of another fire in the making, but the bell stopped. Her heart was pounding in reaction to the horrid recollections of yesterday's disaster, and her hands were frozen on the ship's railing. She felt lightheaded again, as she tried to suppress those inescapable emotions welling up inside her. She could not wait to put it all behind her and digress into a structured world where she could sleep the night through without fear of the morrow. She dared not think about the pain she was inflicting on Olof, because of the love he had once held for her. Her life along the lower Columbia had reduced her to a coward, a person incapable of picking up the pieces and pretending she could ever hold them together.

∞

Olof had tired of the waiting, wandering and aftermath of the fire. He had reconciled himself to the fact that Ingrid had disappeared. He was worried about the length of her absence, yet he had once been on an odyssey of his own following Henry Hihnala's death, and he supposed she was doing likewise, searching for answers where there were none. He had spoken with everyone who knew his sweet Ingrid, and they also assumed she had been somehow disoriented by Little Henry's death. However, in each case, the topic immediately veered off to address other concerns, because Astoria was still being ravaged in the wake of the fire, and a vigilance committee was taking over where the sheriff had failed. Rightfully so, people were doling out their concern in judicious amounts.

Olof had just finished another search between the cemetery and the ruins of their house. If it was supposed to be Independence Day, no one could prove it by him. He was drenched in sweat. In Ingrid's absence, he was about the business of sifting through the charred remains of their house, extracting a few usable items as he came upon them. On the other end of his circuit, he had managed to get a headstone placed on Little Henry's grave, with the addition: "Born American." He had paid dearly for the haste involved in getting it completed, but he knew Ingrid would be pleased with the sentiment.

It was beginning to come together for Olof, putting the old to rest while preparing to embark on the new. There would never be children such as the twins they had lost, but others would be welcomed, and they, too, would be born American. He nurtured such encouraging visions of the future as he explored the limitations of the past. He was truly amazed by the modest size of the dwelling they had once inhabited. Collapsed on the ground, the diminutive nature of the small rooms was evident, including the living area where he had pushed the twins around and around in the fish-box when he wanted some relief from the outside world. The kitchen now seemed impossibly cramped, and the side-by-side bedrooms incapable of ever having held four occupants comfortably. He was already leaping ahead, thinking how much better it would be in the future. Given time he would construct a house for his family, a larger more spacious home, removed from the probability of fire and the negligence of others.

Olof did not notice Charles Felton, who had also come to look at the remains of the Anderssons' house. His unobtrusive presence had escaped Olof's attention as he went about the job of sifting through the charred boards and restacking them off to the side. Charles Felton had assumed that delivering the young Andersson boy into his father's arms would be the most difficult task ever given him, but as he watched the determined Swede at his work, he realized the message he had to deliver was much worse. He ran his thumbs behind his red suspenders to straighten them and tucked in his shirttails before speaking. He struggled to find words.

"Been looking for you since yesterday afternoon," he said.

Olof wiped his hands on his trousers and stepped free of the ruins. A horse and carriage went by, and the dust kicked up around him. He took a handkerchief from his pocket and wiped his nose, all the while moving in Charles's direction. "What's on your mind?" he replied.

Charles paused a moment, wondering how to make his words go directly to the heart of the matter; it wasn't fair to keep a man in suspense. "My wife said that your wife, Ingrid, that is, left on a schooner bound for San Francisco, and she thought I ought to pass that along."

Olof could not comprehend who had said what to whom, but he did get the message. Ingrid had acted on old threats and was going home to Sweden. Olof nodded his head in acknowledgment. "Thank you for coming by to say as much," he said calmly.

Charles Felton's face was beet red. He turned to go, but paused to say something else. "I'm real sorry," he added, then walked off, relieved to have the matter finished.

Olof, a man of action, realized immediately that sifting the rubble was a waste of his time. His family no longer existed, and he was foolish to pretend otherwise. He walked so quickly as to nearly overtake Charles, going in the same direction. Olof's first stop would be at the moorage where he had tied up his salmon boat, then on to a saloon, to celebrate Henry Hihnala's birthday. That done, he would return to the river and lay out his net. The weather was far too warm to promise him a good catch, but the season ended in August, and then, with the Clatsop Mill lying in ruins, he would have more pressing matters to concern him. Be it comfort or consolation that America offered, he would have to arrive at that answer himself.

Chapter Seven

~ ~ ~ ~ ~ ~ ~ ~ ~ ~ ~ ~ ~ ~ ~ ~ ~ ~ ~

1885

The boardinghouse kitchen was teeming with all the sights and sounds of a Sunday supper in the making: flour-coated chicken sizzling in the frying pan, gravensteins cooking down to the consistency of applesauce beneath trails of spice-laden steam, and freshly churned butter paired up with a crock of blackberry preserves, left in the proximity of lightly browned biscuits in the center of the table. If there was anything Olof missed about a woman's influence on his life, it was this — the way she could minimize the stress of the outside world by creating the sights and smells of home. He grumbled something under his breath as Molly Bochau finished reading aloud the article in *The Daily Astorian*. In his opinion, another strike was an old story revisited; the buttermilk biscuits cooling on the table between them seemed a far more enticing subject, although equally prohibitive. Either way he turned, there was an exorbitant price exacted for moving off center. "Are you sure you won't humor an old woman and at least taste one?" Molly asked a second time. She ably translated the scowl on her visitor's face to mean no and promptly scooted her chair away from the table. She returned to the wood stove and the supper in progress. Olof observed Molly's ease in the kitchen with more respect than in the past; still, no woman could cook like his sweet Ingrid, the very reason for turning down Molly's offer to partake in the biscuits. Denial was an exercise in self-discipline, a barrier that prevented outsiders from inquiring about the viability of his austere lifestyle.

Olof's cravings for the intimacy of his past were quickly upstaged by Molly's preoccupation with the newspaper. It was her Bible, the written word from which she could extract either gospel or gossip. "We all know too much of a good thing brings the riff-raff out of the mountains. It's just the way of the world," Molly remarked offhandedly. Again Olof grumbled, although he was pleased she had verified a goodly portion of his ongoing history. The migrants had returned for the onset of the fishing season, and the battle lines were already drawn. "It happened with the fur trade," she mentioned with a tinge of regret in her voice, "and now it's about to happen to the salmon-canning industry. Sooner or later, the walls of Jericho will come a-tumblin' down around our fair city."

"Vengeance is mine, saith the Lord," Olof quipped.

Molly's back bristled, but she refrained from making a comment. The resignation underlying Olof's remark was disquieting. He wasn't at the end of his rope, but the fraying was becoming noticeable. Molly was both saddened and angered at the changes she saw in her old friend.

Observations were something she meted out with discretion, not wishing to trip over the fine lines of demarcation keeping their friendship at a safe distance. What Molly really wanted to see from Olof was the display of spunk that had once made him invincible, instead of the staid interest he showed in watching her stir flour into pan drippings. There had been times when he would knead her neck with his fingertips and they would speak of the nonsensical nature of the world, but now he was casting her off, much as Ingrid had cast him off. She could observe him over her shoulder, sitting complacently in the chair, getting more estranged by the minute. As the gravy bubbled up and began to thicken, there was a look of frustration on Molly's face. Her old friend would not even be so kind as to taste it, or accept the advice she so desperately wanted to impart. The less-liable recourse seemed to be in adhering to the subject of fishing, the only tangible asset left him. "What's the Scandinavian Packing Company's position on the strike?" she asked.

Olof nearly upset his coffee cup. He dared not admit it, but he had been daydreaming about Hanna Jane and cradling her in his arms while Molly heated goat's milk on that very same stove. The familiarity of the kitchen was coming in upon him, like a flood of regrets he could not dam. "Are you really interested?" he asked with uncertainty. "Interested in the association?"

"Sure am!" Molly replied.

The Scandinavian Packing Company, like most everything in Olof's life, seemed shrouded in inexplicable details, differing somehow from the norm. Like Uppertown, where the cannery was situated, it was comprised mostly of Norwegians, Swedes and Danes, united in their desire to perpetuate a fishing legacy. Furthermore, the packing company was also an association, wherein the members profited individually from its success as a whole. Thus far, the quality of their catch had made them competitive, but the thought of a strike on the river would certainly be a test of the membership's mettle. What would occur when they went against the grain, as they surely would, remained an unknown, yet they were deeply invested. Many of them owned their own boats, and most had taken up permanent residency along the lower Columbia. They were the tenacious gillnetters, not the transient labor who sufficed to keep the number of canneries expanding while placing undue pressure on the salmon runs. Molly would not understand the rationale behind them, however, because she was a woman who believed that as long as a gillnetter was kept fat and happy, God and goodness would certainly see to his survival. Was Olof bitter about a woman's lack of convictions? Yes! It seemed to him that, for all of Molly's unabashed beliefs, she was still driven by fate and, according to Olof, fate didn't have a darn thing to do with any of it. Thus, it was a waste of his time to delve into the question with the consideration it was due. He raised the coffee cup and dedicated his lips to a different subject.

Molly waited a generous amount of time before assuming her query had not met its mark. She took the handle of the frying pan in the folds of her apron and shoved the gravy to the back part of the stove. She returned to the table and picked up the newspaper. Olof grumbled again. "I take that to mean the Scandinavian Packing Company isn't going to back the other gillnetters," she said in exasperation.

Olof rose from his chair and took up his hat in leaving. "Right!" he snarled.

He was halfway through the doorway when Molly made her finally summation. "You know I don't approve of anything that ain't American, so I've got to suppose this Scandinavian company is in name only. And ... and you haven't got Henry to keep you safe on that river anymore, so you be darn careful, and don't go instigatin' fights when you haven't got your wits about you. And as for the biscuits, even a stubborn Swede could use a little meat on his body." Then Molly's lips started to tremble, reacting to all the words left unsaid. She did not know how to put it, but she was going to say it anyway. "You're just not yourself anymore, Olof Andersson. It's due time you knocked that chip off your shoulder before you topple under the weight of it."

Molly's face never changed from year to year. Her eyes continued to bulge forth from the restraining effects of her tightly wound hairdo, demanding settlement before moving on to a new issue. Olof paused for a second, not wishing their meeting to end on such a negative note. Wherever he turned, others mirrored his frustrations. "As far as the Scandinavian Packing Company goes," he offered sincerely, "it's named for the fishermen who fish for it, just like the other canneries are named for their owners. If there is pride in a name, a man oughta wear it."

Molly's expression remained unchanged, and Olof went outdoors.

Perhaps Molly's outpouring had done some good, because it set Olof to thinking. Perhaps he was at the end of his rope and, like the slabwood road leading away from the boardinghouse, structuring his future along the lines of least resistance. The impending strike was something he dared not take too lightly or delve into too deeply. The fishermen's union was becoming more radical, more secretive in its organization, and although he agreed with them in principle, at times their methods were reprehensible. The bomb blast stood out as the most blatant example, followed by the apocalyptic litany occurring thereafter. Perhaps it was maturation thickening his skin; or, having been bitten once, he was wary of the snake. But regardless of the reasons for his change in attitude, he could not bring himself to get upset when the threat of another strike arose. Molly's admonitions were appreciated, albeit too loudly stated. Olof felt secure in casting his lot with the association because it was slow and steady, and those who fished for it were of a common mind. It was a new approach to an old problem, and it demanded a certain amount of resignation on his part.

Because of Scow Bay's proximity, Uppertown (or Upper Astoria) had enjoyed the freedom to develop a separatist attitude, with stores and churches, a post office, school and cemetery established on its own. It was dwarfed by Astoria's sheer size and understated according to Astoria's flamboyant and tempestuous nature, but it was an integral part of the river's workings.

Six canneries were located along the waterfront, each one a viable competitor for the overseas markets. In the prior two years these markets had been fully saturated, bringing a truism to bear upon the now-ninety canneries operating along the Pacific Coast and the thirty-seven operating on the Columbia River: Something had to give. There had been talk among the canners of limiting their production to each cannery's capacity, or dividing the boats evenly among the canneries to level the competition, yet the focus of the change again fell upon the shoulders of the gillnetters. It was a presupposed solution, but low profits from the increased competition could be offset by paying the fishermen less. In Uppertown, however, a permanent population of gillnetters was trying to change this hopeless pattern by interjecting themselves into the equation.

The golden tones of the setting sun were reflected on Arnold Larson's door. Before knocking, Olof stopped to compare the real thing with the reflection. Both the rising and the setting of the sun told him much about the weather and the conditions he would face on the next drift. Tomorrow being the first drift of the season, he observed the glowing orb with keen interest. The sunset was colorful and unabashed due to a cloudless sky. Following an early-morning shower, the spring air was now clear and crisp and the temperature in the mid-forties, all ideal conditions for finding a run of fish moving upriver.

In Ingrid's absence, these were the sensual assurances bringing Olof gratification, temptations both beautiful and alluring and of a substantive nature. He was anxious for the next day's sunrise, anxious to return to the river and get on with the business of living.

Arnold met Olof on the stoop and allowed him entrance to the modest two-story home, typical of those being hastily constructed along Cedar Street. From the landing at the foot of the stairway Olof entered the living area, where an upright piano occupied the otherwise sparsely furnished room. Beyond the piano and a refurbished settee, the remainder of the Larson family was seated around a table, finishing bowls of rice pudding. Before Olof could remove his hat, Arnold Larson was already posing the problem.

Arnold was forthright, and very much the master of his own fate. He was five years older than Olof and had two sons, one seventeen and one nineteen. Arnold did not offer Olof a seat at the table but rested his hands on the back of his vacated chair. "I think we've got a change of plans," he said bluntly. "This first day out, we should team up and leave our boat pullers at home. There could be trouble;

some of the other canneries in Uppertown might go heavy on the strike. I don't want either Jason or John involved."

Olof glanced around the table and caught the concerned look of Mrs. Larson. Olof thought of her as being round eyed and round faced, with the endearing qualities of a totally devoted puppy. She was the last of the Larson family to arrive from the Old Country, and her English was limited to a few words of perfunctory cordialities. Knowing this, Olof shied away from her. He did not much care for the double standard when graduating from one language to another, knowing she could have her say behind closed doors and in public profess her innocence through silence. Also, her name was Ingrid, and perhaps Olof was particularly impatient on this point. Nonetheless, he extended her the courtesy of a nod, certain she had negotiated the deal prior to his acceptance.

Arnold stood about five-foot-eight and weighed one hundred and seventy pounds. He had a light complexion which blended well with the sandy hues of his beard. His hair was beginning to thin on top, above his square forehead. Everything about Arnold Larson appeared to be fairly distributed, except for his excessive concern for his sons' welfare. This discussion would not have taken place two years ago, before Ingrid Larson's arrival.

Molly Bochau was correct in this one instance, because without Henry Hihnala at his side, Olof was obliged to follow the lead of others. He left the Larsons' house without uttering a word, much as he had in the past, when the threat of a strike was looming.

April 13, 1885

The river was disconcertingly serene the second week into the strike. Some of the canneries were up and running, but many more sat idle. A staged march through Uppertown prevented Olof from making his early-morning drift and, although the event was peacefully orchestrated, he was too versed in the ensuing speeches not to see the folly of the participants. As usual, the real problems were glossed over, and the gillnetters proved as quick to wield their swords of defiance as were the canners to shield themselves behind a wall of indifference. With the markets seemingly saturated, it was an exercise in futility to suppose the canners could not hold out until the gillnetters eventually conceded. Olof stood by and revisited his past until Olavi Pustinen forced his way through the crowd and came to the forefront. His eyes then turned to his young apprentice, Jason: "This has been going on for ten years now, and until both the canners and gillnetters weed out their own ranks, nothing will ever come of it." Enough said, Olof split the crowd and led his boat puller back to the business of fishing.

The Scandinavian Packing Company was the last in the cannery row, the one farthest from Astoria and nearest to Tongue Point, a highly visible, forested land mass jutting into the river, used as a navigational aid for all vessels traveling the river. This day, like the week of days before it, the Scandinavian Packing Company was about the enterprise of fishing, regardless. Late in the afternoon, Jason brought the boat around to be unloaded at the receiving dock and, thanks to Olof's skill as a fisherman, there were many chinook salmon to be counted. Ed Mattson was usually the man stationed on the end of the dock, a congenial fellow always with a tally sheet in hand, prepared to receive the fish, get them on ice, and receipt the transaction. This day, however, it was necessary to tie up alongside and wait for his appearance. Occasionally, if something was amiss inside the cannery building itself, such delays occurred. Between the processes involved in gutting the fish, packing them in tins, and placing them in the retort for canning, the fish changed hands many times. The cannery, though simple in principle, was a maze of twists and turns. Ed Mattson could have his hands full, overseeing the separate parts so they would ease together as a whole.

Olof motioned to Jason to climb the ladder. "We'll begin lifting them dockside," he ordered. Jason was capable of fulfilling this request, proving that both fear and affection were at times great motivators. Sometimes the sandy-haired youngster was in awe of the scarred fisherman and all the tales surrounding him, and at other times he was admittedly fearful, mistrustful of the sordid stories concerning the drowning of the first boat puller and the death of the Mongolians. Unbeknownst to Olof, the youthful apprentices were a second generation in the making, comparing notes and evaluating the captains for whom they worked. Most of the time Jason felt insignificant in Olof's presence, poorly equipped to do much else than obey. Olof's awesome appearance was more than a legend. When his green eyes looked in Jason's direction, Jason either jumped to, or wilted.

He and Olof were working in harmony, rapidly unloading the salmon onto the raised receiving dock. Olof filled a lowered box from the bowels of the boat, and Jason winched it upward to exhume the contents. The scene was nearly picture perfect. In the background, Tongue Point stood out as a reference point on the horizon. Between it and the piles supporting the end of the receiving station, a lonely salmon boat with sails raised could be seen moving upriver. A slight chop on the Columbia's surface highlighted the various hues of the river's creative urges, faded blues and golds awash over earthy greens and browns. Olof's salmon boat was nestled in against the piles, the flood tide gently rocking it while holding it in position. Both fishing partners, wearing their shiny black knee-high boots, appeared absorbed in an activity with which they were completely familiar. One was doing a balancing act as the fish were lifted upward; the other appeared solemnly critical of the goings-on below. Between the two levels of operation perhaps there was a gap of eight feet. Six rungs on the vertical ladder spanned the distance uniformly, arriving at a point on the platform where a man with paper in hand was supposed to be tallying the catch.

When the tallyman finally arrived dockside without a tally sheet in his hand, he was grinning from ear to ear, amused that somebody else was performing his duties. The third box-load was about to be winched upward when he gave Jason a violent shove in the chest and let his presence be known. A glance from Olof confirmed the man was a stranger, certainly not one of the members of the association, and certainly not someone he wished to do business with.

"What the hell do you think you're doing?" Olof roared, but the cunning smile remained on the stranger's face, and Jason had no other option than to give him a wide berth.

The man's appearance, somewhat abject yet rugged, was very typical of the lower river denizens; he could have been a gillnetter from a neighboring cannery, a local farmer come to the river's edge for a breath of fresh air, or a curious millworker taking a break from the monotony of high-pitched saw blades buzzing in his ears. But at the moment, Olof had no idea what he was about, except that he had laid a hand on his youthful partner, an act that did not set well with him.

"I suppose you think you've got a mighty fine catch there," the stranger said jokingly, but in Olof's estimation his catch was not a laughing matter, nor was the man's sarcasm. He thought about climbing the ladder and taking the man to task; instead he stayed where he was. In the building directly behind the stranger there were many voices. Olof assumed incorrectly that they belonged to members of the association. It was not until the fish that had been loaded dockside started cascading into the river that Olof came to grips with the imminent threat. He had never witnessed such a thing, but he was seeing it now. A bizarre expression on young Jason's face best represented the outlandishness of the situation. More strangers had arrived dockside, and all of them were engaged in jettisoning Olof's fish.

"Let my boat puller pass," Olof said assertively. "He's still a boy."

The seventeen-year-old threw his shoulders back and stood his ground, but his knees were about to cave in from the quaking. The instant the words were out of his mouth, Olof was aware of the mistake he'd made by placing his youthful partner in such an untenable, face-losing situation. "I said to get out of here!" he hollered at Jason ferociously, a rude rebuke, meant to free the youngster from any false ideas of allegiance. He repeated himself: "I said to hightail it, right now!"

Jason's already pale visage was awash with uncertainty, and he had seemingly melted into his clothing and become something inert. All totaled, seven men had appeared from the recesses of the building and were gathered where Jason cowered. A distinctive voice came from the interior of the receiving station, giving Olof good reason to pause. He could not immediately attach a name to the voice, but he knew he had a good fight on his hands. Intuitively, he thought of the gun stowed in the bow of the boat. In the mere seconds it took to turn in that direction, two men had joined him aboard and were attempting to restrain him. An assailant took him by the arm and tried to wrest it against his back. It was a painful maneuver, and Olof howled before wrenching himself free. For a split second his hands clenched on the enemy's throat, but then he saw the look of terror in the man's eyes and changed his mind. Instead, he took the man by the upper body and threw him overboard, breaching the river's surface with a tremendous splash. He turned immediately to do the same to the other, but he had lost ground to the multitude who were now swarming his boat, tossing his catch overboard. His boat was taking on water over the gunnals as the unknown army continued their work. Two more men struck the water's surface as Olof forced his way toward the gun. Olof was one man short of reaching his objective when the entire affair ended as abruptly as it had begun.

Arnold Larson was standing dockside with Astoria's sheriff. Ed Mattson and a good dozen of the association's gillnetters had joined them, whereupon the sheriff drew his gun and discharged it in the air.

"Do you want to press charges?"

Sheriff Evans asked the question repeatedly, but even with the boat regaining its stability beneath him, Olof remained in upheaval. His face was a fiery accompaniment for his beard and hair, and every ounce of him was pulsating from the blood racing through his veins. His fists were knotted tightly, predisposed to finishing what he'd begun. The assailants were unexpectedly meek; three of them stood in arm's reach of their intended victim with pathetic looks of remorse on their faces, and four others were in the process of climbing the ladder. Along the dock and within his boat, all eyes were fixed on Olof expectant of a reply. It was so obvious to all of them, yet it remained a puzzlement to Olof.

"All I want is to get a fair shot at each of them," he finally responded. "What's the use of them spending the night in jail? I'm not going to get my fish back."

Arnold could interpret the consternation on Olof's face, having been the one to play the lead part in a story without a recognizable plot. "Olof and I need to have a little talk," he suggested to the sheriff.

It was beyond Olof's scope of life experiences to grasp the reasoning behind litigating the matter: that which could have a questionable outcome would be better settled here and now. As they stood in conference under the eaves of the main cannery building, removed from the others, he and Arnold argued.

Olof was indignant. He was an eye-for-an-eye and a tooth-for-a-tooth man and could not get it through his head why Arnold had gone for the sheriff instead of lending him a hand. He felt betrayed. "It's like this," Arnold replied coolly, "it began long before you came into the receiving dock, and it was planned and paid for by the strikers, all meant to keep us off the river." Here Olof attempted to interrupt, but Arnold Larson laid a hand on his shoulder, intent on having Olof's undivided attention. Olof wanted to pull away, yet, out of deference to Arnold he did not. His face remained beet red, but his thoughts were beginning to return to normal. Sometimes, a good fist fight had rejuvenating properties. "Go on," he grumbled.

"When I arrived with John, two loiterers had made it as far as the receiving dock. Ed Mattson was getting antsy, having them hanging around. After I counted out, he suggested to me that, as the other fishermen came in off the river, we should keep an eye on their whereabouts. Even then, Ed had the notion something was brewing. They looked like troublemakers to all of us, evasive when spoken to and not giving any indication as to their business here. Then four others showed up, and they went wandering off toward another cannery. It was then we all smelled trouble, assuming they were strikers, about to wreak havoc on the company. That's when Ed suggested I go for the sheriff. None of us had the vaguest idea what was on their minds, but with their numbers growing, it seemed like the best thing to do at the time. We half-expected them to try torching the place. Tossing your fish overboard came as a complete surprise."

Olof glared at the gillnetter, then turned and pierced the water's surface with a wad of Scandinavian dynamite. In spite of his respect for Arnold, the conspiratorial hubbub was an excuse for leaving a job unfinished. "In the old days," he explained, "Henry and I would have simply done them in, and if we were to get the short end of the stick, we'd take it in the jaw. The law of the sea and the land are quite different," he protested, "and I can't see what's to be gained by taking it in front of a judge."

Arnold was visibly annoyed. This was not what he had expected of Swede Olof. He was the most determined fisherman on the river, and of all the fishermen, he should have been willing to stand up for the Scandinavian Packing Company. Arnold began pacing back and forth across the same stretch of dock for several minutes. He truly liked Olof Andersson, but the man could be bullheaded and old-worldish. "We have a chance here," he stammered, "an opportunity to stop the strikers from interfering with our fishing. If we let it slip through our fingers, they'll come back, expecting to do more damage. It's only with the law on our side that we can knock some of these transients off the river." Arnold's voice was noticeably less strident as he aired the last thing weighing on his mind. "Either way, I heard how you tried to keep Jason out of harm's way, and for that, I'll always be beholden to you. He's a youngster, a little wet behind the ears." Arnold started moving off, leaving Olof to sort out his options.

"I still don't see the point in it!" Olof called out.

"Just show up in court on the appointed day," Arnold replied.

For a long while, Olof stood and observed the river in solitude, hoping for something there which might assist him in reaching the right decision. The sea gulls were noisy overhead, in pursuit of the silvery fish carcasses beginning to reappear along the cannery's eastern perimeter. The incoming tide had moved the salmon beneath the cannery docks, to tempt the birds, the sole beneficiaries of Olof's loss. He looked contemptuously at the seven men who had come to feed upon his success. He was incapable of comprehending the intricacies of the battle just waged, but a war was in evidence. He was finally able to put a name to the voice he had heard coming from within the receiving station, sufficient reason for Olof to pursue any avenue available to him.

April 22, 1885

District Attorney Price was of a serious mind, befitting the controlled environment of his courtroom. He was clean-shaven, distinguished by grey inflections around the temples, and meant to be the one wearing a blue pinstriped suit, a fashionable foreign import of exceptional quality. The only perplexing detractor from his image was the silk cobalt-blue necktie, tied haphazardly and on a par with something a barkeep might wear.

Across the aisle, Defense Attorney Chas Carter presented a more informal image. He wore muttonchop whiskers; his hair had been allowed to grow slightly beyond the barber's best judgment, descending from a center part and cupping itself over the tops of his ears; and his suit was unsuitably wrinkled, perhaps a ploy to contrast himself with the neatly groomed defendants. As his eyes wandered around the courtroom, his upper body was constantly in motion. If he was not shifting papers, his hands were busy rearranging anything available to him, including the loose hair falling against his face and the alignment of his chair according to the table. Unlike the district attorney, he was consumed by details, the most obvious of which being the three unoccupied chairs at his immediate right.

Molly Bochau made her way up the courthouse steps on one large swallow of air, her corset giving her distress. She elbowed her way through the unsightly crowd of curious drunkards gathered in the foyer. Since they had chosen to fortify themselves with the false courage of whiskey, she offered no apology for prodding them with the tip of her black parasol, a useful accessory apart from her funereal garb. As the proprietress of a boardinghouse, Molly viewed such miscreants as common incorrigibles. She had become inured to their foul breath and bad manners and would certainly say as much if confronted.

At first John Lord could not believe his eyes. He removed his wire-rimmed spectacles and rubbed the lenses between the nonabrasive folds of his handkerchief. He recognized the prosecuting witness in this case, but surely it couldn't be Olof Andersson! With the spectacles resettled over the bridge of his nose he looked again, and just as quickly his pencil was jotting down notes in rapid succession.

The room was filled to capacity and beyond. When one of the sheriff's deputies tried to block Molly's entrance, she never even flinched. She moved him aside forcibly with her folded parasol and kept going, her eyes guiding her through the crowd congesting the center aisle. As soon as she recognized Olof's red hair, she stepped to a bench seat and started lowering herself into a six-inch space. John Lord raised his eyebrows as he saw this bustle-bottomed woman coming at him. "Ma'am," he sputtered, "ma'am, I don't believe there is sufficient room."

"Then make it!" Molly retorted. "Can't you see this old lady is tired of standin'?"

John Lord, still a bachelor, found the proximity of Molly's left buttock on his right thigh sweat inducing. He dearly wanted to comply with the woman's wishes, but the crowded bench refused to permit it. Grunts and groans echoed his very sentiments as the boardinghouse matron took her place, two rows behind Olof Andersson.

As a daily occurrence for thirty years, the courthouse had sufficed to dispense justice according to the normal bill of fare: drunkenness, profane and abusive language, and fighting. The fines therefrom averaged five dollars, and the time spent in jail varied from one to ten days, depending upon the orneriness of the accused. Drunkenness being so common along the bawdy waterfront, most five-dollar fines were forfeitures, and the guilty left, free to find more useful ways to spend their earnings. This particular trial was out of the ordinary, however, bringing different precedents to the forefront concerning individual freedoms. Every gillnetter along the river was anxious to learn the verdict, hoping it might somehow dislodge the logjams impeding the fishing industry. In accordance with the interest in the trial, the old courtroom was splitting at the seams, having never been intended to house such controversy.

The room was poorly ventilated, and the body odors were strong. The fishing element was in a majority, and John Lord had yet to divest himself of certain biases. If he dared elaborate on the word "stank," he would add that the courtroom was mostly filled with vagrant troublemakers, expecting their pound of flesh. That was how he saw it, anyway, with Olof Andersson the prosecuting witness in this case. Perhaps the flagrant Swede had not been involved in the murder of the Mongolians, but he was not a man of high credibility. The grand jury would certainly dismiss the matter, and all the hubbub would come to an end.

Bill Price and Olof had been operating under a truce, exchanging information in brevity and keeping everything on a level of civility. Olof's concern about the division of land and sea according to law remained the most obvious point of contention, but the attorney had suffered through the radical lecture, remaining completely non-argumentative. Olof professed ignorance with regard to court procedures but had accepted the tenet to speak only when spoken to, the one solid underpinning in their relationship. Simply put, they could win if Olof would refrain from orations concerning the biases of his background and refrain from acting out.

Olof had been duly warned, but when the three tardy defendants came down the aisle, he could not help himself. He stood up, making himself known to the man whose voice he had heard coming from within the receiving building, Olavi Pustinen.

As a matter of courtesy, Chas Carter was already standing, allowing the remainder of his clients to file in behind him. With all the last-minute details having finally fallen into place, he had assumed a look of composure. Before Olavi would file past and assume the vacant chair, however, he stopped in the center of the aisle and spit on the floor, all the while eyeing Olof with a smirk on his face. In spite of the prior warnings, Olof reacted. He lunged forward toward Olavi, his right hip contacting Bill Price in the process. The movement of Olof's lower body shoved the prosecuting attorney's chair into the aisle, whereupon the occupant planted his feet and grabbed the armrests to keep from being thrown to the floor. He was caught in the middle of a fight in the making. Shouts of encouragement came from around the room, Molly Bochau being the most vocal.

"Nail the traitor!" she shouted at the top of her lungs. She, too, was on her feet, prepared to throw a punch if Olof was not. "Get the buzzard while he's still fair for the pluckin'!" she bellowed. The entire room exploded in an uproar, shouts bouncing off the walls and bodies in movement. Everyone had his own axe to grind.

Olof, nevertheless, read the moment of confrontation for what it was: a setup. Olavi was tempting him, luring him back into his trap for reasons unknown to Olof. Olof studied his opponent and wondered why they had never established the underlying reason for their personal feud. It had gone on for a decade and had to be based on more than the bad chemistry between them. Olof really needed to hear what

Olavi had to say in his own defense, in order to defeat the man at his own game. If he faltered now, Olof would be placing that chance in jeopardy. He started backing off, regardless of the jeers being lauded in his direction. He closed his ears upon the vulgar interpretations of his heritage, and diverted all his courage into addressing Bill Price's certain remonstrances. The district attorney looked somewhat peaked, surprised, perhaps, that Olof had refrained from delivering the first punch.

John Lord was on the verge of taking the folds of Molly Bochau's skirt in his hands and yanking her back into her seat. He was sorely tempted to fall out of character. He reached, then stopped, aware of the crowd's effect upon him. Their momentum was both infectious and inebriating, causing him to think along unfamiliar lines. He just could not do it, nevertheless, and phrased his request with all the civility he could muster. "Ma'am, I think the worst is over. I don't believe they've killed each other, and if they did, I wouldn't suppose it would matter much."

Molly relaxed into her seat. "A damn shame," she grumped. "Olof had the opportunity and blew it. The river would be a whole lot cleaner without scum like Olavi Pustinen rinsin' his dirty laundry in it."

John Lord could not resist, his opinions being so far afield. "I fail to see the difference. According to Ma'am, how does one draw a line between the two hooligans and discern the good from the bad?"

It was only the seriousness in the inquirer's voice that kept Molly from laughing aloud. "You're either funnin' me," she exclaimed, "or your mind has been touched by an excessive amount of whiskey. Everyone knows the difference between a cheat and a liar, and an upstanding citizen."

"Is that what this is all about, a cheat and a liar tossing an upstanding citizen's salmon overboard?"

"That, and trying to do away with him a few times in the past. They don't see eye to eye on the politics of gill-netting, and surely never will. Olof's on the side of the real fishermen, not the ones who come and go each season 'cause the canners keep bringing them in by the shipload. They're the rowdy ones, the ones who take any job available so's to visit the brothels and get pickled on booze. Don't get me wrong; most of the gillnetters partake on occasion, but they ain't dangerous, if you get my drift, and don't go around causing trouble for the pleasure in it. You can tell the good ones from the bad ones real easy, if you look closely. Some of them take pride in what they do and love the river; others just come to burn through the money the canners give them. They leave their nasty scars and then move on."

"How do you know so much about Olof Andersson?" John Lord asked. His interest was more than casual.

"He used to live at my boardinghouse, him and his partner Henry Hihnala. Together, they made the best team on the river. Very seldom failed to bring in a good catch, unless, of course, something else got them sidetracked."

"Like the disappearance of all those Mongolians?"

"Exactly so. The ones who did it were sitting all around the supper table, whilst Olof and Henry were counting heads and figuring out how they were going to come out of this one alive. 'Cept Ingrid was sittin' there, and Olof wasn't about to start a row. Those bad'ns got away just that once, but sometimes it's better to let nature take its course. Some of them died in the big storm that hit the river in 1880, and an old score was settled. Unfortunately, Henry Hihnala went the same way. A person's got to miss Henry Hihnala; he had a cheery heart and was a damn good boat puller."

John Lord began jotting down notes, and Molly looked over her shoulder, curious about the unusual hobby enjoyed by the talkative stranger. "You scribin' a letter there, Mister?"

Judge Larry Graham found the condition of his courtroom intolerable. Twice his arrival at the bench had been announced, and twice it had gone unnoticed. He raised his gavel and struck it repeatedly on the hardwood surface with the wide arc of a carpenter determined to drive a nail in the fewest possible strokes. From the front of the courtroom to the rear, conversations dropped off, and the cautious took stock of the man who was in charge of such a controversial meeting. Rapidly, he garnered the respect of most. His face was stern, with frown lines etched across his forehead. His jawline was deep and his chin set well forward. His eyebrows were thick and bushy, infused with the same white capping his head. His eyes were brown, and below them vertical indentations creased his cheeks. If he were to smile, it would go against his very grain. He was ageless, yet aged.

He remained standing, his black robe flowing around him. "I want the aisles cleared," he said with authority. The timbre of his voice was forceful, and at the back of the room, people obeyed. Slowly the extra bodies cleared the room, and he nodded to the sheriff making his way toward the door, to close it. He promptly took his seat and motioned to the sheriff's deputy to allow the jurors entrance. They filed into the room in silence, and occupied the twelve seats cordoned off by a wooden rail. Judge Graham addressed them directly as he delivered his instructions.

"This is a preliminary process, meant to test the body of evidence and find it either sufficient, or insufficient, to hold the defendants over for trial. The prosecuting attorney in this case will tell you why he believes the evidence is sufficient, and the defense attorney will explain why it is insufficient. As a grand jury, your job is to decide whether or not pursuing the matter is a waste of the people's time."

From the back of the room, an errant comment interrupted. "You're damn right it's a waste of our time! The whole damn thing is a waste of our time!"

Judge Graham immediately sought out the offender and held him accountable through eye contact. His gavel struck the bench only once. "Have that man escorted from the premises," he commanded. All heads turned as the sheriff left his post at the door and started down the aisle. The judge was now using his gavel to point out the offender, but the guilty had turned his head toward the wall rather than rising to meet the challenge. A few guffaws echoed throughout the crowd, and the judge's gavel again met the bench's surface. "Take him by the neck and throw him in jail!"

"Ahhs" circulated among the crowd, and the white-haired gentleman at the bench returned to the business at hand, allowing the murmurs to die of their own accord.

Bill Price took the judge's dislike for long, drawn-out speeches into account. He went directly to the heart of the matter, explaining to the jury that there were two cases being given unto their consideration, one involving seven men charged with the malicious destruction of property, and the other involving three men charged for their participation in a riot. It was the state's contention that these three men had conspired to instigate the crime carried out by the other seven and should be held culpable. The prosecutor briefly outlined the events surrounding the forfeiture of Olof Andersson's fish and cited the list of witnesses willing to testify as to the evolution of the crime, but then he ran up against the expected roadblock: linking the two groups of defendants together. In order to get Olavi Pustinen and his cronies indicted, he had to rely on Olof Andersson to keep his wits about him and impress the jury with a credible tale. That done, the real issue would arise concerning the rights of the strikers versus those who chose not to strike. He knew it could be a landmark case, if only Olof Andersson would cooperate.

"Put your right hand on the Bible and raise your left hand."

Olof followed all the instructions, then settled into the witness chair. It was slightly elevated, giving him a good view of those in attendance. It was very different from addressing a mob of irate gillnetters, yet the explosive nature of the situation was much the same. The line of demarcation was drawn down the center aisle, with the members of the association sitting behind the prosecution, and those who favored the strikers seated behind the table designated for the defense.

"Do you recognize any of the defendants?"

"Yes, sir. One."

"Can you point him out?"

Olof obliged, indicating Olavi Pustinen.

"Where do you know him from?"

"Union meetings."

"Are you and Mr. Pustinen good friends?"

Olof scowled. The prosecuting attorney continued. "I assume that to mean you and he are on opposite sides of the fence, so to speak."

"Objection!"

"Sustained. Please refrain from leading the witness."

"If you and Olavi Pustinen are neither friends nor foes, how would you describe your relationship?"

"Don't have one. He hates my guts, and I hate his."

"Objection!"

"Sustained. Inform your witness to speak only for himself."

"You said you hate Mr. Pustinen's guts. Can you tell us why?"

Olof became animated. "He's a strikemaker and a strikebreaker, and he sets off bombs when things aren't going in his direction!"

"Objection!"

"Sustained! Attorney Price, please warn your witness to avoid things not in evidence!"

For a few minutes, Bill Price paced back and forth in front of the bench, allowing time for his witness's allegations to impact the jury.

Unfortunately, he'd outstayed Judge Graham's patience. "Strike those last comments from the record, and the jury is instructed to disregard them."

Olof's eyes left Bill Price and settled upon the jury box. In the end, these would be the twelve people who would have to separate truth from fiction. Olof's hand came off his lap, and his fingertips traveled the length of his scar. The jurors were staring at him with either fear or awe, as Ingrid used to do, when trying to divine the whole from the halves. For their edification, he could justify the scar, but when it came to the fiery red hair and emerald green eyes, he was at a loss. He cupped his hand around his beard and stroked it. A female juror twisted nervously in her chair. He had once resembled Christ, and now he resembled an issuance from hell. The distinctive nature of his hair coloring and eyes was inherited from his mother, the only person who might possibly be capable of comprehending his distress at that moment.

It had gone without saying that Anders Niklasson, Olof's father, firmly believed his Irish-Catholic wife, Noreen Murdoch, would be as acceptable as a breath of fresh air amongst the otherwise complacent villagers. But even as a child, Olof could detect the subtle shunning. His grandmother, Bengta Nilsdotter, proved to be the most fertile of the objectors. During the long fishing expeditions when the men were absent from the village, she would interject herself into things not her business, starting little brush fires in an otherwise peaceful home.

Olof's Farmor (grandmother) Bengta was well versed in the Lutheran Bible, and she would leave it open on the table where Olof's mor (mother) kneaded bread, scrubbed dirt from turnips, mended clothing, and set out the dinner plates. Noreen Murdoch had a Bible of her own, and she would lay it aside Farmor Bengta's, a sign when enough was enough. She also fretted over her husband's long absences, a point sometimes well taken, and other times overlooked. It was not until Olof was ten years old that he actually heard his farmor taking his mor to task, but it came as no surprise, and the words of degradation impacted him equally. The Bibles were out and ready for battle. His mother was standing over the table, peeling potatoes, and his Farmor Bengta was seated across from her, crocheting. It was late in the afternoon, the time the fishing fleet would return, if it was to return at all that day.

"I know you're always worried when the men are at sea," Noreen replied calmly, "but I, too, feel the same. One must learn to trust in the wisdom of our fishermen and not dwell on doubts."

Olof's farmor was a formidable woman, with the gradual addition of fifty pounds. She also was extremely tall, an attribute inherited by her son and grandson. She was fleshy while angular, an odd combination for a farmor and, regardless of her weight, her posture was as upright as a flagpole. Olof recognized her immediately when he came through the door, having finished with the endless chore of finding something suitable to stoke the fire. He was about to remove his outerwear when Farmor Bengta leapt to her feet.

"There is nothing said by a red-headed foreigner that can bring me comfort!" she snarled.

Always self-conscious about her hair, Noreen pulled it back from her face. Most often she kept it braided like the other women in the village, but today she had just washed it, and it was more profuse than normal and full of the vibrant color which annoyed her mother-in-law so. "I'm sorry if I spoke out of turn," Noreen answered simply. "You're welcome to your beliefs, as certainly as I am entitled to mine."

Even in Swedish, Olof's mother had a way with words. Her green eyes would flash like beacons of wisdom, and Olof thought the matter finished. He began uncoiling the knitted scarf from around his neck, believing this brush fire had been doused.

But Farmor Bengta took a very unusual pose, resting her hands on her hips and leaning into her daughter-in-law's face. Her message was meant to be cutting. "If they weren't ever to come back, what would you do? You have no family here."

Olof stopped dead in his tracks, the scarf a heap on the floor. His farmor had said something to strike a raw nerve in him, and his childish reticence was no longer a factor. Why should his grandmother tell such a lie to his mother? They were all Swedes under his father's roof, or so he'd thought. He watched his mother's face for her reaction.

He was certain she would cry, like she did so frequently when Anders was long overdue; yet this time she did not. Her face became flushed and fiery, and her green eyes lowered themselves upon his Farmor Bengta. She was angry, not sad. Olof could feel the same emotion building inside of him, and he came forth, not knowing why.

"Farmor Bengta," he said very crisply. "My far will always return from the sea, and you shouldn't worry my mor with such nonsense." Olof couldn't believe the words coming from his lips, but he had said them, and he was willing to stand by them.

"It's all right, Olof," his mother said sternly, "this is no concern of yours."

Farmor Bengta rose from her seat and took her Bible firmly in her grasp. "The red hair is surely a sign of the devil," she said to Noreen, but the comment spilled over on Olof as well. Nothing was said for several minutes, but as Bengta Nilsdotter turned to leave, Olof moved aside, not wishing her hand to fall on his shoulder in her usual gesture of familiarity. At the moment, Olof felt very estranged from his farmor, and he would forever have to look at her differently. With both pride and prejudice to guide her, she marched from the house, her Bible pressed firmly to her chest.

Alone now, Noreen spoke to her son harshly. "She's an old woman, and must be excused for her fears. She meant no harm by pointing out our differences, but it would be easier for her if there were none. She's worried that if something happened to Anders, I would elect to take you back to Ireland with me. In that respect, your farmor is a very foolish woman. Once you've left the place of your birth, life moves along too rapidly to turn back the clock. You'll forever be a Swede according to your upbringing, yet the color of your hair will remain as a test of your tenacity. Count your blessings for being somewhat different, because looking at the world with a different slant will hold you apart from the crowds. One has to keep focused on doing the right thing, my brave Olof, and pray, the best way one knows how, that it will account for something when tested against the rigors of time. When your farmor returns, apologize to her. A fight over the color of your hair isn't worth the loss that comes with winning."

The defense attorney was fascinated by the range of emotions crossing the witness's face. Chas Carter was being paid an exorbitant fee to break this man, yet he was not certain Olof Andersson was at all fragile. As Bill Price paced back and forth in front of the judge, the tension was building. Perhaps the district attorney could get at the heart of the matter, but Chas Carter doubted it. There was no link between the canner who paid for the defense of Olavi Pustinen and his henchman, and the outcome of this trial. It was a dirty little secret, known only to himself, Olavi and one of Astoria's more respected citizens. Olof was simply the fall guy, a dupe who would ultimately fail the credibility test. He was definitely rough around the edges, and the jury was eyeing him like an untrustworthy stranger in their midst. Chas Carter expected things to end here. After all, that was why he was receiving a healthy retainer.

After rebuking himself for having made such a big blunder by outstaying the judge's patience, Bill Price returned to his prime witness. Tempo was everything at this point, and the far-off look in Olof Andersson's eyes didn't bode well for rapid-fire responses. Mr. Price cleared his throat several times, but his question was slow in coming: "You said something about a bomb blast; could you elaborate on this point?"

"Objection!" "Sustained. Can you stick to the case at hand?" "Yes, sir."

Bill Price could not condemn Olof for his failure to respond. Chas Carter was quick on his feet, shooting down each stab in the dark, while the prosecuting attorney was wasting Judge Graham's time, a mistake wholly of his own doing. He needed to place more confidence in his key witness: "On the day in question, Mr. Andersson, when your fish were thrown overboard, can you establish the whereabouts of the defendants at that time?"

There was no objection raised, and all eyes focused on Olof. He intended to do his best and temper the excitement in his responses. "I can," he replied confidently.

At this point, Bill Price returned to face the jury. "The state can supply additional witnesses to substantiate the malicious activities of seven of the defendants, but the activities of the three ringleaders remains in doubt. Here, Mr. Andersson's observations become germane." Still facing the jurors, Bill Price tossed another question back at the witness. "Mr. Andersson, you said you could place all of the defendants at the scene of the crime. How's that?"

Olof stared directly at Olavi Pustinen as he gave his answer. "I heard him," he replied, "and I'd know that voice anywhere. Remember, we've had our separate says on several occasions."

The entire left quadrant of the courtroom supporting the defense rose to its feet. Boos and guffaws filled the room. Judge Graham's gavel struck the bench forcibly. "Either be seated, or I'll have the courtroom cleared!" he threatened. Molly Bochau leaned over and spoke in John Lord's ear: "Olof's gonna get him now! He's gonna flush the rat from the woodpile! There's more here than meets the eye, and Swede Olof's finally gonna get his pound of flesh."

Chas Carter was also on his feet, wishing to approach the bench. The ground rules needed to be altered, quickly. A few minutes earlier he had been watching Bill Price repeating the mistake of pressing the judge's patience; now it was his turn to accept the woes of his own shortsightedness. He had been firmly in favor of keeping personal histories out of the debate in order to prevent Olavi's sordid strike activities from being drawn into this preliminary session. Now his hands were tied, unable to discredit the state's main witness by drawing on an equally questionable background. He was sweating profusely when the judge denied his request, and he realized that this case was probably going to trial. His secret benefactor would not be at all pleased — still, there was one escape clause left to those who practiced the law of the land, and he'd be very sure to implement it.

May 20, 1885

He had followed the string of events starting in April, yet John Lord was worried that his final accounting had missed the mark. His article would be picked up and shared by dozens of other newspapers; hence, it was imperative to avoid the inexplicable while producing something substantive for all truth-seekers to ponder. The law had been faithfully observed, yet in some ways had come up short. Nothing was ever cut and dried, particularly when it was linked to the goings-on along the Columbia.

TRIAL OF TEN:
The Outcome of the Late Disturbance
On April 13th Sheriff Evans and Chief of
Police Babbit were called to Uppertown and on

going there arrested seven men who were engaged in throwing fish out of Olof Andersson's boat, he at the time being engaged in fishing for the Scandinavian Packing Company. They were lodged in the county jail, complaints having been made out in Judge Graham's office charging them with malicious destruction of property.

A crowd of noisy men came down from Uppertown that evening to release the prisoners. The prisoners were not released. They were given a preliminary examination before the judge next morning and held in bonds of $100 each to appear before the grand jury. On the 22nd that body indicted them, and also indicted three others for alleged participation in a riot. Yesterday the last-mentioned three came into court and pleaded guilty; the other seven pleaded not guilty and stood their trial. They were defended by Chas Carter, his argument being in effect that the indictment was defective in not charging them with unlawful conduct, and that what they had done on the 13th was only in pursuance of the object they sought to accomplish and had not resulted in personal injury to the prosecuting witness. He argued that there was no riot in the popular acceptation of the term and that the usual accompaniments of a riot were wanting. Mr. Carter made a very able plea, and did all that counsel could do to clear his clients from the charges preferred against them.

District Attorney Price replied in an argument of equal length, the question being did the defendants use force, coercion or intimidation in making the prosecuting witness desist from his lawful employment.

This, the district attorney argued was the case, and he asked for a conviction on the grounds that while any man has a right to cease work and strike if he wants to, he has no right to compel others to quit work or interfere with them in their daily avocation. The case went to the jury at half-past three: upon retiring they took a ballot resulting four for conviction and eight for acquittal; after further deliberation they brought in a verdict of guilty. The prescribed penalty for the offense of which the accused were found guilty varies from a fine of from $50 to $500, or from three months' to one year's imprisonment in the county jail.

At the close counsel for the defense gave notice of intention to file motion for a new trial this morning.

The case has attracted considerable attention owing to the circumstances subsequent to the arrest. The whole thing boiled down amounts to just this: a man has a perfect right to do as he pleases, so long as he doesn't interfere with another man's right to do as he pleases. Considerable sympathy is felt for the men who are convicted, partly on the ground that they were not the ringleaders in the affair. The trial and its result may have the effect of a salutary lesson to those who need a reminder that the law cannot be defied and the lawbreaker go unpunished, we suppose.

Chapter Eight

~ ~

Norgersund, Sweden
1887

Ola Jeppsson was extremely kind, soft-spoken and well-meaning, so it was easy to understand why Hanna had elected to wed his younger brother Ored. Ola was convincing in pitching the same proposition to Ingrid, but Ingrid could not commit to a man for his kindness alone and casually assume a niche vacated by the death of a first wife. It went against the grain. Besides, Ingrid was still married, although her presumptuous suitor failed to understand the relevancy of such a distant cause, placing it second to his own designs. It did seem plausible that these two mature adults shared much in common, but Ingrid had experienced marriage for what it was: a tremendous risk, not to be taken lightly. She quickly rephrased her refusal to coincide with her staunch beliefs in country and family, alluding to her immediate responsibilities embodied therein; yet Ola's brown eyes could be pitiable, leading Ingrid to conclude that a marriage of convenience was an acceptable outcome if it inspired such dogged determination. She had to delve deeper, citing her obligation to the small school she had begun, as well as the public trust which had never before been given to a woman. She was committed to staying on course this time, but temporarily her logic was lost on a man who bathed himself in the outpouring of her protestations. The years spent in Astoria were beyond Ola's capacity to understand and lent little credibility to Ingrid's insistence on remaining independent.

What had begun as a marriage proposal was rapidly deteriorating into a test of wills, causing Ingrid to wonder why this offer was being foisted upon her so unexpectedly. Hanna and Ored were only three days wed and Ingrid's acquaintance with Ola barely established. If the proposal was to be made in front of her family and Ored alike, she deserved more information. "You have no children to concern yourself with," Ingrid said frankly, "so what's the hurry? Your wife left this world only a few months ago, Ola Jeppsson. A respectful period of mourning might be in order."

For whatever reason, Brita Hansdotter, Ingrid's mother, reared back in her seat. The chair legs creaked as all four supports resettled on the floor, but her hands never moved from her lap, and the glazed-over look in her eyes never varied. Ingrid supposed it was her duty to infer something from her mother's mix into this burdensome conversation, but Brita Hansdotter was tough to read. She used to verbalize an opinion on most everything, but now she had little to say concerning the outcome of such important matters. The pure white scarf covering her hair attested to the tidiness she exacted out of life, yet the skin folds below her cheekbones said something else of her existence. Ingrid could only assume Brita's impetuous reaction was one of disapproval, but as far as Ingrid's American experiences were concerned, being skeptical of a man's motives was a necessary evil. Brita continued to reject the concept of being one's own person, as if being independent made Ingrid too unaccountable and exempt from the daily suffering incurred by womanhood, a by-product of living Ingrid understood all too well.

Nils Gustav Petersson, Ingrid's father, was adrift on a separate sea, trying to bring a personal saga to a palatable end. Ingrid thought his complacency acceptable. He was aging quickly, each season on the Baltic having taken its toll. He kept his fingers bent around the table's edge, and on occasion a wracking cough would cause him to grip down on the worn surface. The knuckled hands which had fashioned so much from so little, including the table, were expressively tired. Staying in touch had become a conscious effort. Ingrid's parents were old before their time, and Ingrid was rapidly following suit.

Ola was becoming flushed. Like most people with ulterior motives, his were bound to rise to the surface. He looked over at Ored and Hanna, who were seated on the narrow bench below the triple-paned window, and the three of them communicated with their eyes. Obviously, something was transpiring amongst them, and Ingrid was determined to get to the bottom of it before it exceeded her patience.

Ola Jeppsson fit the village norm for a middle-aged widower whose wife had endowed him with a modicum of social graces. He was both pious and pliant, respectful of his elders, and publicly heedful of the gentler sex. Still, Ingrid knew he could change into someone he probably was not when uncomfortably attired for courting. She eyed him more cautiously, cognizant of the self-indulging reticence he had been superimposing on this family gathering. For the sake of his own argument, he was in control, causing consternation where there really was no cause for it. Ingrid didn't intend to marry this confident optimist, in spite of old-world politics.

"Well?"

Hanna had interrupted. With the distinction of a recent bride to encourage her enthusiasm, she was reaching far beyond the parameters of good sense. Ingrid could recall those same feelings of empowerment, instances when she believed marriage to be a pathway of intervention, a rising from the ranks to a higher level of influence. As it was said of her and Olof, Hanna and Ored did make a handsome couple and would surely bear handsome children, but that old wives' tale failed to tell the entire truth. Appearances counted for little when the world started spinning off-center, a crucial lesson, perhaps, ineffectually imparted upon Hanna.

Intuitively, Ingrid wanted this meeting to draw to a rapid closure before anything damaging transpired. She was grateful when Hanna rose to her feet but was wholly unprepared for the ensuing announcement. "We really shouldn't have sprung it on sweet Ingrid as a total surprise," Hanna apologized, "but we wanted so desperately for her to come with us." In a symbolic gesture, she hastened across the room and placed Ola's hand upon Ingrid's. Ola's palm was cold and clammy, not at all the sultry communication Ingrid should expect of a an ardent suitor.

Hanna's words were only beginning to make a substantial impression on Ingrid, but they were stridently clear to her parents. Brita Hansdotter's eyelids were drooping at the corners, while Nils Gustav Petersson had resigned himself to observing the collection of plates displayed on the open shelves above the hutch. One generation was surely withdrawing itself from another. Ingrid tolerated the next display of emotionalism because she had performed it herself, inspired by a false sense of security in the benefits of change.

Hanna dropped to her knees and spoke to the bewilderment in Ingrid's eyes. "We're going to America," she professed calmly, "the Midwest, a place where we can grow crops and raise our children. God willing, they'll be yours and Ola's, too."

Put so succinctly, Ingrid could almost believe in Hanna's remake of an old fairy tale; still, it seemed a cruel joke when drawn out to this extent. Olof had been correct in this particular instance, predicting that Hanna would grow up with or without her assistance, ultimately, to make her own decisions. It was not what Ingrid had expected from her younger sister; on the other hand, making assumptions had always been one of Ingrid's fatal flaws. "I suppose a bride is due a few pranks," she said calmly to Hanna, "but I guess I'm getting too old to understand the value in playing the wretched fool." She withdrew her hand from beneath Ola's and stood. She remained a beautiful woman, but her cold indifference set her apart.

Her father was halfway out the door with his coat flung over his shoulder, and Brita Hansdotter was staring across the room, the stress too much to reconcile. It was a strange turn of events, and Ingrid felt somehow both the betrayed and the betrayer. She had either opened the door for Hanna's departure or had closed it upon herself. Either way, she was again being entertained by her own stupidity, acting on the pretense that she could be a positive influence on the lives of others.

She turned to face Ola Jeppsson. She was now trembling. The anger in his eyes was to be expected but was completely unfounded. "Nej, Ola," she repeated herself, "I won't marry you because there is no basis for it. I've taken that path and have come to understand my limitations. When and if you get to America, even love may not be sufficient to assist you in the resettlement of your expectations." She was going to stop there, but her bluntness seemed too cursive. Her voice softened. "There are women who'd be willing to dream your dreams and escape into your fantasy land, but I've had my share of fantasies and would eventually prove a burden to your aspirations. But it was a fair offer, Ola Jeppsson, and the refusal is not intended as a personal insult."

Ingrid turned to Hanna to make her final comment. "I wish you and Ored no ill will in going to America, but my heart will pine for you each day as I imagine the hardships and heartaches you will surely encounter. The creation of a new life is a gradual process, whereby truth and trust must sift from one level to another. In America, they referred to Swedes as simple, God-fearing people. Be leery of those who offer such platitudes, and don't make the mistake of believing them yourself."

∞

In the worst of times, orderliness and tradition had been capable of binding this Swedish village together. The old had been maintained, and the new groomed to fit within a pattern of least resistance. The dirt paths were worn smooth and level, each one a needed easement leading to a neighbor's nearby cottage home. All the window casings were painted white to match the winter starkness, and the sidings were of warmer hues to absorb the summer sunshine. Until of late, there were few surprises amidst this passive setting. Nothing had aroused it from its sluggish stupor until America had become an outlet for those with far-reaching visions, and men like Olof Andersson had come forth to begin the process of emigration.

"You haven't written to him yet?" Ingrid's hostess asked.

"No." It was a worrisome matter to Ingrid, one better dropped. The man whom she had divorced by distance remained an integral part of her life; thus, scribbling her final regrets on paper seemed an insurmountable chore. She could put it off another day, month or year, if need be. In the interim, her neighbor kept her informed.

The tea tasted good and had a calming effect on Ingrid. Pella Jönsson suggested a second cup, but Ingrid was cognizant of the imposition. In comparison to the New World, Sweden was a country continually set upon by hard times, thus the great exodus and the growing number of families split asunder. Ingrid had to remember that, or else Hanna's decision to move to America could do her irreparable damage.

She set aside the teacup to take Pella's one-year-old son, John, in her arms. He was a fitful child, while three-year-old Herman was calm and complacent, happy to eavesdrop on a conversation concerning his papa. Alfred, the eldest of the three brothers, was about the business of stoking the fire, but he was listening over his shoulder, wanting to learn the latest.

Pers Jönsson, or Pete North, as he was called in America, worked for a dairy farm in the Young's Bay area, a watery indentation just west of Astoria. His chosen occupation kept him apart from gillnetting, an option not unusual for those whose hopes of a fishing career had been dashed by the paltry returns of the Baltic. Yet he managed to return to Sweden for months at a time and plant the seed for another child. Ten years ago it would have seemed an unthinkable arrangement, but the world was a different place, and people were on the move.

"Nej," Pella shook her head and said, "news from the Columbia is never good. Pers is glad to give it a wide berth, because so many of them perish."

Ingrid was versed in the death toll exacted on the gill-netters, but it was the politics that had done her the greatest harm and, ironically, now constituted the reason for her continued interest. Through Pers Jönsson's correspondence with his wife, Ingrid had learned of Olof's involvement in an extraordinary trial. She'd lain awake for a month of nights, trying to imagine how Olof had done on the witness chair. It was so unlike him to trust in the law of the land. Perhaps he was changing for the better.

"Get me the newspaper clipping your father sent us," Pella instructed Alfred. "I'm certain Ingrid would be so kind as to translate it for us."

Alfred, five years old, was an interesting composite. He was fair-skinned like his mother with the same sandy hair coloring, but his eyes were deep set like those of his father's and full of mystery. He had the newspaper clipping in his outstretched hand before Ingrid could return the one-year-old to Pella. He appeared pleased with himself. "Alfred's quick on his feet, isn't he," Ingrid commented, but unlike Little Henry he shied away from the visitor's obser-vation and quickly went to stand next to his mother's chair. Ingrid was about to say something as to the differences in their children, but that was a mistake in the making. Her children were dead and buried, a fact that made her lips tremble without even speaking their names. She picked up the clipping from the floor where Alfred had dropped it and began translating the fairly recent article.

Of the 154 pound nets now infusing and confusing the lower Columbia River, a certain percentage have been deemed to be illegally placed and therefore hazardous to the navigation of the gillnetters. With such findings to support them, the Columbia River Fishermen's Protective Union is waging both a subtle and substantive war against the Washington Fishermen's Association, the organized entity representing the trapmen. The gillnetters believe that impounding salmon in traps is an ungodly way of catching fish, and that the proliferation of such contraptions around Baker Bay, admittedly a prime fishing ground at the mouth of the Columbia, cannot be tolerated. So far, the frequent cutting of pound nets in the night by the Protective Union's scow has gone without recourse, but last week's "fish fight" could lead to increased hostilities. While the canners argue that the pound nets ensure them the freshest catch at the lowest cost, the gillnetters concern themselves with the heightened competition. For the sake of the fishing industry, we hope both sides can find an equitable solution before these small skirmishes expand into full-fledged war.

∽

"Oiy!" Ingrid concluded abruptly. "This may be the end of Swede Olof."

Pella understood the concern on Ingrid's face. It was difficult, having a foot in two worlds and no way to adequately bridge the gap.

Astoria, Oregon
May, 1887

Olof wasn't surprised. Unionism was becoming as radical a proposition as were the institutions it hoped to dethrone. The constitution read: "No liquor dealer, gambler, politician, capitalist, lawyer, agent for capitalists, nor persons holding office, whether under national, state or municipal government shall under any consideration become members." Such limitations were isolators and, according to the Finnish being spoken at the meeting, history revisited. He didn't want to join, but according to the latest threat imposed upon the gillnetters by the trapmen, he needed to be a player, and to be a player he had to align himself with like-minded supporters. He cringed at the idea of working alongside Olavi Pustinen, but the devil was always lodged in the details, and the betterment of the situation a product of the process. Ingrid could have accused him of being unprincipled in the matter and not adhering to his own lofty ideals, but being principled had yet to make a difference, and as far as the trapmen were concerned, the union's resources were his only means of fighting back. At the conclusion of a twenty-one-hour meeting, Olof headed for the nearest tavern to rejuvenate himself and prepare for the next episodic adventure in freeing the Columbia from this most recent insinuation.

∞

In the fifteen years Olof had fished the river, he had seen the number of gillnet boats more than quadruple, the canning industry become so avaricious as to fall on its haunches a few times just to salivate over its successes, and now, the advent of the fish trappers. There was no logic behind any of it, other than greed — a precursor to certain disaster. The Columbia, as Olof knew it, was being disemboweled before his very eyes as an opportunistic industry continued on a rampage to blight its beauty. The piles and nets webbing Baker Bay were more than a blockade for the salmon entering the river; they violated the river's natural ebb and flow. They also opposed Olof's sense of fair play, and he intended to go so far as to battle his own countrymen in this matter by making another disparate stand.

"You should get yourself another wife instead," Molly Bochau quipped. "Perhaps your frustration is due to something other than the trapmen."

Perron Bochau, Molly's husband, did not have an opinion one way or the other on Olof's marital status. He rested his arm over the chair back and continued to puff on his pipe. Olof's stated dilemma was a more compelling topic. As one of the diehard fur trappers, Perron could draw many parallels. "The higher the profits, the more determined the competition," he commented. "Someday it'll all be dried up and the problem will be settled for sure. As long as there is a market, men will march with the fever, cutting new trails and tamin' the wilderness until humanity is visible on every horizon. It's a sorry state of affairs that a man's got to feed his belly; otherwise, things could stay as they were."

Olof had to agree with him, but the problem along the Columbia was hardly moot. What the fur trappers had done to the Pacific Northwest was a fair example of the overharvesting of natural resources to supply foreign markets, yet Perron's stories were riddled with inconsistencies. When hindsight was applied as an excuse, the witness's credibility came into question.

Molly finished peeling the potatoes and took a seat across the table from her husband. "He's going to stay this time," she said to Olof.

Olof did not know what to make of the remark; it sounded more like a spur-of-the-moment decision than one given lengthy consideration. Perron was an unknown entity, a part of Molly's past resurfacing. They were an unlikely couple, however, Molly being rooted and Perron a drifter. He was rough around the edges and fingered the whiskey bottle on the table with too much familiarity.

If Molly was asking Olof's opinion, he dared not reply. In his case, marriage had ended in a disappointment, and in Molly's case the same could very well hold true. Once a man got an itch to follow one particular occupation, there was little a woman could do to veer him off course.

"Best get back to Uppertown," Olof said, rising. He left the shot glass drained and took his hat from the table.

"Anyone from the Scandinavian Packing Company on your side?" Molly asked.

"What they don't know won't hurt them," Olof replied gruffly. His voice had an edge of defiance to it, too rebellious to sound objective. "They've got families to worry about, and I don't. It's better they stay clear of this one."

Molly appeared extremely agitated. She rose to escort him outside and have her say in the privacy afforded by the porch. "I got a passel of my own problems right now," she said cryptically, "but yours are going to get a lot bigger. I read in the newspaper that the legislature is keeping a close eye on what's happenin' with the gillnetters, and you ain't got Henry to shove you out of harm's way. I know I've said that before, but goin' it alone ain't always the best answer. It could be you just haven't got the longevity to keep saving all these people from themselves; could be a another wife is a better answer."

Molly paused to take a deep breath and experience the same view preventing Olof's attention from resting solely upon her. The river was partially obstructed by a three-story house in the building, and the sea gulls had retreated nearer the water, no longer a busy orchestra in the background of the comings and goings of the boardinghouse patrons. Adapting seemed inevitable. "I realize Perron ain't much," Molly continued, "but I suppose he's all I got. Time comes when you've got to admit defeat and start existing like everyone else. The world is a rotten place when it comes right down to it, full of potholes to break your body and disappointments to break your heart. Most of them trapmen are just tryin' to make a living. Don't go bustin' no bodies, unless the need be to save your own."

∞

Recently evolved on the East Coast and spirited to the West, the fish trap was a very simple concept and easy to implement. A series of piles were driven and a net stretched across the river's current. The natural instincts of the salmon caused them to swim against the downstream current, and once they encountered the webbed netting, they would follow it, trying to elude the barrier. The salmon were then led successively through more piles and nets defining the leads, heart, pot, and spiller of the trap, their instincts preventing them from backing out. Finally corralled, they were ready for harvesting at the trapman's leisure.

Backing out was not an option when Olof left for Baker Bay on Monday night. He was accompanied by Thomas Bergman, one of the four volunteers who had assisted Henry and him in ridding the Columbia River of

Danny Bell, the tenacious kidnapper. The remainder of the small flotilla sailing north-northwest was also manned by gillnetters who were schooled in the risk-return relationship. The presence of traps had ultimately closed off much of the prime fishing grounds from the salmon boats, and additional lives had been lost as unwary gillnetters ventured too near the bar in order to intercept the incoming runs. It was proving to be ruinous competition, erupting, oddly enough, from the recent influx of immigrant farmers and, sadly enough, inclusive of many newcomers who shared Olof's native tongue. It irked him incessantly. The observance of his personal beliefs was being ridiculed by those of his native land, so if there was any solace to be gained by Ingrid's abandonment, it was in knowing she would not be privy to this bizarre situation.

Six boats overshot the head of the drift and kept going. Rain had settled itself across Clatsop County and southern Washington for the better part of a week, another passing squall line did little to impede their progress. Beneath the umbrella of rain the river remained remarkably calm. A light on the easternmost tip of Sand Island came upon them quickly, a beacon of caution emerging from the darkness and drizzle. This light was a navigational aid, placed on the island to warn of the proliferation of traps. To Olof it represented a travesty — an earthly intervention disturbing a grave part of his past. He had once stood where the light now illuminated the darkness and supposed the fate of the hapless Mongolians; just as he would now encourage the darkness as a way of keeping the river's wildness a scintillating secret. But all that had been defiled.

The bay protecting the island from the Washington shore was infused with piles, piercing the water's surface with the same rigidity and copiousness as the quills on a porcupine. It could never return to its pristine state, when Olof had lived the odyssey in search of Henry Hihnala. On the south side of the island, however, the encroachment of piles into the free-flowing current had to be halted. It was all too conceivable that on a stormy night, the river's unpredictable surges would force a gillnetter into the traps. Olof had dreamt of it repeatedly, reliving the unforeseeable storm that had taken Henry Hihnala's life. It went without saying his occupation required leeway, and the traps were an abridgement to that leeway. The law of the land was again in violation of the river's integrity and, according to Olof's personal history, it only continued to worsen.

The union's recently enlisted snag puller was lying off the southwest portion of the island. Here the traps were three deep and jutted well into a deep channel, and here the night's work should commence. The small steamer had come from upriver, retired as a passenger carrier because of its diminutive size. It started complaining long before the first pile could be extracted, shooting steam clouds in the air and rolling from side to side on the flat-bottomed hull. The captain and crew of this calm water vessel had their hands full, as did the gillnetters who had come to assist them.

"Maybe we oughta wear the masks the committeeman gave us," Thomas Bergman suggested.

Thanks to the persuasive powers of men such as Olavi Pustinen, the rules were never clear and the outcome always murky. Olof took the mask Thomas handed him and tossed it in the river. Thomas Bergman was of a similar mind. In agreement he stuffed the idea of anonymity into the pocket of his raincoat and returned to the work at hand. "Maybe this will change them landlubbers' minds," he remarked casually, "but I sure hate destroying all this hard-to-come-by netting."

Olof knew the pitfalls of unwarranted sympathy. He pulled the long-bladed knife from its sheath and started whacking through the barrier with unbridled ferocity. "The trapmen make as much as we do, undercut our prices to the canners, make a mockery of fishing, and clog up the river with their ungodly contraptions. In the end, they could very well be the end of us," Olof snapped.

The steamer lacked adequate power. A pile driver had done an exemplary job of embedding the trap supports deep in the riverbed, and another passing squall halted its progress altogether. The six salmon boats were too busy with their separately assigned tasks to notice that their escort was falling short on its promises.

Olavi scratched his head as he watched from the wheelhouse. He was disgruntled. Not only were the gillnetters from Ilwaco tardy in their arrival, but the captain of the steamer had been correct all along. It would require a stronger head of steam than this boat could muster to attack the thick forest of piles. Olavi poured the final draught of coffee from his thermos, having admitted defeat. "We'll try it another night," he said over his shoulder.

The captain did not appear to be the kind of man who would give up easily if the cause were a rational one. He was heavyset with a thick growth of beard that enhanced a very powerful jawline. His skin was abrasive from the drying effects of the weather, and beneath the black peacoat dignified with gold buttons, his shoulders were broad and his chest hefty.

"I warned you," he cautioned Olavi. His presentation was throaty and his words inflected with sincerity. "I said that working this churning river so near the ocean would be a far sight different from ferrying a few passengers between Portland and Oregon City."

Olavi never even flinched. "You'll get your money, one way or the other."

Captain Sorensen studied his passenger for a minute. "What about them gillnetters out there we're supposed to be guarding? If we're going to pull up stakes, we ought to give them plenty of lead time. Our crew's been armed like you requested. We should follow them back, not the other way around. They've got to rely on sails and oars, so we could at least provide a little insurance."

The captain's beneficence was far down the list of Olavi's concerns. He could stare into the night and see that the gillnetting contingent from Ilwaco was not going to materialize, meaning his efforts to lure the Washington state fishermen into the conflict had failed and would not headline tomorrow's news as a manifestation of the union's growing strength. He swore under his breath and got to his feet. "Let's take her home, Cap'n Sorensen," he ordered.

Two things were occurring simultaneously. The steamer was moving away from the island as a fleet of boats was approaching via the narrow channel reaching into the river from Ilwaco. A gunshot rang out, hitting its mark and shattering a window in the steamer's wheelhouse.

It was then Olof raised his head and became aware of his surroundings. Something was amiss. The bulky steamer, like a ghostly apparition, had merged with the distance and disappeared into the night. Oars continued driving through the water, and the lead boat of the approaching flotilla of insurgents could be seen to the west. Thomas Bergman took the cigarette he had been nursing through the dampness and tossed it overboard.

Olof wanted to say something, but words were unnecessary. They were sitting ducks. The outcome of the trial had not changed Olavi Pustinen one iota: the cause

remained more imperative than the individuals it suppos-
edly represented.

"We know they're armed," Thomas Bergman
suggested. "We should just get the hell out of here!"

Olof was not so certain. Five other gillnet boats were
out there somewhere, and only two of them could be seen,
silhouetted against the backdrop of a moonless rain-
scudded sky. He wondered what was going through the
minds of his fellow compatriots and, without the steamer to
assist them, what they would deem the most plausible
course of action.

"Let's go have it out with the trapmen," Olof said
brashly, "and face them fair and square. I didn't care much
for sneaking around, anyway."

With Henry at the oars, it would have been a done
deal. Instead, Thomas hesitated, and Olof withdrew a
whiskey bottle from the bow of the boat.

∞

The farmer Jonas Gunnarsson Hallberg had been born
in the village of Holje in the parish of Jämshög. If he had
nurtured a particular dream to help motivate himself
through the infancy of his life, it was in owning a parcel of
arable land and going about the business of raising crops.
He had succeeded thus far in the acquisition of acreage, but
the payment for all he intended to erect thereon waited upon
the success of his fish trap. Two years of uncertainty seemed
like an eternity to a man in his mid-twenties, and he was
anxious to bring his rights to fruition.

Of the thirty men involved in this evening's battle
against the gillnetters, his opinion was probably the most
subjective. He loaded the gun and fired toward the light in
the steamer's wheelhouse, convinced his actions were

justified. By hitting the mark, his self-confidence grew proportionally.

"We'll get the rest of them now," Jonas gloated to the other occupants of the boat. "We'll blow them off this river and send them packing." His words carried beyond the realm of comfort and moved into invisible reaches. He took a seat, and the oarsman continued moving the lead boat into the maze of traps.

Olof handed the whiskey bottle off to Thomas Bergman. He could not understand the words coming through the darkness, but they were ample warning. He started rowing, moving away from the dangerous confines of the traps. He knew his pursuers would spot the salmon boat very soon, but he had to trust the other gillnetters to outmaneuver them.

One advantage of spending nights on the river was the enhancement of the senses. A gillnetter could see through the darkness and hear through the quiet. Thomas Bergman took a swig of the whiskey and then sat as still as stone. The sound of the oar blades cutting cleanly through the water was hardly perceptible. The river's current sloshing against both the boat's hull and the network of piles was far more discernible. Escape was never a viable option. Olof was only buying the gillnetters some time to slip into position.

A shot pierced the air. Olof knew it was meant for him. He could see a man pointing the weapon in his direction. "Stop where you are!" came the challenge.

Olof obeyed. He pulled in the oars and left the boat to divine its own heading. He was still buying on margin, capable of locating only five of the six salmon boats. The scene was confusing, because it appeared two gillnet boats were off the stern of the low-water boat approaching him.

The lead boat was obviously a trapman's fish retrieval scow, the others still begging anonymity.

Olof stood as the approaching boat came alongside. It carried six armed men, two of whom quickly reached out and brought Olof's boat next to theirs. "We're taking you in tow," Jonas announced proudly. "We'll let the law deal with the likes of you."

Olof handed Jonas the bowline. He said nothing in his defense nor did he attempt to dispute Jonas's sovereignty. Instead, he offered the fish trapper a piece of advice. "Better ride with us, youngun, or you just might see us slippin' away into the night. Or we might shoot you in the back with one of these." Olof held out his gun for all to see. "Or maybe, as a trapman, you expect to die of a bullet wound for staking out a river that wasn't yours to claim in the first place. I'd think about it long and hard before I started encroaching on another man's territory. The river belongs to fishermen, not farmers. I'd no more imagine drawing a gun and driving you off your land than you should be thinking about taking my salmon boat in tow. Each should stick to his own and not go trespassing against his neighbor."

Olof's words of warning had a sobering effect on Jonas. He wanted to take the gun from Olof's hand and prove good on his demands, but something told him it would not be wise. If he were trespassing on his countryman's territory, there would be hell to pay in his own conscience. He stood aside as another trapman usurped his leadership. "We've got licenses to fish this island," the man announced haughtily, "and you gillnetters have no rights whatsoever. You're a bunch of drifters, thinking you own something you haven't paid for."

Olof could barely contain himself. The gun was in his hand, but the shot fired came from the darkness. Someone aboard the scow had been struck, thus the battle begun. In those moments of realization, Thomas shoved off from the scow, using an oar as a wedge against a trapman's grip. Jonas fired at Thomas, lodging a bullet in his shoulder. Another salmon boat had come out of the darkness, and gunfire was being exchanged in a wild melée. Havoc reigned for a few precious seconds, and Olof laid to the oars. A squall line came upon them as a blessing from Mother Nature, and sheets of rain brought an end to the futile volleys.

The entire scenario was vaguely re-enacted in the newspaper: From Ilwaco came reports of destruction of property, amounting to $40,000. The men who destroyed the traps were masked, and it is said that they are residents of Astoria. One man was reported killed, one wounded. It is directly asserted that the men who did Monday night's work are fishermen who view with jealousy the encroachment of traps.

Late Summer, 1893

Putting the boardinghouse up for sale said more of Molly's failing condition than anything else. "You wouldn't consider settling down and earning an honest living, would you?" Molly asked Olof. The suggestion had been offered in jest, but the humor was lost on him. For all intents and purposes, he had settled down. "What about Perron?" Olof grumbled. "Seems he has a stake in this business."

The question itself drained more energy from Molly's tired visage. "Never did and never will. Can't remove a fur trapper from his wilderness, anymore than you can keep a gillnetter off the river. We decided it was better to die apart than to live together in misery. Perron ain't got no use for civilization. He always said as much, so there's no reason to call him a liar."

Olof watched Molly rise from the kitchen table and move toward the wood stove. There was labor expended in each and every step, yet there was no keeping her from her routine. She opened the oven door and left it hanging on the hinges until she could locate a pair of hot pads. She then lifted out the roasting pan and placed it atop the stove. She stopped to catch her breath before closing the oven door. A process she had once made to appear so simple was becoming a chore.

Without being asked, Olof left his chair and removed the chickens from the pan. Molly moved toward the pantry to get the flour. Olof stood aside as Molly stirred the flour into the drippings. The boiled potatoes were simmering on the back of the stove, but the absence of buttermilk biscuits was a marked change. "How are you doing with all the boarders?" Olof queried.

"Same as always," Molly replied. "Some pay their rent on time, and others dodge the issue. I still send the rowdy ones packing, however, 'cause there ain't no man who's going to give me any guff. And how about you, Olof, they still causing you grief?"

Aware of what Molly was alluding to, Olof took his cue to let silence intervene. News traveled fast up and down the river, and this time it was sickening. The legislature had sided with the trapmen and those who employed another contraption called the fishwheel. It was wrong, but Olof no longer wished to fight it. If they deemed it responsible to categorize him as a lawless drifter, coming for a fishing season and then moving on, it was okay by him. People could be blind to the truth, even if it was close enough to bite them. It was better to give it all a wide berth. Olof walked by the table and picked up his hat. He was about to make his exit when Molly stopped him cold.

"Before you go sneakin' out on this old woman, I suggest you see what came for you in the mail. I hope it don't break your heart anymore than it's already been broken."

The letter was from Ingrid.

It made no sense, but Olof dared not open it until he had gotten to his boat. There he had every intention of reading it, but he cast off instead. He kept kidding himself that he could wait, but he had used up all the patience available to him. He dropped the sail before approaching the small fishing dock servicing the town of Frankfort, Washington, and read the letter as the current moved him along.

> Dearest Olof,
>
> I know it has been years for the both of us, I hope years well spent. I don't pretend that this letter will be of interest to you, the assumption being that you've remarried, or at least, moved on. I have done neither, finding my time better dedicated to the care of my family and the teaching of school. It is enough for me. Nils Gustav Petersson died in the spring, and Brita Hansdotter remains a sorrowful widow. I do what I can to guide her through these later years, hoping my attentiveness suffices. When she is gone, the past will be at peace. I hope you are well and content.
>
> Ingrid Andersson.

Chapter Nine

~ ~ ~ ~ ~ ~ ~ ~ ~ ~ ~ ~ ~ ~ ~ ~ ~ ~ ~

March, 1896

Money wasn't everything in life, but as Samuel L. Wright could attest, it did precede most everything else. He placed his hand over his wine glass and slipped the server a dollar bill. He didn't intend to make waves, just remain lucid.

Beyond the rain-streaked windows protecting this private lounge from a typical spring deluge, the riverbank appeared wild and uninhabited, but that would change as the sternwheeler progressed downriver, as would the tenor of this meeting. Things always changed while remaining within the same context, like a few grey hairs growing into a majority unnoticed. As a cannery owner and millionaire, Mr. Wright could predict what would occur next because the dictates presupposed by his accumulation of wealth would speak for him.

"I suspect we all in agree about the 'combine,'" Thadeus Bowman suggested from the head of the table.

It went without saying who had nodded in the affirmative. Sam took the platter of smoked oysters and held it in reserve as his mind searched for the proper phrasing of the joke meant to accompany it. Every action and reaction were rote: another year, another meeting, another drink, and another platter of smoked oysters to generate a wanton distraction.

"Maybe a 'combine' isn't a good idea on the Columbia," Sam said.

Seven gentlemen, the kingpins of the lower Columbia canning industry, turned their heads. Sam had no idea why he had offered the comment; it had just slipped out.

The man who had always conducted these meetings was quick to override the remark. "Some of us who merged to form the Alaska Packing Association," Thadeus Bowman readily pointed out, "found it a profitable arrangement. If we combine our resources on the lower river in a similar fashion, we can manage both supply and demand. Competition among ourselves isn't the answer. We need to control both the market and the production; otherwise, our investments will be at risk."

The waiter continued around the table, keeping all but one of the wine glasses filled.

A rebuttal put so succinctly by one of the originators of their canning industry was the sign of a propitious move in the offing, yet Sam did not like the sound of it. He passed the oyster platter off to Harold Stinson, seated on his left. Harold was Sam's mentor and benefactor, perhaps the only participant in this unusual congress for whom he felt any compulsory admiration. The rest of them had moved beyond the realms of the Columbia, rolling their profits into other exploits. Neither Harold nor Sam had expanded their concerns to include the salmon runs along the Pacific Coast or had invested in the burgeoning opportunities connected with the railroad and timber industries. In the company of such dynamic examples of entrepreneurs, both Harold Stinson and Sam L. Wright were small-time players.

"I see you didn't take any," the recipient said jokingly as he received the platter of oysters. "Not feeling well, Sam? Or just not up to it?"

Harold Stinson's lightheartedness had the desired effect. The camaraderie around the table reconnected, and Sam's faux pas was overlooked. With the exception of Sam and Harold, each of the packers in attendance accepted the hors d'oeuvre course as simple foreplay, preceding the ultimate coupling destined to take place. Still, any hypothetical outcome could never be 100 percent, in spite of Mr. Stinson's cementing relations.

Harold Stinson's father had owned a fishery proper, an enterprise involved in salting salmon and packing them in barrels. He'd met with limited success due to shipping problems, unstable markets and shortages of both barrels and salt, yet it remained a better living than devised by most. In his maturity, Harold had foreseen the need to convert the barreling establishment into a cannery. The old days had come to an end. He had partaken in the growth, including the unbridled competition which had eventually altered the river's character. Harold Stinson, at the age of sixty-five, had perseverance to his credit, yet like the ancient Chinook Indians who had once provided the salmon for his father's fishery, he was of a different breed and of an entirely different perspective. He was the only one seated at the formal luncheon informally attired. He was casual in his personal habits, but not casual in his personal convictions.

Sam L. Wright was completely indebted to Harold Stinson for his acceptance into this elitist gathering of men. The canning process, jealously guarded by a few, had revealed itself through the graduated steps of employment provided by Harold, beginning with the rudimentary duties of a bookkeeper and culminating in the prestigious position of cannery manager. Through Harold's unselfishness, Sam's rise had not stopped there. He had gotten his own financing due to Harold's influence and branched out on his own.

Of the eight men seated at the table, three of them had matriculated through a similar history. As teachers, pupils and competitors their lives were all intertwined, and with the exception of Thadeus Bowman and Harold Stinson, each had a few chits that would become payable as the trip progressed.

The sound of the paddle wheel driving relentlessly through the water could be misleading. It made a man feel empowered, imbuing him with the sensation that he could press on unchallenged. As the prime rib was being served, Sam watched the city of Kalama passing on the starboard side of the sternwheeler. Normally it would be a scheduled stop, but this was no ordinary trip, and the sternwheeler kept churning up the Columbia's surface with a vengeance. Their conscripted vessel would project its rolling wake against the opposing shores until reaching Eagle Cliff, its first port of call and the birthplace of the Columbia River canning industry, fifty miles inland from the Pacific Ocean. By then, it would all be settled.

In the interim, Sam finally addressed the container of horseradish sauce for what it was and plopped two spoonfuls next to three generous slices of beef. The mixed vegetables were swimming in the hot juices, and he intended to consume his serving before his stomach gave

him fits. Out of the corner of his eye he saw the man at the
head of the table raise a napkin to his lips. It was too late.

Thadeus Bowman was a man of distinction. Like
others of comparable status and upbringing, he wore a
three-piece suit with the top of his vest also showing lapels.
His shirt was traditionally white, but the collar was
narrower than most, probably influenced by a recent
European trend. He maintained a stylish mustache, but
unlike six of the eight men at the table, his chin was clean
shaved. His eyebrows were darker than the graying hair
pomaded back from his forehead. His eyes were brown, and
the pockets of skin beneath them slightly puffy. He was of
average height and could be considered thin. He looked
younger than Harold Stinson, but such a comparison was
completely subjective. Thadeus Bowman was an East Coast
import and Harold Stinson a West Coast native, thus shaped
by different environments. They represented the two
opposing views at the table and would do so with gusto.

"How do you feel about a strike?" Thadeus Bowman
asked. His question had been thrown out to the group, but it
was meant to inspire himself. He continued: "The gillnetters
seem committed to five cents a pound, but I can probably
hold out until they drop to four. We're heavy on the market
right now. Will it be a problem for any of you? Other than
Mr. Wright and Mr. Stinson, we've all got seiners and
trapmen who'll work for whatever we offer. The union has
been busy inquiring as to the viability of our paying five
cents as opposed to four, getting facts and figures on the
stock market, and what our brokers are asking. I don't think
it will cause a problem with the public's perception,
however, because as the union tries to pick us apart, they'll
be fighting internally. The Scandinavian Packing Company
has already talked to me about the marketing possibilities

for their product — supposing we will assist them, so to speak. Even those who are against us will eventually join us. With the 'combine' in mind, this strike might prove to be the last we ever have to weather."

The main speaker finished sharing his thoughts on the subject and resumed eating. Sam, however, had lost his appetite. He was not necessarily opposed to trading in his autonomy for the sake of the industry, but the means and the ends were both questionable. "Mr. Stinson and I are dependent upon the gillnetters as our sole source of salmon," he noted emphatically, "and if you can bring the Scandinavian Packing Company to its knees for the same dependency, then why aren't we just as vulnerable?"

"Ethics," Thadeus Bowman replied handily. "It's ethics that brings us together to discuss our plight openly, and it is ethics that separates the winners from the losers. Because you rely solely on rogue gillnetters, you put your own selves at risk. The 'combine' will solve your problem of vulnerability in the future, trust me."

"Why?" Harold Stinson spoke up. "We could have solved these problems years ago, if we'd trusted one another." Harold came forward in his chair and rested his forearms on the table's edge. He was a large man. "So, explain to me, Mr. Bowman, what's changed? Another year of turmoil is going to disrupt the lower river, and more lives will be lost, and more good people will be broken. You speak of the rogue gillnetters from personal experience, I'm certain. As for Mr. Wright, myself, and businesses such as the Scandinavian Packing Company, we don't enlist transients, rely on farmers or have horse seiners do our bidding. The increased competition we're currently facing is due to the expeditious thinking of men such as yourself. The problem won't correct itself by packaging it in different terms. It's time the canners began eliminating the dictatorial practices that continually wreak havoc upon our own industry. The dedicated fishermen, thanks to your enterprising nature, might very well lose their homes."

Thadeus Bowman dropped a fist on the table. "Then let them lose their shacks!" he exploded. "Who in the heck invited them here, anyway?"

Harold Stinson remained calm. "You did, Mr. Bowman, and Harry there, and Mr. Branson seated to your right, and Edward Stone, who is staring at me incredulously from across the table. None of you has any innocence in the matter. From the very beginning, the single motivating factor was the accumulation of capital. It never mattered how the salmon found their way into your packing concerns, just so long as they kept coming. Do you recall when we were forced to pay the gillnetters not to fish? That was because the transient fishermen came in by the boatloads, just to ensure that your season would be a profitable one. Then the traps, barring the mouth of the river, another insurance policy meant to further cheapen the price of labor." Harold paused for a minute, the cheeks above his pure-white beard were flushed, a reflection of a rapidly beating heart. "The horse seiners possibly represent the final destructive measure to be enlisted against the river. When we're all gone, which is inevitable, the river will be poor and the memories of its wealth vanished. The money isn't worth it, gentlemen, because we've bequeathed an impoverished future upon those very people who've promoted our success. It has to stop here and now. I can't justify another strike, knowing we have the power to avert it."

Edward Stone was the one to pick up the gauntlet. Sam could guess as to where the conversation was headed, having taken this detour during similar discussions. "Some of us have invested in fish hatcheries for the sake of the industry," Mr. Stone said in a slowed and steadied rhythm. "I'm not so certain one can presuppose the rape of the Columbia is inevitable; furthermore, I don't want to be held accountable for the debits without taking credit for the benefits our industry has brought to this region. Without us, there would be no jobs for the immigrants; without us, the merchants would surely fold. For all of your accusations, Mr. Stinson, I'm afraid they are rooted in feelings of guilt I fail to share. Our products have provided an inexpensive food source for many of our overseas brethren. As our costs become inflated, their capability to pay goes down. It's to our credit that we've withstood all the pressures thus far."

As the dishes were being cleared from the table, the meeting adjourned temporarily. Sam walked over to the windows and leaned against the brass railing to accept the swells of a passing steamer, headed upriver. Six of the eight diners had gathered in a separate conclave next to the bar. Harold Stinson had taken his coat and gone outside to walk the decks alone. Sam watched his elderly mentor strolling along the upper deck, wondering what it would be like to be burdened with such determination. Sam had never adopted that particular quality under Harold Stinson's tutelage, and had never understood the symbiotic relationship which bound a man morally to the success of his business. Sam L. Wright enjoyed the opportunities provided by the river but was incapable of living up to the singularity they demanded. Walking the decks on a brisk day to inhale the air and view the forested hills in passing couldn't harden him. He started making his way back to the table as the waiter returned to the lounge with the individual dessert plates compacted on a large platter.

"What do you think of the pie?" Mr. Branson inquired.

"It's very good," Sam replied, "but not as good as Lorraine's lemon chiffon. I don't know what it is about home cooking, but everything else falls a little short." All heads around the table nodded. Sam was relieved that this once, they were in total agreement. "The ice cream, however, is superb," he added. "Lorraine has yet to try her hand at putting together such a delicacy." At the moment, Sam missed his wife and children. He had left them at their first home in Portland, while he'd gone marching off to war on the lower river.

Mr. Bowman interrupted the silence while the coffee was being poured. "Although the Columbia River Packers Association remains in its infancy," he said bluntly, "it's going to happen. Those wishing to join will be welcomed; those abstaining will survive as the competition. Certain canneries will remain operative and others will act as fish-receiving stations or warehousing facilities for ice and equipment. We'll employ gillnetters, trapmen and horse seiners alike, looking for the best possible combination. Stock will be issued and reasonable compensation paid to those who wish to participate. Positions will be made available to those packers wanting to stay actively involved. It will be a large organization and should dominate the industry."

Harold Stinson was extremely agitated. "It sounds like a squeeze play to me," he growled. "With so many canneries running on margin, the strike will take them to their knees, and then the 'combine' will come in for the kill. I have to respect your business acumen, Mr. Bowman, but not the intent behind it. There is something less than satisfying about this solution, because it's aimed at forcing me out of business."

Nothing was said of the canning industry following Harold Stinson's appraisal of the situation. Sam L. Wright turned inwardly to consider his own options and evaluate the importance he placed on his accrued million. Evidently, Harold Stinson would forfeit his elitist position to keep his cannery running — but it was different for Sam. He had never really been on either side but had admired Harold for those selfless qualities that few men could ever possess. It was time for Sam to bow out graciously, hoping to salvage what he could when the Columbia River Packers Association came to fruition. It was an amicable compromise for a fatalist. He lifted his hand in the air and snapped his fingers. "Waiter!" he called out loudly. "Is there any wine left in that bottle you were pouring?"

∞

Olof was not one for making promises he could not keep, but the house he was building was another matter. It was a contractual obligation he had made with himself, based on the slim possibility Ingrid would return. It was slow going due to the graduated steps restricted by a tight budget, but he finally had the structure roughed in, and the efforts of his labors were beginning to surface. It was a two-story dwelling with a raised porch affording a panoramic view of the river, and it was protected from the encroachment of civilization on three sides by natural vegetation. Below it was adequate space for a garden. It was a tremendous undertaking by most standards, but the standards he was adhering to were strictly his. For his own sense of accomplishment, he had more than doubled the square footage of the house that his family had occupied in Astoria, and for Ingrid's approval he had incorporated much of it into a formal room meant for entertaining her guests.

"You may have it completely finished this summer," Arnold Larson remarked as he off-loaded another bundle of shingles from the boat, "because it doesn't look like this strike is going to be a short one. If we get into June, the association could go bankrupt. Many possibilities are surfacing, and a lot of determined talk can be heard in Uppertown. The meeting tomorrow afternoon is going to be a big one, drawing gillnetters from as far away as Eagle Cliff."

Olof only had to lift his head and look across the river's surface to see the truth of Arnold's statement. The number of salmon boats heading into Astoria was astounding. The total complement of the Butterfly Fleet was on the lower river, making itself known. It should have been inspirational for Olof to see the commitment implied by such a gathering, but he knew better. Striking wasn't the answer, and he did not want to have any part of it. He stopped to wipe the sweat from his brow before joining Arnold dockside. "Going to help me lug these up to the house?" Olof asked.

Arnold stood amid the bundles on the dock, observing Olof's nonchalant mannerisms with disbelief. Olof appeared so unruffled as to raise Arnold's ire. "If the strike brings more hardship on my family," Arnold said vehemently, "we'll all be leaving. The boys need more than a season of fishing to carry them through the winter. Hard to believe, but I'm a grandfather five times over. Both John and Jacob are talking about selling their boat and moving on to land somewhere upriver. If they up and move their families, Ingrid will want to follow. She's gotten real fond of being a grandmother. Besides, if this strike fails, I won't be making payments on my house, anyway."

The concern on Arnold's pale visage was very real, but Olof supposed he and the other gathering gillnetters were amassing on another dead-end road. The canners would ultimately win this bout, considering all the resources they had managed to garner. "A strike isn't the answer," he replied bluntly, "and I hope to heck the union sees that before it repeats an old mistake. Striking has never gotten the gillnetters anywhere. If it didn't work twenty years ago, it sure isn't going to work now. Until both the packers and the gillnetters are willing to cull out their own ranks, strikes will only serve to keep the river muddied."

Arnold was completely befuddled. "I would think that having committed yourself to land and property, you'd comprehend the seriousness of this strike! There's not going to be any crossing over on this one! The Scandinavian Packing Company is going to get shut down like all the rest of the canneries! We're finally talking war!"

Olof bent from the waist and nestled a bundle of shakes under either armpit. He felt compelled to respond to Arnold's fervent plea, yet the words of explanation were not available to him. He headed down the dock, leaving Arnold to reach his own conclusions.

"What the heck's the matter with you?" Arnold called after him.

A wood stove and two stiff-backed chairs were in the kitchen, representing the total complement of comforts Olof had thus far added to the interior of his house. A can of hardtack sat on the seat of one chair, and a burlap sack of potatoes leaned up against the leg of another. Living alone and fending for himself had definitely altered his lifestyle. The consumption of starchy foods had furthermore expanded his waistline. He was not the fine figure of a man Ingrid had slept with, nor the brash young darer who had presumed to right all the wrongs along the lower Columbia. He had his hands full just living one small dream, without having it constantly threatened. At times he rued the day he had ever set foot on a salmon boat, and at other times he simply rued his own being. Due to his fearsome visage, guarded privacy, and the added girth around his waist, the children playing along Frankfort's waterfront had coined the name "Pot" Anderson to taunt him. The double 's' in his name had been dropped for reasons of convention. Whether he acknowledged it or not, he was considered a recluse by many who sidestepped him in their passing. He was an isolated man on land, and in his singularity had to assess the rationale for going to war. For whom was he fighting?

When Olof lay down on the floor and pulled the covers over him, the luxury of sleep awaited him. He rolled over on his side to extinguish the lantern and any lingering recollections of Arnold's shrill remonstrances. He intended to remain neutral this time around, but there was the crumpled and faded newspaper where it had lain alongside Ingrid's six letters, telling him how impossible such a decision would be. He raised up and used an elbow for support, drawn by the newspaper's allure. On the second page he had circled two items, one concerning the fishing industry and the other about Molly Bochau. Molly's obituary was short and to the point, but the puzzling bit of information continued to stand out, revealing how she had been born to a respected East Coast family. Why that fact stood out in Olof's mind he was not certain, but it had to do with himself and the tremendous departure he, too, had made from what had been expected of him.

Olof moved on to the second article titled: "As to the Transfer of Canneries to an English Syndicate." Six years earlier, when the article had appeared, the syndication of the canneries had not occurred, but through the wiles of an astute journalist who had covered the story, Olof's suspicions had finally been put in print. The journalist, while exploring the pros and cons affecting the local economy if such a syndicate were to buy out the canneries, had stumbled across the truth. The reason for the great disparity between the wealth of the river and the poverty of its denizens had been succinctly stated: It was notoriously the fact that the profits of the cannery industry, in all the years, had been skimmed off and taken elsewhere for expenditure and investment.

Olof read the quote several times before setting the newspaper aside and rolling down the wick on the lantern. In the old days, he would have curled up with the truth and fallen fast asleep resolved. Now, parting himself from his problems with the brief interruption of sleep was a task all its own.

April 8, 1896

It was a strange morning. A hailstorm impeded Olof's progress until he was midriver, at which time the sun shone and a rainbow stretched from the hills above Uppertown and touched down near Taylor Sands, forming a colorful arch above the western end of Woody Island Channel. Well inside Tongue Point dark clouds regathered overhead, and a rainstorm followed him into Astoria. As Olof was docking, the sun reappeared and he made his way up the slickened ladder rungs to start his trek through civilization. The willows were green with leaves along the riverbank, and the fruit trees were in full bloom in the corner lots. By the time he had joined the crowd of gillnetters headed for Fisher's Hall, he had stripped off his rain gear and was enjoying the springtime warmth.

The crowd was beyond any dimensions he had ever imagined. Fisher's Hall, boasting the largest room in

Astoria, was incapable of housing the assemblage. A block away, Olof began elbowing his way toward the entrance. He had seen it all before. He spotted some of his fellow gill-netters from the Scandinavian Packing Company, but he felt the need to go it alone, because he was singular in the vast history supporting his convictions. The confusion he evoked by his mere physical appearance allowed him passage. He heard a few grumbles as he disrupted an occasional gathering of conversationalists, but never a challenge.

The Columbia River Fishermen's Union had been reinstated for this convention, but the extremism had been squelched. No one questioned his right to be there, although he had yet to join. By his body language alone, it was evident he was the captain of his own fate.

The meeting was called to order in English. Over his shoulder, Olof saw a few recent emigrants depart the room. That was to be expected. A few left, a few filled in from the crowd milling around outside. Hopefully, the chaff would be separated from the wheat before the real debates began.

The chairman was an Astorian and employee of the Branson Cannery. The Branson Cannery was central to many of the problems facing the gillnetters and, therefore, the chairman's point of view very germane. Being one of the real risk takers, Olof was interested in what he would have to say. For once, the Fishermen's Union had made a good choice in their leadership.

Carl Hansen was nervous facing a crowd of hundreds, and for a moment when the assemblage had quieted and all eyes were focused upon him, he started to falter. His mind had not gone blank; quite the opposite, it was extremely cluttered. He took a deep breath and spoke as loudly as he could. "The Fishermen's Union, in executive session, has come to the conclusion that five cents a pound is a fair price for salmon, and the members should fish for nothing less. But, realizing that there are many others who perhaps should be consulted in the matter, it was decided to call this mass meeting of fishermen of all classes on the river to discuss the proposition of the packers. They are standing firm on four cents and are unwilling to negotiate."

In prior years Olof would have anticipated jeers and guffaws to interrupt at this point, yet everyone in the room refrained from making their frustrations known. Another speaker, the Secretary of the Union, had taken up the chairman's slack by proposing to read several letters from the cannerymen. His voice was confident upon reaching the end of the third: "Owing to the condition of the market on canned goods, it is impossible to stand the price of five cents per pound on raw material. Edward Stone."

Now, the gillnetters were getting a little restless. "What's the point?" someone hollered out from the back of the room.

The secretary was the one to answer. "The point is, I can disprove those figures using market quotations from a New York newspaper."

With the exception of Olof, everyone listened attentively. The secretary had done an admirable job of breaking down the facts and figures available to him, but this was not the argument Olof wanted to hear. He had expected it, but it was not the central issue at hand. It was sufficient to unite the gillnetters, however, because a vote was taken to stand on five cents, and the 'yeas' were thundering.

"Now we get to the crux of the matter," Carl Hansen responded, "because if we intend to shut down the river, we need to do it completely."

"Finally," Olof grumbled under his breath, "we'll see if this strike has any legs to it." A handful of gillnetters crowded around him heard the comment; a few even cast disparaging looks in his direction. Olof never flinched. Thus far the entire meeting was history revisited.

Carl Hansen continued. "Everyone will be allowed to fish for his own consumption, but no one will be allowed to provide fish to the markets or private individuals, boats or other consumers. To make certain of this, there will be a group formed to look after the fishermen. Further, no trapman or horse seiner will be permitted to sell their fish upon any market, and to ensure they obey this closure, two other groups will be formed to monitor their activities. Individual cannerymen are not to be allowed to employ non-union fishermen or any other fishermen, even if they should be willing to pay five cents per pound, unless every cannery on the river agrees to that price."

At this point, the chairman's speech was interrupted. "There are many fishermen upriver who'll fish for the four cents!" someone cried out. "And what about the fish-wheels?" another uncertain voice added. "Who's going to keep an eye on them?"

Olof studied Carl Hansen's face very carefully. These questions were fair, although never fairly dealt with. Olof hoped the chairman could see the answer, but the frown on his face said something different. Olof started parting the crowd, making his way to the front of the room. Presently the jeers and guffaws started, but Olof was immune to the mockery.

His fist struck the podium squarely. "The real problem lies with the transient fishermen," he said gruffly. "There will never be peace on this river, until they're weeded out. Like the trapmen, horse seiners and fishwheels, they provide a means to an end for the canners. They are like poison in our blood, sapping our strength as they eat away at the river. We can supply all the fish the canners require and more, but that doesn't stop them from bringing in their seasonal workers to muddy the waters and damage our reputations. We need to go to the canners on this; we need to make it perfectly clear that we're willing to hold out as long as they're determined to employ drifters to do our jobs."

"That was a real pretty speech," Olavi Pustinen commented.

Olof hadn't noticed him standing there, within arm's reach, watching the entire situation. A flashback of the first union meeting Olof had ever attended came to mind, and the instinctive mistrust resurfaced. Nevertheless, Olof was not going to yield the floor. He had more criticism to level against the canners, including the methods they had fostered to denigrate the role of the gillnetters; further, he had a handful of canners in mind, including Thadeus Bowman and his cronies, who needed to be exposed for their financial shenanigans. He had worked it all out — a plan to return dignity to the lower Columbia. He started to speak, but he felt a heavy hand fall on his shoulder. "I appreciate your views, but our plan is inclusive of all your concerns," Carl Hansen assured him.

But they had not taken it all under advisement. Talking both to the chairman and the assemblage alike, he remained at the podium to make his point. "It always starts out well and good, but then the defectors take over. It's like dry rot creeping through the hull of a ship: no one takes notice until a storm is brewing, and by then it's too late. The transient fishermen are already here, knitting nets and working around the boat yards. It won't be long before a packer starts sending them out at night, and more will follow. A man who has to keep his family fed will be tempted, and by then it's impossible to sort the good from the bad. The canners will have won, and we'll be back exactly where we started, thinking about another strike while they're off spending the profits in parts unknown."

"That's a real sorry picture you're painting there," Olavi interjected, "but I don't believe these men here are going to be tempted. Am I right? Aren't we going to hold out for five cents or nothing? All the way to August 10? The day the canners are forced to put their businesses on notice?"

The room exploded in voluminous approval, but Olof was not finished. He turned to Olavi Pustinen, a grimace on his face. "I'm right about this," he snarled, "and you know it!"

The crowd's continued approval gave Olavi the edge he needed. The clapping and yelling was earsplitting. He leaned into Olof's face and whispered. "Seems like the score is never settled between us, is it? You cost me a month's pay in court, and then managed to escape from the trapmen. You're a good student, Olof Andersson, but not smart enough to figure out what's going on along this river. At least you got one part of it right: eventually everyone falls prey to temptation."

May 8, 1896

Three hundred gillnetters, mostly the old-timers, had volunteered to try it Olof's way. They would split out in groups to canvass all the canners, but Olof had elected to approach Thadeus Bowman from a different angle. Mr. Bowman was the legend, the one who could very well turn the tide or halt the entire process in its tracks, but he was as slippery as an eel. Olof carried a copy of the proposal in his pocket as he stood on the wide porch surrounding the gracious Victorian home, but referral to it was unnecessary. He knocked several times before a Chinese maid admitted him into the parlor, a luxurious setting decorated in all hues of pink with rich browns invested in both the Oriental rug and throw pillows, and brass lamp fixtures framing a window view of the Columbia. She looked at him skeptically before leaving him seated on the settee. Since no questions had been asked, he knew the networking capabilities of the packers were functioning. Up and down the river, similar visits were occurring.

"Where are the rest of your followers?" Thadeus said as he approached Olof from behind the settee. He felt very secure, taking his uninvited visitor by surprise.

Olof stood and turned. They were within inches of each other, yet the packing czar was the one to back off. Olof was wearing a dark-brown suit he had purchased for Molly's funeral. His hair had been cut short and parted to one side, and were it not for the nasty scar disfiguring his face, he thought himself quite presentable for a proper visit. Between Ingrid's civilizing influences and Olof's knowledge of battle strategy, he was prepared.

He extended a hand and introduced himself. "I'm Olof Anderson, a fisherman from the Scandinavian Packing Company, here on business. Pleased to make your acquaintance."

Attired in a casual dressing gown, Thadeus was completely taken aback. According to his own suppositions, the union should have sent out two or three dozen men to rant and rave around the perimeter of his property, not a lonely representative who had the gall to bid himself entrance. A one-on-one confrontation would be harder to handle, particularly since they had elected to send someone who was both impressive and imposing. He found himself gawking at Olof's scar and tremendous stature and almost afraid to concentrate on the emerald-green eyes. At that moment, he felt ill-equipped to entertain any arguments.

Olof retracted his offer of a handshake and got right to the heart of the matter. "We would like you take back the twine that you've distributed to your transient fishermen. We expect you to give them credit for their labor, at fair wages, spent in knitting this twine into nets or repairing old ones. In return, the remaining fishermen will be willing to fish for four cents. It's a fair offer, Mr. Bowman, meant to bring peace to the Columbia. The time has come that this thing be settled fair and square."

Thadeus Bowman was speechless. His visitor's words made such sense he found it difficult to defend his own position. "Tea?" he muttered. "I'll have the maid bring us some tea."

"Tea is unnecessary," Olof replied. "I didn't come here to take up your time, I just wanted to know if you're willing to put an end to this senseless strike, and if not, why?"

"I believe you've empowered me with too much influence," Thadeus replied. "I'm not the only canner on this river. Your Scandinavian Packing Company is in agreement with us, too. Four cents is all we can afford to pay."

Olof did not immediately see the advantage of towering a head above his adversary, but Thadeus Bowman did. He finished his statement and retired to the settee, leaving Olof to explore the social graces involved. Ingrid would have called his host rude, but Olof thought him wily. He remained where he was, standing in the middle of the room, the center of attention. He was reminded of the coy barkeep on the scow who had evaded his questions until the shanghaiers had gotten into position. "An answer is all I require," Olof said flatly. "Your business problems are your own."

"I suppose I could convene a meeting of the other canners and look into your proposal," Thadeus Bowman replied, "but you've got to understand, I'm not alone in this."

Mr. Bowman's pattern of evasiveness was exactly what Olof now expected of him. Having delivered his message, Olof could very well take his leave at this juncture, or he could press the issue and expunge the venom threatening his very survival. He took the hat he held in his hands and turned it by the brim. Like Little Henry, he studied his options, then opened his window of opportunity.

"You've always had this river by the throat, squeezing the guts out of it and taking the profits to other places while repressing the local economy. And they blame it on men such as myself. I'm not new to the wars waged on this river, and I'm well aware of who's been behind them. For years, I've had the notion that men such as yourself would tire of the raping and pillaging and move on to something more dignified. Yet you hang on, returning for the season along with your drifters. A man such as myself gets frustrated over the likes of you. Every time I see what you've done to the Columbia, my stomach gets tied up in knots, and when I think of the death and destruction you've caused, hate and disgust overcome me." Olof looked down at his hands and saw how they were crushing the crown of his hat. He was a man of strong convictions.

For the first time in his life, Thadeus Bowman felt intimidated. "You get out of my house, you gillnetter!" he cursed.

Olof's chest was heaving. The temptation was there to lay his hands on this man's throat and twist until something snapped. For a fleeting second, Olof could visualize Danny

Bell coming up from the Columbia's depths and recall his own irrational desire to hold the unscrupulous shanghaier's head beneath the surface. Was he capable of it? At that moment, Olof experienced the same uncertainty.

"When I came here years ago, it didn't much matter how the next man led his life, because rubbing elbows wasn't a common occurrence. And it wasn't the money exacted from the river that mattered, it was the freedom it inspired by its possibilities. There were so many salmon, a man could believe the Columbia would sustain hundreds of years of history without losing an ounce of its energy. It was the pot at the end of the rainbow for someone who'd grown up mindful of such riches.

"Money's never mattered much to me, just the freedom to earn it by fishing. The real gillnetters are at the heart of this river because they accept it during the good times and the bad, and they respect it as one would a great competitor. And that's where we part company, Thadeus Bowman. It seems you're so removed from the natural ebb and flow of things that you judge your worth by the amount of money to be made, rather than appreciating the source from whence it came.

"I feel pity for you, Thadeus Bowman," Olof said, "because you fall prey to your own greed. You don't win a man's admiration by denying the truth of his words. I hope you'll take the petition into consideration, but I have my sincere doubts. It's a fair offer, and that's why it probably falls short of your expectations. Unfortunately, war has become such a way of life along the river that some are blind to the true cost of it."

Olof took his leave before Thadeus could comprehend how close he had come to knocking on death's door.

∞

The number of occupants in the cemetery had grown, as had the salal which was beginning to encroach upon the headstone marking the unoccupied grave next to Molly Bochau's and the twins'. The setting was in keeping with the insinuation of loneliness gradually creeping into Olof's life. Henry would understand, because he'd experienced what it had been like to fight for oneself only. Olof knelt down and tugged at the grass growing between Hanna Jane's and Little Henry's headstones. It seemed important that they never be separated by anything. Olof's feelings of separation were eating at his guts, destroying the continuity of anything positive remaining him.

"I'm building a house, regardless of the strike," he muttered. Any response would have been welcomed, but the quiet was even more assuring. The people he had loved would offer no criticism, bring no fault to bear upon the futility of his daily endeavors. "We could have taken Mr. Thadeus Bowman by the shoulders and shook some sense into him," Olof continued, "but it would have done no good. He's only got whatever good sense God gave him, and it doesn't seem like it's plentiful. The river will guard its treasures regardless, and it will always need fishermen. Going back isn't a choice," he said gruffly, "because I don't know how to take a piece of ground with me. Ingrid did, but I don't."

With his brief apology made for his inadequacies, Olof stood upright and took in the view that had so enamored Little Henry. Like Olof, the wild and untamed was gradually giving ground. Midriver on Desdemona Sands, a barn was being erected so the horse seiners could expand their influence. The number of traps on the river was approaching four hundred, literally disrupting the river's contours with their intervention. A new suburb referred to as Finntown was growing on Astoria's western perimeter, and Uppertown was relinquishing its distinctive flavor as more and more structures were filling in the landscape. In such a short length of time, the law of the land had literally overcome the natural course of the river. Astoria continued to grow into the water, as other towns along the Washington shore came to greet her. The industry was breathtaking, but not so breathtaking as that which supported it. For his own sense of well-being, Olof had to remember that. The past could be buried but never forgotten, and for what it was worth, he had had his chance at divining the future. He could do no more.

∞

John Lord knew this was to be the biggest news event to occur along the lower river but putting it all in perspective would be a far greater challenge. He removed his visor and tossed it in the wastebasket. He expended a bit more energy cleaning the lenses of his glasses and drumming his fingers on the desktop. He had burned the midnight oil many times in his life, yet this article had taken him well into the midmorning hours, and there was still no ending to the story. "It Looks Like a Compromise" headed John's insightful summation, but he felt his optimism premature. Half of the article was clearly stated and the remainder a series of maybes. The union members had presented a logical and reasonable compromise which could ultimately negate the ongoing strike and, according to Harold Stinson, their petition should be accepted. But Thadeus Bowman had employed too much rhetoric during a brief interview to promise anything definitive. For the sake of the local economy, John Lord hoped Harold Stinson represented the consensus of the canners. Just this once, the editor was sympathetic to the gillnetters and very wishful that his talents could ease their plight:

> Like nearly every other line of business, that of fishing in the waters of the Columbia has to a certain extent been overdone. This, at least, was the import of the overtures made yesterday by the fishermen to the packers. As is well known, there has been considerable talk among fishermen to the effect that there are too many men engaged in the business to make it profitable to all. There seemed to be quite a sentiment in favor of some means of reducing the number of men fishing on the river. Butchers, bakers, grocers, drygoods men, lawyers, doctors and even the farmers have passed through the same experience, and many of them are today suffering from too much competition. From all appearances, the same competition will last to the end of time. The fittest survive. Philanthropists and scientists seem to agree that there is room for everybody in the world, but it is said that only a small proportion are happy in their choice of an avocation or line of business. Sooner or later the error is discovered. Hence it is that many failures result, and sometimes when it is too late people learn that it would have been better to have confined their work to a different sphere.

> Yesterday a committee of about three hundred fishermen called at the Branson, Bowman, Stone, Wright, and other canneries, and submitted a proposition which, if accepted by the packers, will probably settle the strike on the Columbia River. It was proposed that the cannerymen should agree to take back the twine which they had distributed to a large

number of fishermen, composed principally of the floating element of the craft, who have no home ties in the city, and who only come here during the season to work. It is estimated that about 25 percent of the men on the river are composed of this class, and that few of them are native born or naturalized citizens. A demand was made that the cannerymen reimburse those who have already been involved in the knitting and repairing of nets. The men stated that if this arrangement could be made, it would result in about 25 percent of the fishermen now here leaving the river and going into other lines of work. The balance of the fishermen, or the 75 percent remaining in the union, are prepared to work for the four cents proposed by the canners.

Up to a late hour last night, none of the cannerymen had made any reply to the proposition from the fishermen. It is hoped that a meeting of the packers will be called today and that the question will be decided. The matter is an important one and deserves careful consideration by all parties concerned. The general business of the city is suffering to a certain extent on account of the strike. Packers claim that because of the condition of Eastern markets and general business throughout the East and Middle West, it is impossible for them to put up salmon and pay out five cents for the raw material. One of the most prominent cannerymen on the river said last night to an Astorian representative that the proposition made by the fishermen involved much more than appeared on the surface. "It is really in the nature of a compromise, for if the cannerymen accept it, take back the nets and twine of the men who will leave the business, and pay them besides for their labor in knitting the nets for their own use, it will mean that we will have to carry a very large amount of dead capital. The way things are at present, we cannot afford to pay five cents for raw fish, and I do not believe that the vast number of fishermen on the river can, as a body, make anything at four cents a pound. If the number of men is materially reduced, the balance can no doubt make wages at four cents. If five hundred should leave tomorrow and engage on the railroad, or in other work, I think it would be better all around and that the remainder would be enabled to make something this season, while the packers could afford to start their canneries and put up the fish. There would be little profit to either side, but it would keep matters going until better times come. I have not decided, so far as I am individually concerned, what I shall do in the matter, but will of course consult with the other cannerymen. We shall no doubt have a meeting in a day or two.

Thadeus Bowman motioned to Sam L. White to close the curtains so the passersby would refrain from peering through the hotel lobby windows. The meeting attendees could do without the publicity. Since the gillnetters had laid their offer on the table, public opinion had shifted. Astorians were edgy, not having the gillnetters' currency floating among their establishments. With the fishing industry shut down, people had the time to give the situation considerable thought, and many of them were sympathetic to the union.

"Let's get right down to business," Thadeus said abruptly. "It seems our good intentions are at stake, as well as our good names. I've given thought to the union's offer and found it failed several tests. I hope you're all in agreement. For one thing, it ties our hands in the future. Without the seasonal fishermen to rely on, what's to keep the union from running our businesses, setting the price for fish every year, and putting our market shares at risk? Further, we have the trapmen and horse seiners to take into consideration. They could possibly be our mainstay in the future. Their equipment costs less and requires less manpower. They also work for less. If we sign the petition as it stands, we'll be at the beck and call of a foreign element. Regardless of what the union professes, it isn't as American as apple pie. Think about that, gentlemen, before you sign over your industry to the rabble."

Harold Stinson refused to bite. He wanted to hear what the others would say and find out just how far they'd fallen into Bowman's pockets. Bowman owned the path to the markets and could control the pricing by flooding the markets with canned goods from his Alaskan interests. It was dirty pool, but dirty pool was all that interested Thadeus Bowman. Harold Stinson would reserve his exposé for later.

This meeting had been expanded to include over thirty men who represented twenty canneries. The kingpins were scattered among the audience to provide a guiding influence. The first to raise his objections was one of two Scandinavian Packing Company representatives. Harold Stinson wished the lonely dissenter courage.

"For your sake, you should be glad that your insults fall on deaf ears," the Swede countered. The genuineness involved in his wavering voice was incongruous with the cryptic example set by Thadeus Bowman, and all heads turned to hear his spontaneous rebuttal. "This business you were talking about, maybe we should return to it; time is very valuable, and most people don't have it to waste. Our association packs some of the highest-quality salmon to come upriver; perhaps it is the best label representing the Columbia's salmon. We do that through our fishermen, also the best along the Columbia. We can fish the spring freshets when the river gives up its prime chinook, as the trapmen and horse seiners can't, and we can be relied upon to maintain the good reputation our exported products deserve. If we're willing to reduce the number among us who aren't the best at their trade, I suggest only foolish men would refuse the offer. I've had my say."

The Swede quickly took his seat, and another speaker rose. This one Harold Stinson knew by heart, Sam L. White, his protégé. "What the representative from the Scandinavian Packing Company said is all well and good," he beamed, "but trust is another matter. In the case of such an association, the risk can be spread out among the participants, but speaking for myself, I've got all my eggs in one basket. Let's face it, the gillnetters aren't the most trustworthy workers to emigrate to America."

Harold Stinson felt a chill run down his spine. He had expected it, yet Sam L. White's defection came as a blow. Those who were privy to the upcoming "combine" were jousting for position. This was Harold's last chance. He cut in on Sam's speech: "What about the Columbia River Packers Association? Is everyone in this room aware that there is going to be a 'combine' formed, one that presupposes influence over the river's entire canning industry? When you vote against the union's proposal because of the power they could possibly exert over your industry, keep that in mind. Some of the gillnetters do have the right idea. They've already discovered that you can cut a pie in only so many pieces and still call it pie."

Chapter Ten

~ ~ ~ ~ ~ ~ ~ ~ ~ ~ ~ ~ ~ ~ ~ ~ ~ ~ ~ ~

June 7, 1896

It was fifty-nine days into the strike and a month to the day that Olof had aired his grievances with Thadeus Bowman. Following the petition's failure it was all evolving in a well-established pattern, including the progression toward violence. As forewarned, some of the non-union fishermen of the migratory class were the first to cross the line, resulting in their disappearance. Upriver, the blood-stained boat with no one aboard began a gradual shifting of public opinion, the assumption being union members were responsible. At the mouth of the river, the cannery at Ilwaco had started production under the protection of the Washington militia. Two steamers, barricaded with railroad ties and armed with cannons, patrolled Baker Bay and Sand Island, meaning the trapmen and horse seiners in the area were also at work. It was a tenuous position for the association to find itself in, the members of the Scandinavian Packing Company being sympathetic with neither side but beholden to both.

"I don't give a hoot," Olof grumbled. "We're not really part of the union any more than we're aligned with the cannerymen. I think we all oughta lay out our nets and see what happens. If we stir up a ruckus, maybe we'll get things off to a good start. Sooner or later the strike will bust itself. Might as well be today as tomorrow. Ain't making payments on my stove by hanging around here."

"You're drunk!" Arnold Larson exclaimed. "Why don't you put a stopper on that bottle until we've all had our say! You keep switching sides, and in my mind that means those are just empty words pouring out of your mouth."

"Got no guts," Olof grumbled. "Had a partner once who knew the value of getting a little tipsy before headin' off to war." Olof leaned into a net rack for support. He was inebriated, more so than usual.

His nineteen-year-old boat puller, Wally Palmberg, was right there to encourage him. He was freckled-faced and lighthearted, a young man who had simply wandered into the cannery two years earlier and Olof had taken under his wing with no questions asked. "My pa used to say that drinking was good for thinning the blood. The thinner the blood, the clearer the thinking. My cap'n here is good at thinking," Wally added, "so you've got to suppose whiskey has some medicinal purposes. At least that's what my pa used to say, before the horse kicked him in the head."

Even the stoic Swede conducting the informal meeting had to join the chorus of spontaneous laughter. Humor was a rare commodity, and in spite of Olof's apparent lack of stability, he did continue to hit the nail on the head. It was only a matter of time before the war of attrition gradually eroded the sobriety of all. "I suppose everybody's got a right to get a little tipsy now and then," Emil Holmes said diplomatically. "We're all getting deeper in debt, thus the question arises, what are we going to do about it? Many of you owe payments on your nets. I don't know how long the cannery can carry you."

The day was beautiful. The dazzling blue sky surrounded every aspect of the physical world, and the sun dropped glitter on the water's surface and made everything it encircled so bright as to be blinding. Heat radiated up from the dock, and the jeweled appearance of the Columbia was at hand, still the fifty gillnetters gathered around the net-racking facilities could not come up with a stimulating solution to free them from their impasse. Some squinted at the salmon boats tied along the dock, others ran their hands over the polished poles that should have been cradling an abundance of nets. The sea gulls lazed quietly on the water's pearly surface, expecting mankind to resume its industry. Apparently, the parades and the petitions had all been for naught.

Ed Mattson, the fish receiver and bookkeeper, was the first to raise his voice and express his opinion. "If the gill-netters went to work at sundown, we might be able to come out even. The books would balance, that is, and everyone would have enough to hold through until the next season. What's your opinion, Emil? You're the one who attended the meeting of the canners. Do you think they'd come after us if we split from the ranks a little early? Some of them are up and running, and I hear they were willing to settle at four-and-a-half cents. If we follow suit, what's to say we don't start a trend?"

Olof had great respect for Emil Holmes. They had locked horns occasionally, but Olof knew him to be fair and consistent. He could be credited with the origination of the Scandinavian Packing Company and had twice as much invested in its operation than did the association members. In other words, he carried the liability for its success or failure while underwriting the common members. He was of good stock, Olof always said of him, because he was on equal footing with the world around him. He stood five-foot-nine and was of a medium build. He was clean-shaven with dark brown, wavy hair. He kept his verbiage to a minimum, but his eyebrows were known to betray him. When he began to speak, they were burrowed in close to his eyes, an indication that he was deeply perplexed.

"We might not have any choice in the future if the strike continues. At the meeting I attended, there was talk of combining several canneries to keep them in operation. It could be our only option, in light of our financial instability. As Ed just mentioned, time is eroding our ability to survive. I don't think the other packers will give us any problems, if we decide to get the cannery operational. They could make it difficult for us to get a fair price on the market, but that's my problem. Yours is to decide if you're willing to oppose the union, knowing I can't promise we won't have to fold in the face of a 'combine.' It's gotten completely out of hand, and at this point I would say nothing is for certain."

June 11, 1896

It was naive to hope their fishing would go unnoticed, yet a small contingent of gillnetters left the docks as dark settled across the river. Under the star-filled sky they lowered their sails and one by one started down the drift. Olof scanned the shore constantly, guessing where and when a possible challenge would come from.

Wally, always filled with youthful enthusiasm and wonderment, was encouraged by Olof's concern. In many respects he emulated Henry Hihnala's trusting qualities. Too, he liked to share his thoughts when nightfall laid a blanket over the river and his curiosity was free to reassert itself.

"How long did you say you've been fishing this river?" he queried. "Where I come from, the trout would swim up the creek by the hundreds, and we'd wade out and try catching them in Ma's basket. Pa'd get fairly riled when he saw how we'd stirred up the water for the cattle. He'd come a runnin' from the barn, thinkin' he could drive us off with a pitchfork. Pa never cared much for fish and crawdads; he believed that the land should suffice for food. Then the neighbors bought the parcel across the creek and settled in. Soon Pa was chasing away their cattle with the pitchfork, and he no longer paid much mind to us younguns. He couldn't tell who'd muddied the water, us or the neighbor's cattle.

"It went on like that for years, before I decided to follow the creek and see just where those fish came from. Pa didn't care, with nine other children to cause him trouble. Plowing the land and fattenin' up the cattle is a love for something I wouldn't wish on any man. Following the river is more to my liking. Someday I intend to follow it around the world and find me a piece of earth where no one's got a claim on it. I figure to have both beef and fish on my table and get rich in the process."

"I'd be a little careful where I'd put my expectations," Olof replied sternly. "If there was really gold at the end of the rainbow, there would be men killing their own mothers to reach their hands in the pot. Been like that since clocks started keeping time."

"Ain't that what we're doing?" Wally asked. "Going out to get our share of salmon before the rest of them knows anything about it?"

Olof searched around in the shadows until his hands slipped around the neck of his whiskey bottle. "If a man lay down with a woman for his own sake, is that the same thing as a husband bedding his wife?"

The comparison was lost on Wally. He watched in bewilderment as Olof leaned into the deck's combing and took a swig from the bottle. "If you have to get liquored up, maybe your heart isn't in fishing anymore," he ventured.

"My heart's in very little these days," Olof replied soberly, "including the giving and the taking of questions. If you didn't want to go fishing tonight, you could have stayed on land."

Wally knew better than crossing one of the old-timers, and he let silence come between them until the residue could settle. He worked the left oar through the water to make certain the boat was properly positioned with the net as they drifted. Olof Anderson's reputation preceded him, and he was a tough man when it came to ineptitude. His confidence in his own surroundings was a curiosity to one who hadn't been born to it.

Wally's appetite for understanding remained insatiable. "I meant to ask you," he said casually, "why do you think the union is about to go bust? Seems like there is enough here for every man, and the canners and the union should get along just fine. My pa said that nothing ever stays the same, but only a fool would bar the path of horses headed for the barn. Makes no sense to me. Are we the horses, or the ones trying to block their path? 'Cause if everything changes at this late date, we ought not be trying to turn the herd."

Olof had to pause and think. Henry Hihnala had never talked such nonsense, but Wally Palmberg was of a different generation. He had never seen the river the way it was, before the horses started stampeding and the inevitability of change started churning up the waters.

"Your pa was right on both accounts," Olof replied, "but the things that get out of hand you can't really touch or feel, and when they mount up against you, you've got to stand and take notice. This river was never meant to be tamed, and the fish weren't meant for any man in particular. Once it started getting divided up like land, then your pa's rules came into play. Before that, it was on its own. When men started deciding who had rights to what part of it, it began to change. Striking is nothing new to the Columbia, but it's as futile as trying to keep your neighbor's cattle away from the stream. There are just too many goddamn people dipping out of the same well and expecting the water to stay pure. People aren't pure, and neither am I. Time changes a man, and like your pa, I've got to start thinking about protecting my own. If you can't stop the herd from stampeding, it's still possible to veer them off course a little."

∽

Olavi was in charge of keeping the gillnetters in tow. The knocking on his door in the middle of the night came as no surprise, yet the false alarms were irritating.

"Keep your voices down and don't wake the girls," Lottie said as she watched her husband pull on his trousers. It was a warm evening, a reprieve from the fog that usually wandered in from the ocean.

Olavi tripped down the stairs to the main floor, opting to greet his visitors bare chested.

The brothers, Ike and Sig Kokkala, were anxious to share their news. They entered the living room without an invitation, their chests heaving. "The Scandinavian Company has sent out its fleet," Ike explained in gasps, "and they're stoking their boilers, getting ready to go into full production. We've got a hundred armed men ready to meet them on the river. All we need is your approval."

Olavi was prepared to give the go-ahead, but then he hesitated. If the union were to make a visible example of disloyalty, here was its opportunity to do so and still bring the defectors back into the fold without warranting bad publicity. "Let's give the Scandinavian Packing Company something it doesn't expect," Olavi remarked. "Let the fishermen return with their catch, and then we'll have a warm welcome waiting for them."

Ike removed his hat and scratched his head. "We've already tried throwing their fish overboard, and that just brought us before a judge. I don't need any more nights in the pokey."

"Get at least five hundred union men to meet us there in the morning," Olavi replied, "and make certain that fifty or more are carrying cans of kerosene."

∞

As he and Wally were racking the net, Olof saw the shadowy figures beginning to grow in numbers along the riverbank. With the sunrise, they continued amassing. They had formed a barricade to impede the fish gutters, and the Chinese bossman reiterated his displeasure in a shrill voice. At first the Chinaman's gibberish was effective in making a mockery of the union's show of force, but what power they intended to wield remained a mystery. Olof instructed Wally to mend the net while he strolled casually in the direction of the bluestone tank.

Arnold's net was finally soaking in the copper sulfate solution, but the beaded sweat on his brow could be assigned to causes other than such an ordinary expenditure of effort. Like all the gillnetters restricted to cannery property, his nerves were beginning to fray at the edges. His feet were embedded in a pile of emptied gunnysacks and his look was distant and unfocused. "Don't think we can take this one to court," he grumbled over his shoulder as Olof came to stand beside him. "This time we've gone too far in trying to establish our independence. Just look at them gathering on the riverbank. They must have us outnumbered twenty to one."

Olof was not much interested in Arnold's statistical analysis. "Who's going to talk with them?" Olof asked. "Better to settle this apart from the cannery. They could shred the nets and sink the boats. Best to catch them off-guard. Maybe we should take a stroll down the dock and see what they've got in mind for us."

"We voted to hold out for five cents or nothing," Arnold replied sheepishly. "I would suppose they intend to get their pound of flesh, because we've settled at four-and-a-half."

The resignation in Arnold's voice did not set well with Olof. He had great regard for his friend, but at the moment no compassion. "We all agreed to go out fishing," Olof asserted himself, "and knew the risks. It's time now to turn the tide and end this foolishness. It's gone on for too many years, and those men need to hear the truth as much as they need to learn of their folly.

If they won't listen, I suppose we'll have to fight it out. That's what it's always come down to — finding out how far the next man will go in stepping over the line he's drawn himself."

"A man such as yourself has nothing else to worry about, does he?" Arnold exclaimed. His face was flushed and his words unsteady. "None of us with family ever intended it to come to this. We just wanted to put food on our tables. You're not much different from the rogues you pretend to fight against, Swede Olof. You're bullheaded and don't possess an ounce of responsible fear to make you genuine. We'd all rather leave here with our lives than to be buried prematurely on account of this profession. I've got two sons looking to me for leadership, wondering what I'm going to do. I'll tell you one thing: I don't intend to die for this cause or any other that will put theirs in jeopardy."

Olof was dumfounded. He shared eye contact with Arnold, but his lips were incapable of refuting the pretense that he had nothing to lose. If he were somehow singularly at fault, he'd have to take responsibility and protect the only family remaining with him. He turned and headed in the direction of the gathering crowd.

"Who's in charge here?" he shouted as he neared the restless men. Whatever delicate grasses that once dignified the sloping easement along the riverbank had been crushed, and the silty sediment underlying it plowed up as a result. Where the dock met the slabwood road, the number of strikers was ten deep. Perhaps five hundred strikers could be tallied in all.

Olavi stepped forward. He was armed with a sinister grin and a can of kerosene. "We're convening a special meeting in two hours," he announced sourly. "It seems that some of our flock has gone astray. We've talked it over and thought we might make an example of the wanderers. It could happen now, tomorrow, or the middle of next week.

What's your pleasure, Swede Olof? Would you like a little bonfire to warm your heart?"

Olof aimed a wad of Scandinavian dynamite at Olavi's feet. He was sorely tempted to start the climactic confrontation Olavi was seeking, but there were the cans of kerosene to take into consideration, as well as the disillusioned men eager to act on the obvious threat. He turned and looked down the raised walkway to the net-racking facilities and the cannery buildings beyond. It could all be gone in the blink of an eye, if he said or did the wrong thing. "We'll all be there," Olof answered steadily, "but the war isn't over until the final battle is won."

"You were never meant to win this war," Olavi replied pompously. "You're an arrogant pretender to a realm that doesn't exist. Get it through your head, Swede Olof, it's always been each man for himself, and you keep thinking there's an army bent on doing your will. Lottie said you were mired in the past with some false sense of immunity to protect you. Let's face it, you've had your chances and wasted them. The only thing you've done for this river was to rid it of Henry Hihnala. Like you, he was a lost cause from the very beginning."

Olof lunged for Olavi, but twenty men threw him to the ground and had him pinned before he could get his hands around Olavi's neck. He could not move, but he could hear. "Give the dumb Swede a few good kicks to the head, and then let him go," Olavi shouted. "He's got a meeting to attend, and we don't want him looking like he's been injured by his fellow gillnetters."

∞

John Lord was usually in command of the truth as he saw it, but with the strike heating up the events were beginning to collide, and staying abreast of the action a hindrance to his collating abilities. He wanted it all to mesh in an orderly fashion, yet even his objectivity was coming into question. The newspaper's owner, a local canner, had just interjected a distasteful variable by inviting more conjecture. He overlooked the four guests crowding his cubicle and shouted out his frustration. "Jonas, hold up on the linotype for the time being; and Anne, take a few notes, if you would!"

The dark-haired woman remained standing while the four members of Astoria's Chamber of Commerce took the only seats available. Anne was attractive, but not compelling enough to bid her entrance into this clannish group.

"I thought you were going to address the union's membership today," John Lord said impatiently.

The four men exchanged glances until the one wearing glasses and a bowler hat came forth with the answer: "They wouldn't let us in at the last minute. Rumor has it the Scandinavian Company's fishermen were about fishing at four-and-a-half cents, but the union put a stop to that. Their gillnetters were invited to the meeting, and we were left standing in the street with our hats in our hands, although we don't suppose they'll experience any success. And that's why we're here, John, to take our argument to the people. We've decided to help those who want to help themselves and have an open meeting at the courthouse tomorrow. We want you to print the notice and encourage all the fishermen to attend. We're planning a parade, with a band and all."

"And what if that doesn't work, gentlemen?" John Lord inquired. "Where do you go from there? What's happening behind the scenes that you're not telling me about?"

"We've spoken to the governor about sending in troops, if this thing doesn't resolve itself. Our businesses are going broke, and tension is in the air. With the report of a cannery being burned four nights ago, we're all getting understandably nervous. We don't want everything to go up in flames before this thing is settled. Like the gillnetters from the Scandinavian Company, many of us only want to return to profitable endeavors."

"It was a bonfire, not a cannery," John corrected his guest, "and we don't know who started it, or why. Couldn't put a finger on it. But I do know from a good source that the cannerymen are also eager to return to normal. I suppose their winter fat is beginning to wear a little thin."

Anne Tilstrom dropped her pencil, and it went rolling across the floor. A look of amazement crossed her face, and all eyes turned. She was new to the business, but such a comment repeated in the wrong circles could obviously endanger the editor's employment. She rummaged nervously through the stacks of paper on John's desk looking for a writing implement, while he appeared comfortable with his assessment. It was then that the door opened and another visitor joined the gathering: Carl Hansen, the Chairman of the Columbia River Fishermen's Protective Union. He appeared down at the mouth and spent. John Lord rose and offered him his chair. He took it without so much as a nod of appreciation.

"Is the strike over?" John Lord asked curtly.

"No, but it's moving in that direction." Carl glanced around at the four well-known citizens of Astoria and made his apologies. "Sorry about excluding you from our meeting, but we had other concerns to settle, and that's why I'm here. We had a little run-in with some of our member-ship from the Scandinavian Packing Company and, unfortunately, they've promised to do the honorable thing. If the cannerymen fail to settle at five cents within four days, many of them will be leaving, some taking their families and moving elsewhere. One of them said he'd forsake his dreams if it would save the river, and by God, he put his promise on the table. Not only is the union going to lose its best gillnetters, but much of the heart and soul of it, too."

Carl Hansen paused a second, unnerved by the unexpected blow Olof Andersson had landed by bringing each one of the union's membership up for review. Thirty men had walked directly out of the meeting to catch the steamer bound for San Francisco. A dozen more were on their way back to their homes intent upon gathering up their belongings, settling their debts, and heading for Portland. It had come as a rude awakening to many that a man's word was still influential.

Carl cleared his throat. "Further, the union pledges to deliver to the respective canneries all the salmon we catch at five cents per pound, provided the canneries are willing to pay two-thirds when delivered, with the balance to be deducted until all debts are paid. If debts are still owing at the end of the season, then the canners can keep the nets in storage until the following spring. We are resolved to working with them, not against them. There should be a lasting partnership here."

In unison, John and Anne watched the five men rise in silence to go their separate ways. John had some lingering thoughts to share with his attractive co-worker, and he turned to address her with the confidence of one who had finally been introduced to the truth. "I must use this moment to borrow from Hawthorne," he said solemnly, studying her brown eyes for approval. "It is my opinion that a man's soul may be buried and perish under a dung-heap, or in a furrow of the field, just as well as under a pile of money."

June 16, 1896

Olof entertained no false hopes that the cannerymen would settle and, in a way, accepting his own edict was like having the weight of the world lifted from his shoulders. If nothing changed in the next few hours, the Columbia River would no longer be his problem or his passion, and he would have come by the divorce with an ease never apparent in the marriage. He arrived at the cemetery midmorning to offer his firm and lasting apologies for all the changes superseding his will, intent upon expressing his farewells in a manner understandable to all. But as he removed his hat to have his final say, he realized how extreme the forfeiture. "Never planned on leaving the river," he stammered, "but I've always tried to live up to my end of a bargain. Now that it's come down to my word against theirs, it's time to pay with everything I've held dear. Doesn't sound fair, but you, too, have experienced the lack of fairness in this world. I guess we're all meant to go our separate ways eventually, leaving behind us the ones we cherished most and supposing that's an even trade for living costly dreams."

Olof concluded his apology by kneeling down to dutifully remove the grasses growing between the twins' headstones. The parched blades were so firmly rooted in the hard clayish soil that frustration quickly overcame him. He rose off his haunches and knocked the dirt from his trousers with a slap of his hat. He started down the roadway, focusing his eyes on the ruts rather than the remarkable view. He was trying to divert all his powers of concentration upon Alaska, his decided destination, and failed to see the steamer *Harvest Queen* rounding Tongue Point with flags flying and her decks crowded with soldiers.

Wally still had the twenty dollars Olof had given him, as well as ample time to spend in figuring out how his indomitable cap'n had fallen prey to politics. He dropped down on his knees and, using the bluestone tank to support his back, slid his legs out from underneath him until they were flat against the dock's surface. He gazed out upon the river's placid surface and wondered where it should take him next. He wasn't so certain that he wanted to follow the river anymore, having seen where such dreams could end. Olof's boat was tugging on the pulleys a few feet off the end of the dock, but the song it played was sorrowful, a plea to return to the work for which it was intended.

Movements were measured, yet purposeless, in and around the series of docks. The canners had won hands down, denying the gillnetters any recourse other than making good on their promise. Everything was unraveling, and the very men who valued their word would be the ones to lose. It was an odd concept for young Wally Palmberg to grasp.

The sea gulls caught his attention. At first it was a few birds involved in practicing the rites of their pecking order by moving from pile to pile and dethroning those of a lesser stature; then dozens took flight, and the sky was filled with raucous disorder. Wally regarded their antics as ordinary play until the steamer came into view around Tongue Point, and he understood their consternation. He covered the distance between the cannery building and the fish-receiving dock with youthful agility. Others had joined him to view the arrival of the Oregon National Guard. "Whose side do you suppose they're on?" one of the gillnetters asked sarcastically.

"Ours," Emil Holmes replied as he parted the crowd. "They've come to provide protection for the gillnetters who want to return to work, even though it may be too late."

Exhausted men orchestrated a spontaneous welcome, Wally Palmberg included. He took his hat and flung it in the air, then dove headfirst into the fast-moving current to retrieve it. For the moment, at least, he was forgetful of the lasting scars in light of the unusual pomp and circumstance to suddenly invade the lower river. Yet, as the steamer came alongside the Scandinavian Packing Company to offer their support, men such as Arnold Larson were boarding the steamer *Telephone,* bound for Portland, while others were considering places as far away as Alaska.

Four days later, the union accepted the canners' compromise offer of four-and-a-half cents, with both sides claiming victory. A hundred days had consumed the energies of all and, for what it was worth, gillnetting was resumed.

Early Spring, 1899

The afternoon was blustery, threatening rain squalls as thick clouds went whipping across the river's surface. The chill in the air indicated that winter was hanging on, yet the calendar said otherwise. The weather was fickle when it was on the cusp, traveling back and forth between two extremes, changing radically. One minute a sheeting rain could be heard beating on the building's exterior; five minutes later a door could open and sunshine would invade the cannery on a gust of wind.

"Come on, Pot, hand over the bottle," Wally kidded. "An honorable man shares when he has more reserves than the rest. My pa used to call it being neighborly." His arm remained stretched across the fish-gutting table, but all recognized the beseeching as an innocent jest, meant to provoke the old-timer.

Olof "Pot" Anderson replied. "But I don't consider myself an honorable man since I failed to leave when issued the invitation, and if I recall correctly, your pa didn't give a hoot about the neighbors. It's called planning ahead, youngun! When you come to a party, you oughta supply your own entertainment."

"Gosh, Pot, I was just poking fun! Emil Holmes supplied a whole case of moonshine for this occasion. Suppose he feels a little guilty?"

"Not as guilty as I feel for not gettin' when the gettin' was good!"

Many laughed, but the deal was done, and the Scandinavian Packing Company was now the Scandinavian Station, an adjunct to the Columbia River Packers Association. The label was lost, and with it, the pride accompanying the accomplishment. The farewell party resembled a wake, the survivors each hesitant to witness the final nail being hammered in the departed's coffin.

The building's destitute appearance confirmed the triumph of one era over another. The dusty shelves on the west wall held only a half-dozen label boxes, and where there would have been pallets loaded with tins, only broken boards littered the floor. Bolts in the floor marked the location of the metal machinery that had once occupied a third of the interior. The doors leading out to the loading dock were blocked by fish-boxes stacked helter-skelter, and the windows, where the Chinese fish-gutters used to convene in private, had been usurped by a spider's intricate webbing. Voices and footsteps were resonant, while all else seemed to die awry in the vacated surroundings.

Wally extended himself clear across the hole in the table where the fish guts used to be discarded, and laid a hand on Olof's. "Why the heck do you think Emil Holmes invited us here?" he asked. "We all know the cannery has folded, and none of us can do better than break even. He can't be paying off any shares, seeing as how there aren't any left to pay. Suppose there's more to this party than meets the eye?"

"Your pa must have told you that there's always more than meets the eye — either justice or injustice — and the thin difference is what they'll write on your grave. A man shouldn't have to live so much history during such a short period of time, because it plays havoc with his innards. I suspect that's what Emil brought us here to say."

The large doors screeched on the rollers, and all heads turned to see Emil Holmes and Ed Mattson enter the building through the fish-receiving area. In the naked surroundings, Emil was as bereft of credibility as the rest of them, and Ed walked unsteadily without familiar points of reference to guide him. Emil's eyebrows were pinched, an indication of something left unsaid. He walked around the table and lifted a whiskey bottle from the box. He opened it, took a full swig and drew his hand across his mouth before speaking.

He scanned the faces of the men who had once worked for him and with him and cleared his throat. "I know this can't be a real jovial gathering," he began nervously, "but I wanted to speak to all of you before you decided to stay on with the 'combine' or to move elsewhere. Change isn't always easy to accept, but eventually it's staring us all in the face. As you can see, that time has come, because the packing aspect of this company has been gutted."

Olof lifted a fist and slammed it down on the table. "Get to the point," he growled. "We all got our own problems. Is the CRPA looking to keep us on, or not ? And if so, what kind of offer they gonna make? Don't much like the idea of fishing for a 'combine.' Sounds like we're coming in second best to the trapmen and the horse seiners. Don't cotton to the idea of fishing for men like Thadeus Bowman, either. Might just take my boat elsewhere, and see if I can't get a better deal."

"I'm not surprised you feel that way, Olof Anderson," Emil replied, "and that's why the whiskey — to ease the pain a little."

"Brought my own!" Olof quipped. "Not expectin' to be beholden to no one, particularly not someone who's willing to give up on this river."

Emil thought it time to answer Olof's challenge. He took another swig of whiskey and set the bottle on the table aside Olof's. "It's just business, pure and simple," he responded bluntly. "That's the way things work in America. Competition got too keen on the river, and you old-timers have to learn to live with it. Things aren't the way they were, and in many respects I see that as a blessing. You can take your boat anywhere you want, but you can't turn back the hands of time. The CRPA will maintain the profitability of this place, and for that bit of assurance you should be grateful."

Olof's green eyes were alive with passion. "There isn't anything about gillnetting to encourage the need in me to feel grateful. From day one, it's been dangerous, thankless work, and I don't see as how your CRPA can promise me anything different."

All eyes looked to Emil, eager for his response. His shoulders seemed to relax beneath his flannel shirt, and he stepped around the bench and sat down next to Wally, facing Olof. "You know, I have to agree with you. The cannery business is risky, but not as risky as drifting the Columbia when the winds are at full gale, and the air off the river so stinging as to freeze the blood in one's veins. The interesting thing about taking risks, nevertheless, is how few men actually survive them all. And that's why you can insult me, Olof Anderson, and I'll just sit here and take it."

Olof was dumfounded. It took him a few minutes to accept the recognition given him. "Well, I've always thought you a reasonable man," he said as he lifted his bottle. "I suppose we all ought to drink to that, and the partin' of our ways."

"I predicted as much," Emil replied, "and that's why I wanted to say something before the fishing season starts. First of all, regardless of Olof's opinion to the contrary, the Scandinavian Station will survive into perpetuity with its integrity intact." Here many of the gillnetters started talking among themselves, relieved to know that they were welcome on their own turf, regardless of the stark changes. "Harold Stinson was one of the canners to rely solely on gillnetters, but unfortunately, his label is off the market. Like us, the hundred-day strike took him to his knees, and rumor has it he's suffered a stroke. Union Fish, on the other hand, is looking to add membership to its cooperative. I can't guess as to their future success, but they did manage to come together on the heels of the strike. It's a known fact that their membership is mostly Finnish with strong ties to the union, whether or not that would make any difference." Emil paused, always uncertain as to where any gillnetter stood on the issue of the union. It had left a bad taste in the mouths of many, but the power it now wielded was almost impervious. He thought he was being diplomatic in pursuing the subject. "The Finnish community is really behind Union Fish, and if anyone is interested in signing on with their organization, I believe the man to see is Olavi Pustinen. He dropped by one day, wanting to buy some of our inventory. He said something about bygones being bygones, seeing as how the war had been convincingly won. He didn't make a lot of sense, but seemed real sure of himself and the future of the Union Fishermen's Cooperative Packing Company."

Olof leapt to his feet, overturning the bench. *"Gud in himmel!"* he blasphemed. "That Olavi Pustinen keeps pushing his luck! He shoves at this old Swede like the mule's gone and died! It's time the real war is waged and won," he declared to all the startled faces. "He's rubbed my face in the dirt for the last time!"

Wally tried struggling with Olof, but he could barely keep his footing on the dock's rain-slickened surface, let alone protect himself from the violent outpouring of curses. He had never seen his cap'n go off the deep end like this, nor act on some inexplicable insanity which seemed to be nurturing it. "That's not even your boat!" Wally hollered as Olof lifted the overturned rowboat and dumped it into the river below. "Ain't got time to rig mine!" Olof retorted. "I've got business to attend to — a person I've got to see. Gonna settle it once and for all. The war ain't over until one side ain't standing!"

Olof's mind was jumping from one event to another, trying to piece together all the clues and discover why Olavi should have succeeded where he had failed; but the intense dislike between them continued to cloud his already polluted thinking, and his anger was too intense to command. "Get me some oars and oar locks!" he hollered at Wally, then he grabbed the uppermost ladder rung with his left hand and dropped feet first into the unstable craft below.

Wally watched as the rowboat remained upright following such an unconventional boarding technique, and just as amazingly, the virgin bottle of whiskey clenched in Olof's right hand remained intact. It even appeared that the falling weight hadn't done the boat any structural damage, but night was beginning to cover any obvious mistakes; and Wally's perceptions, too, had been altered by the free-flowing whiskey. He stood abreast the dock's edge and tried to restrict Olof's activities with his usual levity. "How far do you suppose to get in a rowboat?" he asked sarcastically. "Ain't got the arm strength to oar that thing all the way to Frankfort, seein' as how night is falling, and the sky's full of rain just waitin' to pour. My pa would say that you're acting on whiskey talk, and whiskey talk can lead a man into a passel of troubles. That's exactly how the horse managed to kick him in the head."

This time Wally's frivolity brought no laughter. It was apparent Olof's determination could not be tempered. He held the boat to the dock by clinging to a ladder rung, and the extremely choppy wave action did nothing to sway him. "I wanted oars," he said gruffly, "lest you want to find another cap'n who'll put up with your prattle."

Wally did as he was asked and stood quietly by as the small boat disappeared into the leading edge of a fast-moving squall. Nightfall was equally convincing in its approach, and he could hear the old-timer's voice long after he had lost sight of the boat.

Olof cursed the rowboat's lack of integrity as he threw his upper body into the oars and water cascaded over the toes of his boots in a chilling rush; next, he cursed the foul weather and the occluding darkness which combined to make his destination even more obscure; and finally, he cursed his own lack of coordination when the blade of an oar caught a pile and swung the bow of the boat into the moss-covered supports beneath the fish-receiving dock. A swell dropped him from a height of three feet, and he swore at his nemesis as he fought to return the oar to the oar lock. "You back-stabbing Finn! Ain't fit for a pig, let alone bedding Henry Hihnala's wife! By Gud, it's been a long road that can twist and turn in so many directions and not see an end!"

The wind and rain beyond the Scandinavian Station's perimeter mounted an offense equal to that of the water's churning surface. In the small rowboat, it took every ounce of Olof's strength to gain ground against the combined elements. Sitting backside to his destination and the storm as well, the weather felt like a brick wall pressing against his body. The rain poured from the brim of his hat in a hundred rivulets, blinding him. But what he couldn't see, he could understand. He wasn't alone on this final odyssey. Henry Hihnala had come to join and encourage his progress.

A half-hour later, he had to stop his frenetic rowing to ease the muscle cramps in his upper body. "Only take a second, Olavi. I'm still coming after you. Don't go and get your hopes up, you conniver. Me and my partner need to rest a minute." Left to its own devices, the boat immediately swung broadside with the roll of the waves; nonetheless, Olof was able to fish the whiskey bottle from the ankle-deep water surrounding his feet. He popped the cork and poured a fourth of it down his throat. He started coughing. "Can't you hold the boat steady, Henry?" he complained. "Got enough to do here without capsizing; gotta figure which part of Olavi's body is the most precious to him before I start whittling away at it."

He was still struggling for air as the boat careened into the bottom of a deep trough, and water poured over the combing along the port side. Suddenly his words were apologetic in tone, meant to smooth over old differences. "Seems Olavi married Lottie after you disappeared. Notice I said disappeared, because I've always held out hope that you'd made it to shore and had just kept walking. You were right about Lottie — she wasn't worth the marrying. Maybe she and Olavi make a good pair, except I intend to slit the throat of whichever of them is handy. I don't suppose you'll mind. Sorry I didn't see it coming, but I didn't see a lot of things comin'."

The waves continued to curl over the rowboat's narrow decking and jump the combing, but in spite of the imminent danger, Olof took up only one oar and tried working the boat into the waves so he was facing his Waterloo square on. He squinted into the wind and rain, encouraging the watery pellets, embedded in the darkness, to strike his face. He sounded oddly sure of himself: "A southwester is coming at us, Henry. The storm is still in diapers, only half growed." Again he nursed the bottle toward his lips and poured whiskey until it spilled from the corners of his mouth. This time he was gasping for air. "Suppose I should share, Henry," he choked on the words, "but at times it doesn't seem that passing the bottle gets a fellow very far. You once said, if you haven't got somebody to share your successes with, they don't count for much. Maybe Olavi Pustinen keeps winning this cussed war, 'cause he's got kin to fight for. Us, we've got to bargain with the river for everything we get and then turn around and pay dues on it. The Columbia is the mother of them all, but she don't much see to the care of her children."

The river was seething around the rowboat, turning it in circles, trying to get enough leverage to conclude Olof's strange wanderings. But Olof did not care much, because he was caught in a more personal quandary. There were too many questions about his life left unanswered; too many puzzles concerning his own nature that needed solving. The breakers crashing on Taylor Sands should have provided ample warning, but Olof was not listening. He had given the oars over to Henry's druthers, while he took comfort from the last dregs in the whiskey bottle. The small boat rose up and came crashing down on the island's sandy surface. The waves continued crushing it under tons of surging water, while Olof deliberated over reasons to live. He remained completely passive, even when he and the boat were torn asunder. Unlike Ingrid, the threat of death to him did not seem premature or even fear provoking. He was more shocked than anything, aware that this situation was of his own making. His survival depended wholly upon himself, and as a wave pulled his legs out from beneath him and tried to sweep him off the island, he was not so certain he ought not go. He had to find a reason to fight for himself, but his mind was consumed with visions of Ingrid standing at the end of a plank walkway with the sun streaming off her angelic yellow hair, and while each time he tried to bridge the short distance between them, the water rose up around his ankles to restrict his progress. As long as he stayed on solid footing, she was there waiting for him with arms outstretched.

Until the weather broke and help came the following morning, he survived on that haunting image alone.

Chapter Eleven

~ ~

1900

The Columbia appeared placid beneath the dawning rays of sunshine on this summery Sunday morning, yet making an easy transition from the monotonous roll of the ocean's surface into the river's gaping mouth was inconceivable to someone as distrustful and traveled as Ingrid Andersson. She took in every nuance studiously, wanting to place credence in that which she saw as being remarkable changes. To the south, a five-mile-long jetty of boulders controlled the ebb and flow of the river's tempestuous nature, and where she had once been shipwrecked on the treacherous Middle Sands, the river had purged itself of any remaining evidence. The absence of the sand bar was an inexplicable mystery. She stepped back from the starboard railing of the steamer *Frisco* and allowed an agitated gentleman, burdened with two pieces of luggage, to pass by at a jog. Behind him, a woman in her twenties was enabling a toddler to stand upright while keeping the frantic pace. "Why are you in such a hurry, Jonathan?" the woman called out. "We have plenty of time before reaching Astoria!" The woman smiled apologetically as the toddler lurched into Ingrid's skirt folds. Ingrid placed a hand over her heart and breathed deeply, trying to assess an urgency of a more chronic nature. Mitigating the memories, even with the visual assurances to counteract them, was impossible. She returned to the railing and gripped it firmly. A series of gently sluicing waves was hardly perceptible beneath the steamer's hull; still, she braced herself as the steamer crossed the bar. It was not until she could see Astoria cascading down the hillside and pouring itself across the river's surface that she could accept her surroundings for what they presumed to be at the moment: peaceful and serene.

The inclusion of new homes dotting the Astoria hillside had somewhat quieted the landscape, but the industry along the waterfront appeared to have been built with much the same juxtaposing system of expediency that had characterized it prior to the fire. In a nutshell, much had changed while remaining the same. The city's expansion along the river, filling in the obtuse niches where the cougar and bear had once roamed, merely repeated Astoria's flair for inventiveness.

Ingrid's eyes traveled both the vertical and horizontal lines of the city; they stoped and turned wherever someone had proposed a different idea. The lack of clear directives spoke to Ingrid of things she had experienced in the past, and she was keenly aware of the pitfalls in dwelling on them. Like Jonathan, his wife and child, she joined the amassing crowd preparing to disembark, hopeful that her final destination would provide a respite between the past and the future.

It was late in the afternoon when Ingrid's knees finally buckled under her, and she sat down hard on the steamer trunk. She watched the sternwheeler travel away from Frankfort's dock until it was no larger than a speck on the horizon. She was deplete of energy, and spent of any desire to move beyond her immediate surrounds. A young boy was sitting thirty feet away on the dock, a fishing pole in hand. He was content waiting for a nibble, and she was content, having gotten this far. She removed her white scarf and allowed the wind to tease her hair. It felt good but frivolous, and her eyes lazily followed the progress of a large sailing vessel a hundred yards away, lurching at a forty-five-degree tilt. Like she, it had appeared out of nowhere and was probably headed for home before the river altered its character. Ingrid rose from the steamer trunk and walked over to the youth.

"Do you know where Olof Andersson lives?" she asked.

"No Olof living here," the boy answered impishly. His eyes met hers only briefly before returning to the stillness at the end of his line.

His reply came as quite a blow. Ingrid took her focus off the tow-headed youngster and studied the cozy nesting of homes on the hillside. She realized the possibility, cruel as it may be, that Olof had moved. Six months had intervened since she and he had last corresponded and, worse, she had never said explicitly that she was coming. Her heart sank, and her knees were about to betray her once more. She turned toward the immediate support afforded by the trunk.

"You don't mean the hermit, Pot, do you?" the youngster offered of his own accord. "He lives off the point, but no one goes to visit. They say he's got mean blood in his body and likes to eat his salmon raw. Ma says to stay away from him. He's one of the old-timers and is mighty dangerous. If you're going to go up there, best be warned! The devil put a scar on his face, so we'd know to skedaddle for higher ground, when he comes a sneakin' up. I ain't much for skedaddling myself, but Ma says it's best to give him a wide berth until I'm growed."

"Thank you very much," Ingrid replied calmly.

The long walk up the hillside was a study in self-discipline. She focused on the salal edging the pathway and stopped to admire a perfectly cone-shaped cedar in the center of a yard, rather than dwelling on the youngster's conjectures. She had nowhere else to go other than here, a thought more alarming than being shipwrecked in a storm, or doing battle with the devil in order to reclaim Olof's soul. She stopped short of the stoop and used the pure white scarf to clean the dirt from her shoes. She stuffed it in her pocket and mounted the two introductory steps. She stood at the door for several minutes before even considering knocking, preparing herself to accept whichever of Olof's profiles came to greet her. She heard heavy footsteps and strange grumblings emanating from inside the house. The door opened of its own accord, and there stood Olof, facing her squarely.

They stared at each other with disbelief, neither speaking. Olof's raw edges were very much in evidence, and she felt somehow responsible for his disheveled appearance. She looked down at the thermos he carried in his hands and spoke to it instead. "You were on your way out. I'm sorry."

Olof could not take his eyes off her. She was stunningly beautiful, exactly as he remembered her. He moved a few steps backwards, clearing a path to allow her entrance to the house. He was afraid to extend a hand, afraid to touch the image he was not certain actually existed. "Come in," he said gruffly. "Wasn't expecting company."

Ingrid had not expected a rush of emotions and a warm greeting, but Olof's abruptness came as a slap in the face remembered. Like a child, she became timid before this man of grim proportions. She studied the network of black and blue veining mottling Olof's cheeks and the formidable pot belly at his waist. Accepting the invitation was far more difficult than anticipated: the worst was evident, the best an unknown. "It's a wonderful house, Olof," she remarked while easing her right foot gingerly across the threshold. Her eyes jumped from the bench to the rainwear hanging on the wall, fearful that looking at the food particles embedded in her husband's beard would make her cry.

"Do you still drink tea?" Olof stammered.

"It's unnecessary," Ingrid responded, "but I would certainly accept the offer of a chair. It was a long walk from the dock to this house you've built." As Olof slowly shut the door, Ingrid tried to interpret the reason for his hesitancy. If she could properly read his facial expression, she would say it showed despair. She had to remind herself that she knew nothing of what Olof's motivations had been in creating this strange oasis, perched high above the water's influence. "It's a beautiful walk, however," she capitulated, "and the privacy is certainly worth the effort." She noted two chairs and made her way directly into the spacious kitchen, and there she sat down. She had much to say and no room for error. She approached the problem directly.

"Brita Hansdotter is dead, and I've been freed of my former obligations. The village isn't as you'd remember it, Olof. The younger generation reaches an age where they must choose between the military or America, and most choose America. Before I left, however, I did place flowers on the graves of your parents. It is a shame they died so young, and mine survived so long as to revisit the passage of their youth."

Ingrid had fallen into the ease of her native Swedish tongue, unaware that Olof was no longer capable of understanding it well. He walked across the room to the wood stove and poked around in the hot ashes with a piece of kindling. A small flame erupted, and he reached into the wood box to restore fire from the embers.

Ingrid paused ever so briefly, her eyes following Olof's movements across the room. Once he had settled upon a task, she continued. "You were right about Hanna," she admitted. "She eventually moved to America with her husband, Ored Jeppsson. They have children now, and I suppose no need of me. Hanna writes on occasion, but she sounds happy and content. She's become her own person, and for that I'll always be grateful. It's good to know she has made the right decision. Some of us succeed, where others of us fail. Life is a long lesson, slowly imparted." Ingrid glanced over her shoulder to see Olof dipping a small kettle into a bucket of water. He returned to the stove and set the kettle on the surface. Droplets of water sizzled and popped, but he showed no inclination to offer the briefest of explanations as to what he was doing. She recognized his behavior as being drudgery, something he performed out of necessity in the privacy of his own home. She was no longer familiar with his habits, but she felt awkward being at rest while he managed things second nature to her. She remained seated, nevertheless, as he opened and closed cupboard doors upon barren shelves, searching for something he had apparently misplaced. Olof was slow in his movements, much more methodical than a man fired with youthful passion. He glanced in her direction, and Ingrid returned to her train of thought.

"When Nils Gustav Petersson was nearing death, he would lie on his bed and call out for my mother. When he was lucid, he would argue with her about returning to the sea. It was a gradual process of watching him lapse into a time when I had never existed, and when I did exist, he was confused by my presence and saddened that I had so little. I'd never thought of myself as having so little, until I realized that in the end, the good memories have been given us to outweigh the bad." Ingrid shuffled her feet on the floor and stared out the window facing the Columbia. Her good memories were somewhere between the river and this room, and she was uncertain how to reclaim them. Her voice became gritty, and the speed of her speech slowed, allowing Olof to gain access to the Swedish. "When I used to visit Pella Jönsson and share a cup of tea, I was reminded of the choices I had made in becoming your wife, but I was incapable of resurrecting any instance of our marriage which did not inspire sadness and regret. Even when talking with dearest Hanna about the twins, she was too far removed from their world to grant them credibility. They had lived and died with a history too foreign to understand. Still, the twins survive with me everyday that I wake and walk this world, so I was foolish to abandon their inspiration. I thought I would move blindly through time divesting myself of the pain by helping others, but where there is pain, there should also be comfort. The comfort for me is in coming home. I hoped you would be so kind as to accept me."

Olof laid a hand on Ingrid's shoulder as he set a cup of tea before her. He was speechless, unable to respond in kind. His story was too long to unravel, and sorting out his feelings an improbable venture, ever. "I've got fishing to do tonight," he said casually, as if seventeen years had never intervened. "But I should show you the house," he added frankly, "so you can get acquainted."

Ingrid answered the proposition with a nod. She rose from the chair and set aside the untouched tea; all the while, Olof's hand was resting gently on her shoulder. With the exception of how he had influenced her decision to return, she had addressed everything forthrightly. She stepped free of his hand and turned to face him. The fire in the stove was popping and snapping cheerfully, and the warmth it radiated was a favorable omen. Ingrid saw it as an opportune time to speak her conscience, before Mother Nature and human nature again intervened.

"I had ended up with nothing," she stammered. "Having watched Nils Gustav Petersson in the final throes of life, uttering incoherent phrases about his fishing boat and calling out for Brita Hansdotter, I found myself in a void, a situation as terrifying as any I had encountered in America. Brita Hansdotter's death was a long and lonely process and, being her daughter, I finally understood the relevancy and specialness of the bond from which I'd been created. Through it all, Olof, memories of you and our twins were irrepressible. Whatever I could glean of the happiness due me was rooted here. I don't understand it, but without the worry and rewards you and your river could afford me, I was continually adrift, stranded on the Middle Sands without hope of being saved."

It was Olof's turn to respond in kind, but he did not want to interrupt the dream poised before him. The droplets of the day's departing sun were lingering on Ingrid's hair, and silver wisps were clearly infringing where youth had once prevailed. Like him, she was in the process of accepting reality for what it was, both beautiful and brutal. He could only hope that their time of constant questioning was over, replaced instead by a quiet acceptance of their differences. What he could not say, he hoped to demonstrate with his adoration. He kissed her on the forehead, then led her by the hand to show her the entirety of the home he had purposely built for her and her homecoming.

September, 1905

Ingrid had her routine and was not about to waste an hour of daylight in deviating from it. Olof would not be home again until Wednesday night; thus the baking, the laundry and the garden all required her dedication, as well as the quilters invited into her parlor. She stopped briefly on the raised porch facing the river to scan the horizon for the Butterfly Fleet. It was a ritual repeated constantly over the length of Olof's absences, and although she did not know what to expect from her surveillance, it brought her a modicum of reassurance. Seeing was believing, and the river appeared innocuous beneath a scattering of puffy cumulus clouds.

"Where did Ingrid get to?" Mildred called out impatiently, even though Ingrid's whereabouts were visible beyond the open door. "It must get tiresome, trying to see things invisible to the rest of us!"

Ingrid had to agree with the truth of Mildred's conclusion. Only a white trail above an indistinguishable vessel was keeping her away from her immediate obligations; the salmon boat she was searching for had traveled elsewhere in the accompaniment of its colorful flotilla. She turned on her heels and ducked through the doorway. She was not perspiring but was clearly out of breath when she entered the parlor from the porch.

"Sweetheart, you're too old for that kind of running around," Mildred remarked familiarly. "Better have a seat here and rest your body."

Ingrid stood aside while Mildred, the eldest member of the quilting group, took up her cane and vacated the straight-backed chair opposite the bride's. Ingrid settled in where Mildred had sat. She picked up the threaded needle and started stitching. Meri, the bride for whom the quilt was intended, was rapt in conversation with Karitsa, her mother. Willa, the final member seated at the frame, was busy applying beeswax to a strand of thread. Mildred approached the couch and swept the reddish-gold cat aside with her cane. It hit the floor running and halted abruptly only a few feet away.

"What do you call that cat?" Mildred asked as she lowered her body onto the couch's padded surface.

"Nuisance," Ingrid replied. "Olof can't believe that a cat has any intrinsic value, so we call it Nuisance."

"I must agree with your husband in this instance," Willa replied. "They scratch up the furniture and shred the curtains. They are a darn nuisance to keep track of, kinda like running off to the porch every few minutes to see where your husband's gone to."

Ingrid failed to bat an eye, enjoying the frank opinions expressed by these women. Willa, forty years of age, was of German upbringing and, like her bluntly cropped blonde hair, exhibited practicality. Mildred, as her name implied, was mildly threatening, and exhibiting the characteristics of advanced age, she placed a great deal of credence in having survived sixty years. Karitsa, of Finnish stock, had a flair for keeping things in perspective. She was in her late thirties and, like her daughter Meri, seemed to thrive on simply being accepted.

Mildred laid down her cane, and the reddish-gold cat immediately sought out the depression in her lap. She ran her hand across its back several times, but her strokes were too heavy, and it struck a paw at her. She knocked the cat from her lap but said nothing to disturb the work of the quilters. Mildred, a transplant from Seattle, reminded Ingrid of Molly Bochau in many ways. She was easily obsessed with things not directly concerning her, but had a gift for gab. Her mouth would start working in spasmodic jerks prior to the airing of her thoughts, but eventually they would leap forth: "Did you hear about the man who made a widow out of his wife by getting a fish hook stuck in the palm of his hand? He didn't pay the infection any mind until it spread throughout his body, and by then, it was too late to get him to the hospital. Someday, we'll have to have a doctor in this town. Relying on the riverboats is a far cry from the comforts of civilization."

"What's ailing you today?" Willa asked curtly. "You'll scare young Meri into believing a person doesn't have the capability of caring for herself. She'll have to be self-sufficient being wed. A bottle of witch hazel in the cupboard is a must."

"That and castor oil," Karitsa interrupted. She cast a knowing glance in Meri's direction to make certain the message was driven home. "A good medicine chest always has castor oil, liniment and Lydia Pinkham's Vegetable Compound for Women."

"Which one of them is recommended for rheumatism?" Mildred asked. "It's rheumatism that's bothering me, and a woman my age can't afford any extra aches and pains to slow her down."

"Sloan's Liniment," Ingrid interjected, though she had to think carefully before promising its availability in their small community. "I believe they carry it at the store, Mildred, but are you certain that's all that's bothering you? You look a little peaked today."

If Ingrid had not centered the conversation upon Mildred's health, someone else surely would have. Aches and pains, the bad habits of men, and the futility of the future would all be addressed as the quilting continued.

"Jim Hill's Railroad isn't coming to Frankfort," Mildred cautioned them. She continually dwelt on this theme, having come from a city as large as Seattle to discover the isolation of a small river town. "Frankfort was platted with the promise of being connected to the outside world, and those promises seem to have some value until you get to be my age, when you'd like to cash them in. It's a sorrowful thing if a man can't be held to his word. Frankfort will eventually turn into a ghost town, mark my words. Then we'll all become widows, like that poor woman whose husband never saw fit to apply witch hazel to the palm of his hand."

Meri started tittering, and Karitsa was smiling from ear to ear. "At your age, Mildred, you should have learned to expect less. Having cash is a wishful thought, and as for a man's word, it's just about as reliable as hitching your future to a railroad."

Ingrid could not say as much, but she was in total agreement with Karitsa. Frankfort was as temporal as life itself, and what would happen to it in the future was beyond anyone's reign of influence. America's passion for rapid expansion and unbridled growth was not always for the better: that which could be built could also be the source of ruination. Images of the Clatsop Mill fire came readily to mind. She secured the needle in the fabric and excused herself to stretch her legs and gain control over her thoughts.

The white plume was coming into close proximity beneath the sternwheeler *City of Frankfort.* Meeting it would be a longer walk than Ingrid had anticipated, but no one was going to take umbrage at the length of her absence. She passed Mildred's residence before reaching the dock. It was small and cramped, similar to the house that had been home to the twins. The door was ajar, but it seemed as if no one would bother to investigate its limited contents. The largest house in town belonged to the Andersons, a point of contention with many who did not understand the under-lying cost.

Thoughts of Sloan's Liniment came to mind as Ingrid watched the cargo being unloaded. The owner of Frankfort's only store was busy officiating the process, so Ingrid strolled slowly, hoping to speak with him later. She walked parallel to the sternwheeler, taking casual notice of the passengers who were lining the deck. The majority of them were formally attired, while she was in a simple cotton frock with an apron tied around her waist. As travelers about their own purposes, no one seemed to notice the disparity. She could admire the bonnets and bowlers without appearing obtrusive.

"Ingrid! Ingrid Anderson!"

Ingrid tried to ascertain the source of the hailing, but none of the faces appeared familiar, and no one immediately stepped forward to claim the coquettish voice. Ingrid continued her relaxed stroll, thinking it all a figment of her imagination until a woman appeared at the railing, only three yards away. Ingrid observed her with ambivalence, including the two young women in her company.

"Ingrid, don't you remember me? Lottie Pustinen?"

The small size of the woman was a clue, but the name Pustinen meant nothing. Ingrid blushed profusely, embarrassed by the one-way conversation. "No, I'm sorry I don't," she replied honestly.

Immediately the three women put their heads together to speak in private. The woman who called herself Lottie Pustinen threw an impertinent glance in Ingrid's direction, and Ingrid finally recalled the connection. "Yes, I do remember you," Ingrid called out. "I apologize for the shortness of my memory. How are you?"

Lottie stepped away from her two companions, and Ingrid could see beneath the broad-brimmed bonnet and identify a familiar face. Similarly, Lottie looked Ingrid up and down, then turned her attention to assaying the worth of the small town in the background. Ingrid adjusted her apron, regretful of her casual appearance. Having become the focal point of those passengers who were impatient to depart, however, she quickly stopped her fidgeting. She regained her composure, waiting on Lottie's reply.

"After the drowning of poor Henry Hihnala," Lottie began, "I suffered tremendously. It was merely the fortune, due the unfortunate, saving me from my grief. I met a man named Olavi, the father of my two daughters, Lilian and Lucille." Lottie placed an arm around the waist of each young woman as she continued. "Lilian, of course, stands for purity, while Lucille represents light. I'm very proud of them; they're both beautiful on the outside, as well as on the inside. We're off to see the Lewis and Clark Exposition in Portland. They say neither the wise nor the wealthy would miss it. Have you been?"

Here Lottie paused, expecting Ingrid to either agree, or possibly appear foolish. Time had not altered Lottie one bit.

Ingrid recognized the trap and veered in a different direction. "The name Olavi Pustinen is somehow familiar. Was he a friend of Henry's, or an acquaintance of yours?"

Lottie bit down on her lower lip, and her eyes darted from daughter to daughter.

Memories of a luncheon crossed Ingrid's mind, and the unfounded remarks that had forever blighted their friendship. It had occurred so many years in the past, yet it was obvious Lottie was struggling with the same recollections. Ingrid did not know why, but her inquiry concerning Lottie's husband had struck another raw nerve. "Sorry if I said something to upset you," Ingrid added, "but the name Olavi was familiar. That's all."

"He and Olof never saw eye to eye," Lottie announced forthrightly. "I'm extremely surprised you're — so dishonest about it. Olavi continues to believe in furthering the fishing industry. You can pass that along to Olof. I hope there will be no hard feelings, but soon there will be motorized salmon boats to make Olof's sails obsolete. The times are always changing, and Olavi believes in staying abreast of the times."

Lottie's words struck home in quite a different manner than intended. So much of Olof's history had been lost to Ingrid that it saddened her. She was deserving of Lottie's harsh criticism, because Ingrid had abandoned her own husband for seventeen years. But then again, Lottie might not know that. Ingrid wrung her hands in her apron repeatedly. At the moment, she was extremely vulnerable.

"How are your children doing?" Lottie asked coyly. "I suppose they're both married now and have moved on to greener pastures. The passage of time makes strangers of us all. I suppose you're a grandmother as well. I'm still hoping for sons-in-law."

At first the question did not even register with Ingrid. She just felt old and lonely, distanced by the watery surrounds and the gay activity aboard the festive stern-wheeler. The bonnets and bowlers were oppressive, in light of her failed resources. "Her children," echoed in her head, but the phrase ended there. She could not imagine their faces as adults, only recall a few nursery rhymes to bring them to life. She looked at Lottie squarely, then studied the placating smiles on the faces of Lilian and Lucille. No one was to blame, it was all water under the bridge.

"What's this about motorized salmon boats?" she inquired meekly, but the sternwheeler was already into the current and the conversation abruptly splintered. She covered her ears with her hands as the ship's whistle continued screeching. Her cheeks felt warm beneath a flood of tears, and she knew she could not pretend anymore.

Maybe it was too late but, God forgive her, she had to enjoin the battle. She clenched her fists in rage, and for the first time in her life experienced the need to hurl an insult. "You Finnish whore!" she shouted at the top of her lungs. Her voice was strong and empowered, and she repeated the curse as she wiped away the defiling tear stains with the back of her fists. Over and over she cleansed herself of the torment, and ever so gradually the air quieted, and Frankfort resumed its subordinate positioning in the vast scheme of things happening along the Columbia.

Chapter Twelve

~ ~ ~ ~ ~ ~ ~ ~ ~ ~ ~ ~ ~ ~ ~ ~ ~ ~ ~

April, 1912

The rectangular tin box, with the rust stains slowly eroding the integrity of its bottom, remained in close proximity to the coffee mug while Olof sprinkled sugar on his buttered toast. Ingrid stole glimpses of the indecorous treasure chest as she rinsed the dishes, wondering when Olof would bolt for the door with its contents buried deep in his pocket. There were no secrets left to be divulged, and the recovery of the weathered box from some private storage place aboard Olof's salmon boat verified that accord. They had debated the inevitability of its disclosure for years, aware change was again upon them, and they either adapted or lost footing. Ingrid settled into the chair across from Olof and considered the sadness in his drawn expression. "We have come a long way, but we must keep going," she reiterated softly. "We're only as old as our bodies tell us we should be, and it remains our duty to be self-sufficient. If an engine is what we need to stay competitive, then an engine is the answer. It might make things easier for you, even safer."

Olof downed the lukewarm coffee, and the heavy ceramic mug impacted the table top with a residual thud. "It isn't that, my sweet Ingrid," he replied gruffly, "it's the principle of the thing. The Columbia River Packers Association has taken over the entire river, including the seining sites on Sand Island. And if it wasn't for them, there'd be more arriving to take up the slack. A man can't breathe with such competition, and motorized salmon boats are making it worse. It isn't gillnetting anymore; the fairness has gone out of it. Anybody can pull a salmon from the river and call himself an able fisherman."

Ingrid made one last effort at solving her best friend's dilemma. "I think the war is finally lost, Olof," she said sternly, "and the time has come for us to start thinking about our own survival. We're both over sixty years old, and whatever heads our way, we've got to learn to cope with it. Change is no longer our enemy, but our inability to adapt is. If you think you can manage a motor, I suggest you hightail it across the river and call the deal done."

Olof fingered the tin box as if it were a rare art object, never meant to be tampered with. He turned it several times in his hands before reaching out the money. It was empty when he scooted his chair away from the table. Ingrid watched her husband's shadowy figure dissolve through the doorway, hopeful he would be capable of facing this challenge with the same reserves of courage allowing her to cope with hers. She made her way to the raised porch and leaned into the waist-high railing. As was now the norm, the reach of the river was obscured by an annoying blanket of colorless fog, but in the foreground she could swear to the identity of Olof's salmon boat departing the intimate harbor. She clung to the vision as a sign of her ability to persist.

Charging the frothy channel beneath a chill, windswept sky, Olof toyed with the idea of altering his course and keeping both his pride and prejudices intact. It seemed like a heroic notion at the time, but the era of bluster and bravado were at an end. He curtly reminded himself that a motorized boat could make three drifts to his one, and the competition was keener than ever imagined, with over 2600 salmon boats, 300 traps and 50 haul seines working the river. These statistics were adequate motivators, but it was for Ingrid's sake that he would ultimately make the sacrifice and let go the history associated with a sail. They had agreed on the necessity.

From all outward appearances the Scandinavian Station was, as had been promised by the CRPA, staying abreast. Evidence of its progressive attitude was clearly substantiated by the presence of railroad tracks, keeping it in concert with an impatient society tripping across a haphazard horizon. Olof muscled the eighteen-foot mast from its tabernacle to pass beneath the trestle and cursed the inconvenience as he laid into the oars.

Each slip in the moorage area contained a boat; and the net-racking facilities, with the abutting nets languishing over the poles, resembled white cresting waves rolling across the docks. The bluestone and tanning tanks were beehives of activity, and for a while Olof's arrival went unheeded. He tied up near the boatyard but found no one tending the small building facing Uppertown's shoreline. He sauntered toward the net racking facilities, intent upon locating the fisherman who had the bristol double-ender for sale. He noted two of the old sailing hulls refitted with engines and paused abreast the one moored in the illusive shadows of the old cannery building. The youngster did not see him as he bore into the stranger with an armload of fish.

The jolt took Olof completely by surprise. "Whatcha doin' with them stinking fish?" he bellowed from the shadows.

Peter Lindstrom stopped dead in his tracks. His eyes settled upon a pair of old black boots, rather than addressing the man blocking his passage. He moved to the left to sashay around the stranger, but the black boots shifted sideways as well.

For a wistful instant, Olof was drawn to the boy. His reddish-brown hair was not curly, but there was something about the defiance in his eyes to sting Olof's heart. He knew it was not Little Henry, but he nurtured the likeness.

A chill ran up and down Peter's backbone. His arms weakened, jeopardizing his grip on the slippery cargo. He brought them closer, tucking them under his chin. It was only when he believed that his shad and flounder were no longer in danger that his eyes traveled from the stranger's feet to his face.

"I'm talking to you, youngun!" Olof repeated himself. "Whatcha' doing carrying around them junk fish? If they aren't salmon, they aren't fit to eat."

The man addressing Peter was preposterous. Peter raised the fish even higher, using them as a barrier against the unknown. The stranger was neither Scandinavian, nor Finnish, nor Chinese, nor a Hindu from the lumber mill. His hair was the color of fire and his eyes were a foggy green, much like the opaque glass floats that wandered across the Pacific Ocean from Japan. The contents of Peter's stomach churned several times before he spit out an incredulous "Oiy!"

Olof felt the pangs of rejection throughout his body. He had not intended to scare the youngster, but he was sorely disappointed in the boy's timidity. He had hoped for more from a gillnetter's child, perhaps a little bravery to rekindle old memories. "Those fish stink up the air!" he offered in jest. "Even the sea gulls won't pick at their bones!"

The stranger's breath came at Peter with the force of a furnace, fueled by something putrid. A flush of hot embarrassment reddened Peter's cheeks as he struggled once more with the fish, now sliding sideways in his arms. He bent at the waist to set them down on the narrow dock skirting the cannery's backside, but the black boots appeared lethal, poised to launch his fish into the river.

"Whatcha' afraid of, youngun? Cat got your tongue? Look at me, boy! Can't go through life not knowing what you're about! I recall a time when it took seven men to throw my catch overboard. Ought to at least say something in your own defense, although bartering in junk fish doesn't give a man a lot to brag about. I have to warn you youngun, those fish aren't fit for human consumption. Best set your sights a little higher if you're thinking about becoming a gillnetter."

Slowly Peter obeyed, giving the stranger the benefit of one more cautious appraisal. He could not help but notice the deep scar extending from the left ear lobe to the corner of the lips, which lifted the left side of Olof's face upward, creating a contrived smile and a deep hole below the left cheekbone. The third generation did not know what to make of the first.

"Let the boy pass!" came a stern voice.

Peter heard his father's warning and took it to heart. He lunged straight at Olof's belly with his cargo of fish.

Olof stepped aside this time and allowed his hostage to make a dash for freedom with a frenzied flock of sea gulls in crazed pursuit. Amused by the entire affair, Olof relaxed against the cannery building and began picking the fish scales from the front of his flannel shirt. "Better clean them!" he called after the youngster in flight. The tone of his voice was far less threatening, but the idea of defending an armload of shad and flounder continued to haunt him. It was an indication of the youngster's innate spunk, but more than that, it was also indicative of the river's inability to produce salmon with the same munificence as it had in the past. However disheartening, it was simply history revisiting itself. "Better cut their ugly heads off, lest they stare back at you from the pan!" he added caustically.

With Peter out of harm's way, Dan Lindstrom was about to encounter the same resistance and, possibly, a good deal of frustration. The old-timers, though few and far between, needed to be regarded at arm's length. If they were fired up on whiskey, they could be dangerous, and if they were riled, they could turn. This one he did not recognize, but the arrogance was there to certify the heritage.

"I assume you didn't mean my son any harm," Dan opened the conversation. He was of medium height, lithe and light complected, with brown hair.

Olof stepped out of the shadows to meet the man squarely. He sent a wad of Scandinavian dynamite beyond the boat to split the water's surface. "Is this the one-cylinder, four-Standard that's up for sale?"

Like his son, Dan was momentarily stymied, but it was not the old-timer's visage taking him aback, it was the lilt buried deep in his speech. "You're from Sweden," Dan stammered.

"So many years ago, I can't recall," Olof replied. "Different era, different times. Used to be from here as well. Isn't much of the lower river that I haven't called home."

Dan was at a disadvantage in this man's presence. He did not know what to think, because the old-timer feigned all allegiances. "So you're interested in this boat?" he queried. He sounded incredulous in the asking, in light of all the tales he had heard concerning the old-timers. Most of them were recluses, living from hand to mouth while disparaging all changes. "The CRPA is advancing money to those wishing to buy boats. I suppose you fish for the 'combine' and expect financial assistance."

Olof did not appreciate Dan's supposition but kept his poise. "Like those junk fish your son was carrying, these gasoline engines stink up the air," he replied evasively. "How much are you asking for it? If it's a fair price, the deal is done in cash."

Dan answered, not expecting the money to readily appear from the old-timer's pocket. Olof counted it out quickly, returning a few crumpled bills to his wallet. "Now, how do you operate one of these godforsaken contraptions?" the enigmatic buyer grumbled. "Show me how it moves faster than a sail full of wind, before I change my mind and take my business elsewhere."

May, 1912

Ingrid continued her limited watch over the river. All the while, Nuisance struggled to be set free. She pawed at Ingrid's shawl, getting her claws snagged in the yarn. Repeatedly, Ingrid ran her hand over her back to keep her under control. "We'll wait a little longer for Olof and then go home," she said reassuringly. Nuisance purred briefly, but the tension returned to her body as they neared the edge of the dock. She leapt from Ingrid's arms and ran toward shore. Ingrid collected the ends of her shawl across her chest and continued to scan the abbreviated horizon. Her cataracts were worsening, and what she could not see, her memory had to supply.

The Columbia River was over the banks that morning, spilling the excess runoff from the snow-capped peaks and glacial ridges of the Pacific Northwest into the lower tidelands. The choppy mixture of waves and stirred-in debris along the dock's edge did not bode well for Olof — he should be home by now. Clouds, the wispy consistency of cotton candy, hung low over the river's surface and dangled thread-like appendages from the sullen sky. Between the wispy tails fell blurry sheets of rain moving gradually in Ingrid's direction. Other than a free-floating log pounding up against the side of the dock, the air was void of sound, being completely censured by moisture. Ingrid bent over and placed a hand on the end of the log, attempting to dislodge it. "It's a big one," she mumbled, "and wedged firmly. A fugitive from a log raft. Olof'll have to tow it when he gets home."

Slowly, Ingrid regained her upright posture. She wiped a slimy residue in the gathers of her skirt, and the numbness in her fingertips became evident. It was a worry. "One has to assume Olof has thick enough skin to keep himself warm. Can't imagine an old gillnetter freezing to death." She squinted one last time at the churning water running wild, realizing the futility in extending her vigil: it was up to Olof to make his way home as promised, although a day late.

Halfway across the floating dock, the mist turned to drizzle and then to insistent rain. This moorage area for the fishing boats was not large, but Ingrid's progress was slow and deliberate. Large raindrops pelted her on the head and shoulders, yet she maintained her pace lest she fall and forfeit her usefulness. She crossed the gangplank, guiding herself with the railing. On land, she followed the muddied path to Mildred's.

"Are you sleeping?" she called out softly from beneath the porch's overhang. Through a crack in the door, she encountered escaping heat. She applied pressure to the door, with both palms held flat against its surface. She entered the living room and pivoted around to coax the rectangular barrier across the warped flooring. It stopped short of sealing completely, leaving the same one-inch crack that sufficed to keep an exchange between the inside and outside worlds.

Mildred's house, however, was in no worse repair than many of the others sheltering the diehard residents. By and large, Frankfort was becoming a ghost town, insulated from growth and prosperity by the Columbia. The sternwheelers seldom stopped, the railroad had never come, and there were no roads to entertain the advent of automobiles. The younger generation wanted the conveniences supplied by electricity and telephones, not the barren lifestyle of the past. Only a few hearty fishermen lived in Frankfort and commuted by gillnet boats to the outside world. The hotel without guests and prominent wharf were, for all practical purposes, useless artifacts.

Ingrid took a seat next to Mildred's bed and let her eyes adapt to the prevailing darkness. Her thoughts were as ill-defined as was the world that morning, murky and cluttered with debris. For several minutes she remained in the chair, listening to Mildred's labored breathing. She began to nod off as the cramped yet drafty quarters came in upon her. She yawned, stretched and shuffled off to the kitchen to the stoke the fire, unwilling to succumb to the effects of what she saw as sorrowful resignation.

Mildred awakened. "Who's there?" Her voice was coarse like sandpaper, and it lacked the clear conviction of one truly interested in receiving an answer.

"Ingrid."

"Oh," Mildred managed to say. "Sorry. I'll be up and around in a minute."

Ingrid poked her head through the doorway. "Are you feeling any better?" she asked.

"Not this day," Mildred replied.

"Well, maybe tomorrow," Ingrid said sincerely. "It takes time to fight the croup, if that's what you've got."

"I think He's coming for me," Mildred proposed off-handedly. She continued to struggle with the bed sheets, as if they had a hold on her and not the other way around.

"You say that every day," Ingrid grimaced. "You need to rise and exercise your limbs so it doesn't settle in your chest. And drink your tea."

Mildred smiled as she sat up in bed. "I do complain too much, don't I?"

"You'll lose all your hair if you're not careful," Ingrid bantered, trying to make a joke. But humor did not suit her. "People who sleep too much do get bald spots," she added in all seriousness.

Mildred's laugh was strained, but appreciative of Ingrid's rare attempt at levity. She then wheezed several times, clearing her chest. "I'm afraid to wash what little hair I have left. I'm afraid I'll catch my death, but the way I feel, it could be a blessing."

"Don't go on so!" Ingrid said sharply. "Think of your children and grandchildren. It's almost summer, time for them to arrive for a visit."

Mildred pulled on her housecoat and slippers and trudged slowly into the kitchen, stepping methodically as if expectant of some unforeseen hurdle. In front of the wood stove, she rubbed her hands together to warm them. Here were two mature women, trying to glean some compensation for enduring a worrisome and detached existence. "You're soaked to the skin, sweetheart," Mildred remarked. "I suppose Olof isn't back yet, and it's torturing your soul. The time comes when you've got to put aside your constant worrying, or the worry itself becomes the injustice. Olof'll find some port in this storm, and make his way home when he's able. Mark my words. When God takes away one's life, He's usually just in the doing, and the end comes without complaint."

Ingrid braced herself against the wooden drainboard and thought about the pessimism that could overshadow her life, if she allowed it entrance. The problem with Mildred's advice was that it was foundationless, rooted in life experiences not her own. Mildred knew not of what she spoke, but so few people did. If there were clear patterns to be followed, humankind had confounded them. "Your mind is beginning to get lazy," she refuted Mildred bluntly. "Olof will make his way home, if the river doesn't get in his way. It's that, pure and simple. Whatever God thinks of Olof I'm uncertain, but I do know He'll propose a fair fight because Olof wouldn't have it any other way. In which case, Olof will win."

Mildred was stunned by Ingrid's unexpected zeal: women were supposed to be meek under duress! She shook her head to indicate her extreme displeasure. In spite of the slight variance in their ages, Mildred found it necessary to set Ingrid straight. "One shouldn't pretend to know the Lord's intentions," she cautioned, "or speak so loudly of them."

Ingrid felt the four walls moving away from her as Mildred's face became a blur. She shrugged off the unsettling deception. Her vision liked to play tricks on her, but her mind was reliable when it came to accepting or rejecting the truth. Veracity, as Ingrid saw it, was somewhere betwixt the Bible and the ethereal translations taken therefrom, perhaps, always shifting from one truth seeker to the next, fluid, like the Columbia River.

"I believe we were meant to protect the life God gave us," she replied tartly, "and not succumb prematurely. There are those who aren't given the choice. Drink your tea and warm your heart, Mildred, before you fall prey to your own pessimism."

∞

Olof needed every foreseeable edge to remain competitive. His days of finding off-season employment to supplement his fishing career were over, usurped by younger, more agile generations. Too, the river was full of mischief, flooding the low farmlands and bringing to bear harsh consequences upon anything unsecured. As it rushed over the sand bars and inundated the grassy islands where the waterfowl normally found refuge, the haul seiners and trapmen sat idle, a slight advantage given the gillnetters in light of the prevailing conditions. Olof felt the pressure.

He talked to himself while he and Wally hauled in the net prematurely due to the passage of a ship. "If it isn't one thing, then it's another," he said in disgust. "Running up and down this river trying to find a spot to fish is getting a mite tiresome. Everybody expects to take his half out of the middle." He stopped to catch his breath only after the boat was again up to speed, making its return trip to start another drift.

Wally seemed relaxed as he sat on the fishlocker with the four salmon inside. "You've got to admit, Pot, we wouldn't be getting anywhere against this current in the old salmon boat. My son says, 'Even if you can tally up your total catch using just your fingers and toes, it's better than counting on nuttin'.'"

The wind was sucking the moisture out of Olof's face, and his lips were raw. His tongue could locate thin cuts in the tender flesh, tasting of blood. Still, Wally's comment reminded him of something Henry Hihnala had once said to relieve his worries, at a time when he had been overly distracted by the number of transient fishermen impeding his progress. This situation seemed somehow similar. "How old is this son of yours now? Five? Ten? Fifty? Or, are you sure your pa didn't say that? I can't keep track of the Palmberg clan. Seems everyone, sooner or later, has an unfounded opinion concerning the management of my boat."

Wally's spontaneous laughter was interrupted by an odd break in the choppy water ahead. "Something's a-boilin' off the bow!" he hollered. Olof immediately heeded his partner's warning and steered the boat toward the starboard. Wally braced himself as the boat lurched off course, avoiding a snag of tremendous proportions accompanied by swirling eddies that hinted at the massive network of things passing unseen. Wally breathed a deep sigh of relief and continued to look for anything unusual on the horizon. Olof had already seen it — a log raft, coming right down the middle of the channel. "These are stinking lousy fishing conditions!" he cursed under his breath. Nothing more needed to be said.

Olof and Wally fished for the Altoona cannery, located across a shallow bay from Frankfort on the Washington side of the river. They drifted with other gillnetters from this cannery, many of whom were fighting the same frustration that came with sharing the river with ships, log rafts and debris, none of which afforded them any leeway. Today the litter seemed heavier. When Olof and Wally reached the head of the drift, two other gillnet boats were standing by. The log raft, pulled by a tug, was longer than most. Olof and Wally lay at anchor, waiting their turn at another chance.

The net was out, and they were moving downriver at a vigorous pace set by the fast-moving current. Once in a while, Olof started up the engine to keep the boat and net in sync while remaining on course. He navigated according to solid points of reference along the Washington riverbank, because the breadth of the river to the south was completely distorted by high water. Many of the familiar breakwaters and piles were completely confounded with debris, and the outcropping of islands invisible under tons of rolling river. Wally moved to the bow, scanning the water's surface. The clouds came and went, changing the intensity of light and producing dark shadows where once there had been glare. His eyes were fatigued from remaining on constant alert. The scraping noise came as a complete surprise, and Wally responded to it. "We're hung up on something!" he exclaimed. He leaned over the edge of the boat, trying to glean immediate understanding from the churning river.

Olof saw the net moving freely while the boat was lagging behind, to recreate the essence of a swirling tidepool in the channel's midst. He surmised they were probably piggy-backing a waterlogged snag, mirroring its abbreviated progress as the river struggled to move it gradually toward the ocean. It was so obvious, Olof failed to vocalize his suspicions or the caution required. He assumed there was no chance of mobilizing the boat on a different course: the snag was holding them hostage. He turned toward the net, hoping to retrieve it before it became involved in the length or breadth of the invisible foe, probably a fir tree of immense proportions with a tremendous root system and influential branches. Left to his own devices, Wally was working with a pugh, a one-tined pitchfork, in an effort to disrupt the union.

Wally's cry was short in duration, but a distressed expression remained on his face long after the pugh rushed off with the current. Olof was confused by Wally's scream, and the reason behind the water dripping from his partner's lower arm. He was moving in Wally's direction as the bottom of the boat rolled slightly, and something between the hull and the snag screeched in agony. Wally echoed that screech, falling to his knees as the boat lurched free. Olof was momentarily confounded by the appearance of Wally's mangled wrist and crushed fingers, until a tree limb became visible behind the stern of the boat, and that which had occurred in a matter of seconds became clear.

At first, Wally raised the injured appendage to his chest at the elbow and would not allow Olof to approach it. He huddled over it; still, Olof could see. *"Gud in himmel!"* Olof cursed quietly. He laid a hand on Wally's shoulder, but Wally simply recoiled from his touch. The injured boy's mouth was wide open, and tears were streaming from his eyes. Immediately, Olof reached the knife from its sheath in the bow of the boat and freed the boat from the net with a violent rip. He forced himself toward the engine. His mind was racing a mile a minute, but his feet were slow to follow.

The engine started, but when Olof put it in gear, the entire undercarriage beneath the boat made a tremendous racket, metal against metal, screeching and groaning. Olof shut it off and tried to compose himself. He felt terribly alone. He looked toward the stern for another boat drifting in his wake. There was none. He had to get the attention of the boat ahead, a few hundred yards down the drift. He retraced his steps to the bow and grabbed for the loaded shotgun. He quickly fired both barrels. Although panicky, his wits remained with him. "That will bring somebody," he comforted both himself and the injured. "We'll get you to Astoria, come hell or high water."

"Pa would have said as much," Wally grumbled in pain, "but you're the one who's supposed to have all the answers. Explain to me, Pot, why the river came up and bit me, when I never did it any harm? Just enjoyed it. That's all." Wally's voice was quivering and uncharacteristically distant.

Olof removed his jacket and flannel shirt, stripping down to his long johns. He wadded up the jacket and used it to support Wally's head. Slowly, he wrapped Wally's arm from armpit to fingertips, making certain not to upset the hold that Wally maintained on it. It was impossible to look Wally in the face and promise the freckled optimist that his injuries weren't life-threatening. The closest boat was gradually retrieving its net. Olof swung around on his haunches and searched through his stores more thoroughly. He came upon six shotgun shells. He continually reloaded the gun until all the shells were spent. The gillnet boat was moving in their direction, but too slowly to lessen Olof's fears. He waved the gun in the air before returning to Wally's needs.

The injured boy was now half asleep. A light drizzle was lying over them both like a blanket, and Wally's face felt cold to the touch from the dampness settled on his skin. His eyes were vacant. "You're almost there," Olof assured him. "I've come up against a lot worse when Henry Hihnala and I did a little too much drinking, but back then we could row ourselves ashore. Sorry about the engine; perhaps old fishermen and newfangled contraptions don't mix. Haven't got the touch with it that I used to have with a sail. I know that doesn't help ease the pain much, but we'll still get you fixed up. Olof Anderson is always good on his word."

The immediacy of the situation overwhelmed the unwary captain of the responsive boat. As he came alongside, there was Pot Anderson, exposing his long johns and brandishing a shotgun in the air. He was prepared to curse the old-timer until he spotted Wally Palmberg crumpled in the bow.

Olof growled at the rescuer when tossed a bowline, spitting out orders like a man possessed. "You're not towing me anywhere!" he exploded. "I'll only slow you down! Get Wally to the hospital as soon as possible. A log crushed his hand, and he's trying to sleep it off. Don't let him get too comfortable, but keep him warm. His mind is fading in and out, meaning his courage is running thin about now."

The two men manning the other boat did not have time to object. Olof passed Wally from one boat to the other, supporting him all the way. The direness of the situation was evident in the injured boy's visage. The bewildered cap'n promptly shoved off, leaving Olof to fend for himself.

Olof was out of touch with himself and the world around him. His jacket was there in the bow of the boat, yet bringing it within reach was completely out of the question. The boat was rocking beneath him, and the shoreline was spinning. He sat down on the box, protecting the engine to ease the shaking throughout his body.

"Wally's going to be all right," he assured himself, "but getting home to Ingrid is another matter." His hands came up to support his head as he rested his elbows on his knees. The rain rolled off his long johns down the length of his pant legs. He was a disgrace, the discovery being both amusing and perplexing. He knew little of the mechanical workings of a motorized boat, but it was highly probable that the sinker had done damage to the propeller shaft. He did not want to believe as much, but, as the gillnetters aboard the other boat had suggested, he required a tow. Without a sail, he was finally at the river's mercy. Just like Wally, he was in need of assistance.

The men aboard the river tug observed Olof's plight with disdain. "We'll tow an old drunk like you for a fee, and a fee only," the captain grumbled.

Olof had no idea where he was or where the time had gone, but the sun was barely half its normal self upon the western horizon, and his eyelids felt heavier than the weight of his worry. He secured the rope to a cleat and finally draped the jacket over his shoulders. He was wringing wet and did not much care where the tug took him, so long as there was heat available at its destination. The truth of the matter was, he had no recollection of the empty whiskey bottle wedged between the ribs of the boat, or why he felt so cold that he could not fathom having drained it. The light at the end of the tunnel was going dim.

∞

Dan Lindstrom was dismayed to find one of his refitted bristols tied up next to the boat shed and its new owner blocking the easement to his place of work. The morning light could be deceptive, yet there was no mistaking Olof Anderson's bulky figure. Dan approached him with the same guarded trepidation that had served him in the past. He put down his tool chest before facing Olof. The unexpected visitor was so statuesque, with the wind and rain cavorting around him, Dan thought him asleep on his feet.

"Got a problem with the boat?" he asked straight out.

Olof leaned forward; his expression was dazed. He was shaky on his feet, and his green eyes were unfocused. "Had a run-in with a dead head. Must have done some damage underneath. Needed a tow."

"Probably bent something," Dan replied, mocking the clipped speech. "Get to it tomorrow or the day after. Takes a while to grease up the poles and get a head of steam on the donkey. We'll have to dry dock it to see exactly what damage you've done."

"You're going to do it now," Olof responded convincingly. "I don't have time to waste in arguing. There are places I have to be. A day from now might be too long for my sweet Ingrid; and as for Wally Palmberg, I need to find out."

Olof moved past Dan at a sluggish pace. He was teetering slightly, obviously not in the best of shape. The brim of his rain hat drooped in toward his cheeks, and his arms were as rigid as poles suspended from his shoulders.

"Where you headed to, old-timer?" Dan called after him. He was uncertain as to what he had heard, and how to interpret it as being anything other than pure arrogance.

Olof left the young Swede hanging. His mind was closed on the subject of the boat. Ahead of him loomed his visit to the hospital, a wearisome trek even for those in the best of spirits. Every step he took was arduous. He had no idea what to expect, but he was compelled to face it squarely.

∞

The nurse spotted the long johns clinging to the visitor's neckline, even with the jacket buttoned up snugly. She outpaced him by at least six feet, disconcerted by his overall appearance. She used her left arm to introduce Olof to the proper door and then hurried off. Olof recognized her from the several visits he had made with Ingrid, but this day her pleasant expression was overcome by other considerations. Her white uniform and perky hat stood in stark contrast to Olof's disheveled appearance. He allowed the rainwater to drip from his shoulders and puddle around his black boots, lest he traipse it into Wally's room. Wally would not mind, but the nurse would. Olof removed his hat and made his entrance.

The patient was sitting up in bed, looking pleasantly surprised. Too amused, perhaps, to suggest he had recovered. "Look what the cat drug in," he said jokingly. "Just made it off the river? How's the boat? You must have got it runnin', or else you wouldn't be here. Pa used to say that a little polish can make most anything shine. You don't look like a ray of sunshine, Pot. More like a drowned rat. Hope I didn't put you to too much trouble. The wrist is gonna heal, but it looks like it ain't going to bend in the middle. Two of the fingers been taken off at the nub. Should have quit when the river was still a rollin' in my favor. A man oughta' know when to change directions, otherwise he'll keep drifting, until he falls headlong off the edge. My boy came to the conclusion that it's a good thing his father weren't cut out for gillnetting, but my wife has nothing but tears on her mind. Might be she understands the price paid for the lesson.

"I don't hold any grudges, Pot Anderson, it was my own damn fault! Wasn't born a fisherman like you and wasn't ever meant to pretend otherwise. Never had a second sense about it, never considered the river my ally. Pa used to say that if a man doesn't know how to look out for himself, he's only got himself to blame. I'm real sorry. Feel like I've let you down."

Olof's reservoir of courage was completely exhausted. It was futile to make sense of the senseless, while it was not within Olof to contradict anything Wally had said. If Wally was quitting the river, so be it. He had good reason.

Olof began by addressing the simple fact that Wally was alive. "I'm glad to see you made it," he said sincerely, "and I don't know why it came down to this, but I think your father was right — a man has to look out for himself." Momentarily, Olof's gaze settled upon the cast on Wally's wrist and palm, as well as the supports underlying the three remaining fingers. It made him sick, and he wanted to cry out in pain. "I'm the one who's ultimately to blame, however," he offered in leaving. "Like the net, I should have cut you free years ago."

∞

Peter walked over to where Dan was bent over his workbench and shook him by the elbow. "The strange man is back, and he's drinking whiskey from a paper sack," he informed his father.

"Just stay out of his way, Peter, and he won't do you any harm. He's only an old-timer, doing what he does best by getting liquored up."

"Did he do this?" Peter inquired innocently, pointing to the bent shaft and propeller blades.

Dan did not have to think long and hard before jumping to the obvious conclusion. He had seen the empty bottle in the bottom of the boat. "Yes, Peter," he replied sternly. "They get drunk and riled up. Some of them go off half-cocked and do great ruination. They're too old for the river and unwilling to admit it."

It was pouring rain beyond the confines of the shed, and blasts of wind careened through the gaping portals where Olof's boat was resting on the greased poles. Peter's father was visibly upset by what he perceived to be the truth underlying his frustration, and the inclement weather did not help matters much. He rolled the shaft off the work table, and it struck the floor with enough impact to make indents in the wooden planking. He shoved his son aside and went storming from the boat shed to have a word with Olof Anderson, his irritability apparent.

"I can't pound out the shaft!" he announced flatly. He placed his hands on hips and mustered all the ire available to him. "It all needs to be reworked under extreme heat, and I don't have the equipment here. We put boats together, not rend them apart! What did you expect?"

The weather was whipping up around them, but Olof was unmoved, numbed by the circadian clock beginning to recycle itself. "Do you have a boat I could borrow?" he inquired soberly. "I need to get home before dark. My sweet Ingrid will be fit to be tied."

No, Dan Lindstrom was not about to loan an old-timer a boat. Regardless of the rain pelting him from all directions, he hemmed and hawed, intent upon ending this business deal without incident. "I do have another shaft and propeller," he said threateningly, "but it will cost you a pretty penny."

Olof turned aside to set down his bottle and check out the contents of his wallet. He was worth a grand total of thirty-five dollars, not a cent more. He held it out for Dan to consider, the wind nearly stripping it from his palm. With the forfeiture of his net and his boat in dry dock, he was as destitute and dubious as any freeloader wandering the riverbank. He started laughing, and Dan backed away.

Olof encouraged the boat builder to continue his retreat by raising his voice. "It's been a lot worse than this!" he called after him. "Even for my sweet Ingrid, who bested the Columbia during a high and mighty storm in the 1870s! And for Henry Hihnala, who went overboard when a swell overturned the salmon boat! And for Hanna Jane, who smiled her way through life! And for Little Henry, who was lost in a fire!" Olof's voice was quick to give out. He choked on his last words and could not catch his breath. He lowered both the bottle and the money to consider how incredible he had become, ranting and raving much as his reputation would suggest.

Beneath the roof's overhang, Dan Lindstrom halted his retreat. The old-timer galled him to the core. Still, there was no reason to degrade him. Olof was teetering in the rainswept surrounds of the open walkway, with a wad of one-dollar bills clenched in one hand and a bottle of whiskey in the other. Dan did not feel sure of himself, playing such a pivotal role in a story he knew nothing about. He nudged Peter in the shoulder to get his attention. "Go tell the old-timer we'll fix him up just this once, and then he should take his business elsewhere. But I don't want you falling prey to his wayward tongue. He's just an old fool, full of meaningless prattle."

June 7, 1913

Ingrid placed her right hand on Olof's shoulder to guide her descent. She had become so frail that fielding her weight was akin to receiving a pat on the back, and Olof barely flinched. She dropped to her knees beside her mammoth husband and ran her delicate palms over the cold yet enduring gravestone and transferred the familiar sentiment from her fingertips to her consciousness. It read: Beloved Hanna Jane Andersson, 1877-1880. She commented: "It's strange how someone can live such a brief life and leave such a lasting impression. Her goodness and gaiety remain beacons on a hazy horizon."

Olof pulled two more clumps of grass from the earth and arose, while Ingrid continued her hands-on exploration. The sight of her fingering Little Henry's headstone and the added phrase, Born American, made him uncomfortable, wondering what nostalgic words of remembrance would ensue to further erode his composure. He looked elsewhere, focusing on the activities of the living, a broad arena where he continued to compete.

From Tongue Point to the mouth of the Columbia, change was occurring rapidly. Astoria had become a summer stopover for pleasure seekers, travelers making connections through its harbor on their way to ocean beaches. Railroads and riverboats were the key to this nascent industry, and both could be seen from the heights afforded by the cemetery. A sternwheeler, on a north-northeasterly course, was certainly intended for a juncture with an intriguing railroad, one that meandered on a curious trek along the sandy foundation of the Long Beach Peninsula.

A lengthy train, approaching Astoria from the west, carried vacationers headed for the easy reach of the Oregon beaches. It was a perplexing industry for someone of Olof's work ethic to comprehend, contradicting the harsh realities he had come to expect of the lower river.

"The canners are banding together to eliminate bonuses to the fishermen," he said offhandedly, "and they've made a deal not to hire from one another. They continue to think they own this river!"

Ingrid raised her hand in the air, and Olof lent his assistance. As soon as she was on her feet Olof took her arm and folded it around his. They started walking. "What does that mean to us?" Ingrid asked. "I wouldn't suppose you'd consider changing canneries at this late date. As for the bonuses, we've managed either with or without them, so if there's to be another war along the river, give the responsibility over to the young."

The conciliatory tone in Ingrid's voice was enough to put Olof off, he supposing this was neither the time nor the place to delve into his personal grievances, or provoke a to-do over their financial vulnerability. Instead he became attentive to the uneven ground and guided his wife over the rough spots between the occupied plots, allowing her to make headway using her limited eyesight. Being so encumbered was an experience to temper the strongest of men — a war without recourse. In an effort to quell his mounting frustration, he made casual mention of the hedgerow immediately to Ingrid's left. "What are those funny yellow scrub bushes growing along the fence line?" he inquired.

"I would assume they're Scotch broom, from their pungent aroma," Ingrid replied tartly, "but as for being yellow, I'm afraid I'm at a loss. Besides, you don't really care a hoot about plants, Olof Anderson, you're only trying to put a good light on something terribly bleak. I'm incapable of discerning colors, including the glint in your devilish green eyes. I would hope you're not entertaining any plans to counter the canners' demands or, as you've threatened in the past, doing something foolish to get the younger generation off its duff. We both must learn to accept our limitations. You're no longer spritely, my husband, and I can't see to save you from stumbling across your own deep-seated stubbornness. Remember that."

Olof's arm tightened around hers, and they continued their regulated pace. The rutted dirt eventually turned into a level surface where automobiles traveled up and down the street. It was easier going, and Ingrid's strides increased in both size and speed. Olof relaxed his grip and took a handkerchief from his pocket to wipe his brow. It was extremely humid for a summer's day, an unusual condition along the lower river.

They made it to the hospital's entrance in a timely fashion, but between the second and third steps Ingrid stumbled, catching Olof unawares. She collapsed at the waist, and Olof succeeded in only partially breaking her fall. For several minutes she sat hunched over on the third step with her husband at her side. It was prudent to face the world, now completely enshrouded in irrevocable darkness, with all the fortitude she could muster.

Olof noticed that the sleeve of her blouse had been torn and a few of her hairpins had come loose. He patted her on the knee and said nothing. She had fallen before and had managed to spring back. He took her hand in his as he stood. "We've been through worse," he offered stoically.

"That we have," she agreed softly.

The sultry summer day awaited them following the brief appointment. Olof automatically entwined her arm in his. "Four steps," he cautioned as they made their way to the street. An automobile went by, and a throat-choking dust cloud arose in its wake. Olof shook a fist, while miraculously withholding the expletive ready on the tip of his tongue.

Ingrid followed its progress with her ears, rather than her eyes.

Olof again daubed his forehead with his handkerchief. Ingrid stared off in the distance, completely spent. They went directly to the waterfront, where the gillnet boat was waiting. Olof grasped the top ladder rung and was quickly aboard. He held out his hand and expected Ingrid to accept it.

Ingrid could hear the water lapping against the hull of the boat, but nothing else was available to indicate where Olof had gone. She was bewildered by her blindness. The river was omnipresent in every sound and smell coming to her, and Olof and his boat were adrift in it. She felt herself on the verge of tears. In spite of the tremendous number of obstacles she had overcome, this one was unconscionable.

Olof remained in the boat with his arms outstretched. He heard the plea Ingrid had failed to vocalize, but he did not want to believe it. Ingrid had managed to retain the qualities of both youth and determination in her optimism, thus the opacity in the lenses of her eyes failed to detract from her consummate beauty or subtract from her total being. He was unwilling to give up hope when his hope was still within reach. He climbed two steps and made contact with her fingertips. He was the one now staving off a flood of emotions. "All seats are taken except for one!" he offered in jest.

"I hope it's soft and secure," Ingrid replied demurely. She accepted the gnarled grip of a gillnetter's hand and managed to descend the ladder. Olof guided her to a seat atop the fishlocker and hastened to get them under way.

From Astoria to Uppertown, the chop on the water was arrhythmic. Every so often the boat would dive in a trough, and Ingrid could detect a subtle difference in the engine's running as the watery barrier subsided, and they forged ahead.

"I suppose it's like riding a bucking bronco, at times!" she called back to Olof.

They caught the crest of a wave and the spindrift felt cool upon Ingrid's face. Her first experience with total blindness was both exhilarating and disconcerting. She did not know how to deal with its finality, because it was a puzzle with pieces missing. A train whistle and the clanging of a buoy marker were her only immediate clues. Her mind started wandering. She could observe the twins sitting in a fish-box, while a train went rumbling by. She could feel her feet swelling inside her shoes as the guests departed her house, yet sea gulls circled overhead and made raucous displays to dissuade her discomfort. She gripped down on the fishlocker with tenacity and fought against the singularity so prevalent in her mind's eye. It was a dangerous game she was playing by allowing herself to slip conveniently into the past, when Olof needed her in the future.

Olof did not know where to let his mind wander. Ingrid was totally blind, the canners were up to their old shenanigans, and the river was always filled with the unexpected. Nothing was comfortable on this late-afternoon crossing. Each time Ingrid made a comment over her shoulder, he was incapable of mustering a response. She sounded hysterical, and the rigidity in her upper body made him equally tense. Each wave jolting the boat caused him to overcompensate. He was white-knuckled on the wheel, in a vain attempt to smooth the river's surface. His only attainable goal seemed to be in reaching home safely, before the two of them sank too deeply into despair.

Another glance at the sky further upset Olof's equilibrium. The high cirrus clouds over the river were not a threat, but the thunderheads boiling up above the Coast Range Mountains were. The wind refused to tell him anything by

shifting clockwise, but the river was exceptionally bois-
terous for a late-afternoon trip. They were all mixed
messages. The engine died, and he collected himself. They
had simply run out of gas abreast the Scandinavian Station.

Ingrid clung fiercely to the edge of the fishlocker as
the boat started drifting on its own accord. "What
happened?" she inquired meekly. "Are we home already?"

Olof moved methodically through the process of
remedying the problem. "Don't worry your pretty head
about it" he offered apologetically. "Seems like the cap'n of
this newfangled contraption forgot to feed it."

"I'm not worried," Ingrid replied sharply. "I'm simply
anxious to set my feet on solid ground. With fish to fry and
potatoes to peel, my mind has been playing tricks on me. I
need to apply it to something useful."

A crack of lightning in the distance sent a shiver up
Olof's spine. "You're not afraid of a passing storm, are
you?" he asked bluntly.

"I'm not afraid of anything, anymore," Ingrid replied.

Before restarting the engine, Olof placed a hand on
Ingrid's shoulder. She placed her hand atop his; all that
needed saying had been said.

Olof continued navigating according to a large sand
bar off the port bow, when the first dark cloud obscured the
sun, and the water's surface turned a steely shade of gray.
Soon white caps were parading across an ebony surface.
Momentarily the sun reappeared and his eyes wept from the
glare. He had never seen anything like it, as the sky
imploded and dropped down to touch the river's surface.
For seconds he couldn't draw a breath, anticipating the
unknown. The sky rumbled overhead, and bolts of lightning
careened off the mountains to the south. They were halfway
between the Oregon and Washington shores when the

thunder became deafening, and a hailstorm came across the water like an impenetrable wall of ice pellets. He let loose the wheel to protect Ingrid with his body.

Ingrid experienced the boat rising and falling from tremendous heights. The air had turned icy cold, reminiscent of that occasion when the Bible had fallen from her fingers and come to rest at her feet in her father's fishing boat. "The laws of the land are quite different!" her father had warned her and, like an omen, it was meant to stay with her until this very moment. It had linked her to the choices she had made, either good or bad. She and Olof had moved from one world to the next, always bridging, always trying to extract the best from both. It had been an impossible dream. Ingrid called out for Olof, knowing full well he would never quit the helm until they were safe. She released her hold on the fishlocker when the storm became too much to sustain. The hail was stinging her skin unmercifully when the boat rolled sideways, and a strong hand locked around her wrist. She reminded herself that they were going down together, a fitting gesture after all they had been through.

June 12, 1913

John Lord scoured the newspaper with the same dedication he had once devoted to its preparation. Being retired from his right to edit beforehand, any resulting omissions or oversights irked him. He had never allowed himself the luxury of accepting his displacement, but hindsight was fast becoming his only accessible tool. Unsympathetically, Anne observed him grumbling in his rocking chair. "Don't forget to turn off the lights and latch the screen door," she said in passing. She pecked him on the forehead and disappeared down the hallway.

John squinted through his wire-rimmed glasses and rejoined his obsession with the second page. His eyes ran up and down the left margin until readdressing the three-line mention: Olof and Ingrid Anderson, believed to be of Sweden and residing in Frankfort, died in Monday night's freak storm when their gillnet boat overturned. "That's all?" he muttered.

He folded the newspaper and set it aside, unnerved by what he perceived to be untruths, or truths left unspoken. An entire era had passed by in the wink of an eye, and the Andersons' obituary was proof of its summary dismissal. If it could end here with such abruptness and pretense of simplicity, the river would be purged of all remembrances, and each ensuing generation left without a remarkable history. John looked to the night beyond the window, before reaching for his pen. He prided himself on being a fanatic for leaving no stone unturned, and it was time to set the record straight. He adjusted the pillow to support his head and melded with the chair's contours. What he really wanted to divine from his intended writing was some sense of the American hero as portrayed by Olof Anderson, set against the tumult of the times and meant to shed light on his own confounded generation. For one solid hour the chair rockers creaked across the floor's hardwood surface, and John observed the parade of lights emanating from the gill-netters' net buoys and pilot lights. They reminded him of other parades and other people in passing: times when Astoria was wild and bawdy, and men came together to sort out their differences against the backdrop of the impervious Columbia. He started nodding off, comfortable in his memories.

The twinkling lights spread across the river's surface had vanished with the sunrise, along with the retired writer's good intentions. He smelled bacon frying in the kitchen and heard Anne's footsteps taking her through her paces. The newspaper remained undisturbed on the end table, as well as the pen and ink bottle beside it.

"Did you accomplish anything?" his wife called out from the kitchen.

No, he had not. He had been foolish to pose the question in the first place. The world had moved on, and the qualities defining an American hero from the Columbia River would forever elude him, as would the mien and spirit of the Butterfly Fleet. The natural laws of the river had swept the record clean, probably because they had never come within his grasp to argue otherwise. The era of the sails and oars was over, while he had lived as only a spectator, viewing both its beauty and brutality from afar. Perhaps, like his unsung hero Olof Anderson, life was only meant to convince him of the necessity of positioning oneself, while experiencing the richness of its unfolding from beginning to end. They had existed as contemporaries, he and Olof, but had never known each other's passions. He regretted that.

References and Acknowledgments

~ ~ ~ ~ ~ ~ ~ ~ ~ ~ ~ ~ ~ ~ ~ ~ ~ ~ ~ ~

Astoria Maritime Museum, Clatsop County Historical Society, Astoria Public Library, Flavel House, Columbia County Museum, Oregon Historical Society.

Andrews, Ralph W. and Larssen, A.K., *Fish and Ships.* Seattle: Superior Publishing Co., 1959.

Bruce Weilepp, "Sailing Gillnet Boats of the Columbia River," *National Fisherman,* April 1991, pp. 44-47.

Channel Maps of Columbia River and Willamette River. Portland: National Colortype Co., 1912.

Cumtux, *Clatsop County Historical Society Quarterlies,* Astoria, Oregon:

Alborn, Denise, "The Hindus of Uppertown." Vol. 10, No. 1 – Winter, 1989.

Alborn, Denise, "Shanghai Days in Astoria." Vol. 9, No. 1 – Winter, 1988.

Cameron, Audrey Moberg, "The Dalgity Family." Vol. 10, No. 1 – Winter, 1989.

Dennon, Jim, "Astoria's Streetcars." Part I: Vol. 9, No. 2 – Spring 1989. Part II: Vol. 9, No. 2 – Summer 1989.

Linklater, Elizabeth, "A Child Under Sail." Vol. 9, No. 4 – Fall, 1989.

Marconeri, Cynthia J., "Chinese-Americans in Astoria, Oregon 1880-1930." Vol. 13, No. 3 – Summer, 1993.

Nelson, Harold C., "My Youth on the River." Part III: Vol. 8, No. 2 – Spring, 1988. Part IV: Vol. 9, No. 1 – Winter 1988. Part V: Vol. 10, No. 1 – Winter, 1989. Part VI: Vol. 10, No. 2 – Spring, 1990.

Penner, Liisa, "Upper Astoria." Vol. 13, No. 3 – Summer, 1993.

Niska, Ed, "Astoria's 'Union Fish.'" Vol. 8, No. 2 – Spring, 1988.

"Uniontown – The First 30 Years." Vol. 1, No. 4 – Fall, 1981.

Dodds, Gordon B., *The Salmon King of Oregon; R.D. Hume and the Pacific Fisheries.* The University of North Carolina Press, 1959.

Fadich, Ray, *Last of the Rivermen.* Entiat, WA: Riba Publishing, 1993.

Gibbs, James A., *Pacific Graveyard.* Portland: Binford and Mort, 1964.

Gibbs, Jim, *Windjammers of the Pacific Rim.* West Chester, PA: Schiffer Publishing Ltd., 1987.

Holbrook, Stewart H., *The Columbia, Rivers of America.* Edited by Carl Carmer. New York and Toronto: Rinehart and Co., Inc., 1956.

Hummasti, Paul George, *Finnish Radicals in Astoria, Oregon, 1904-1940.* New York: Arno Press, 1979.

Jekel, Pamela, *Columbia.* New York: Charter Books, 1986.

Kastrup, Allan, *The Swedish Heritage in America.* St. Paul: North Central Publishing Company with the Swedish Council of America, 1975.

Linklater, Eric, *The Ultimate Viking.* London: Macmillan, 1955.

Lorenzen, Lilly, *Of Swedish Ways.* New York: Barnes and Noble, 1978, c. 1964.

Martin, Irene, *Work is Our Joy: The Story of the Columbia River Gillnetter.* Video. Corvallis: Oregon State University, 1989.

McDonald, Lucile, *Coast Country: A History of Southwest Washington.* Portland: Binford and Mort, 1966.

McKinney, Sam, *Reach of Tide/Ring of History.* Portland: Oregon Historical Society Press, 1987.

Miller, Emma Gene, *Clatsop County, Oregon: Its History, Legends and Industries.* Portland: Binford and Mort, 1958.

Moberg, Vilhelm, *The Emigrants.* New York: Simon and Schuster, 1951.

Moberg, Vilhelm, *The Unknown Swedes: A Book About Swedes and America, Past and Present.* Translated and Edited by Roger McKnight. Carbondale and Edwardsville: Southern Illinois University Press, 1988.

Pageant of Old Scandinavia. Translated by Henry Goddard Leach. Princeton: Princeton University Press for the American-Scandinavian Foundation, 1946.

Parrish, Philip, H., *Historic Oregon.* New York: The Macmillan Company, 1955.

Scott, Franklin D., *Sweden: The Nation's History.* Minneapolis: University of Minnesota Press with the American-Scandinavian Foundation, 1977.

Smith, Courtland L., *Salmon Fishers of the Columbia.* Corvallis: Oregon State University Press, 1979.

Tetlow, Roger T. and Graham J. Barbey, *The Story of a Pioneer Columbia River Salmon Packer.* Portland: Binford and Mort, 1990.

Veirs, Kristina (ed.), *Nordic Heritage Northwest.* Seattle: The Writing Works, 1982.

Walker, George F. Walker, *A Slice of Country Life: 1902-1915.* San Francisco: Strawberry Hill Press, 1984.

Youngquist, Erick H., *America Fever: A Swede in the West 1914-1923.* Nashville: Voyageur Publishing Co., Inc., 1988.

To order additional copies of

The Butterfly Fleet

Book: $14.95   Shipping/Handling: $3.50

Call
BookPartners, Inc.
1-800-895-7323